W9-BYR-069

THE DOUBLE V

THE DOUBLE V

How Wars, Protest, and Harry Truman
Desegregated America's Military

RAWN JAMES, JR.

Valparaiso Public Library
103 Jefferson Street
Valparaiso, IN 46383

BLOOMSBURY PRESS

Published by Bloomsbury Press, New York

All papers used by Bloomsbury Press are natural, recyclable products
made from wood grown in well-managed forests. The manufacturing processes
conform to the environmental regulations of the country of origin.

LIBRARY OF CONGRESS CATALOGING-IN-PUBLICATION DATA

James, Rawn.
The double v : how wars, protest, and Harry Truman desegregated
America's military / Rawn James, Jr.—1st U.S. ed.
p.   cm.
Includes bibliographical references and index.
ISBN 978-1-60819-608-1 (alk. paper)
1. United States—Armed Forces—African Americans—History—20th century.
2. Segregation—Law and legislation—United States—History—20th century.
3. African American soldiers—History—20th century. 4. African Americans—Segregation—
History—20th century. 5. World War, 1914–1918—Participation, African American.
6. World War, 1939–1945—Participation, African American. 7. Truman, Harry S., 1884–1972—
Political and social views. 8. United States. President's Committee on Equality of
Treatment and Opportunity in the Armed Services.
I. Title.

UB418.A47J36 2013
355.0089'96073—dc23
2012030030

First U.S. Edition 2013

1 3 5 7 9 10 8 6 4 2

Typeset by Westchester Book Group
Printed in the U.S.A.

The Double V *is dedicated to the memory of my grandfather,*
Cornelius James, Sr., who served in a segregated U.S. Army during
World War II in part so that his sons, Colonel Cornelius James, Jr., M.D.
(U.S. Army, Ret.), Major Ralph James, Sr. (U.S. Army, Ret.),
and Commander Rawn James, Sr. (U.S. Navy, Ret.),
might serve in a better military and live in a fairer nation.

CONTENTS

1

THE CAUSE OF LIBERTY

BY SEPTEMBER 28, 1918, it was plausible that a company of German soldiers, hunkered down in northeastern France and knowing that they would soon be attacked, would send word to the advancing Allied forces that they had suffered enough. One could imagine that the demoralized Germans would rather surrender than offer futile resistance. In the previous few days, the Allied troops had advanced far into Champagne, bringing with them enough artillery, ammunition, tanks, and provisions to inflict extraordinary damage.

The men of the 371st Infantry of the U.S. Ninety-third Division stood poised to take Hill 188 when a German noncommissioned officer approached their camp in surrender. He explained that he led thirty-five men who did not wish "to risk their lives" any further in pursuit of a "lost cause." The Americans took the German soldier into custody. They began to trudge toward the hill.

German infantrymen began rising from their muddy trenches and pulling themselves onto the ramparts, where they raised their arms in surrender. The Americans held their fire.

Suddenly a whistle blew. The surrendering Germans leaped back into their trenches, hoisted arms, and opened fire on the Americans with rifles, machine guns, and mortars.

In an instant more than half of the American soldiers were killed or severely wounded, many killed by a single German machine-gun stand.

Amid the carnage, Corporal Freddie Stowers, a squad leader of Company C, spotted the turret and ordered the surviving men of his squad to join him in firing on the position. In a bloody exchange, they silenced the deadly machine gun.

Through the haze, Stowers spotted another machine-gun position and crawled toward it. His men followed on the ground behind him. From just yards away, they watched as machine-gun fire ripped through his body. Gravely wounded, Stowers continued toward the second German trench. When he could no longer move, he directed his squad to continue toward the target. They crawled past him. He yelled orders and encouragement until he died of his wounds.

Inspired by Stowers's example, the 371st Infantry continued the attack against what senior army officials later called "incredible odds."[1] The Americans took Hill 188 after three gruesome days of trench warfare. Freddie Stowers was buried alongside 133 of his fellow soldiers at the Meuse-Argonne American Cemetery and Memorial in France.

IT WAS 1991 by the time the president of the United States, Congress, and the U.S. Army formally recognized what Corporal Freddie Stowers's commanding officer knew to be true in 1918: The young soldier's actions in the battle that cost him his life were worthy of America's highest military honor.

"He had to be scared," President George H. W. Bush, himself a decorated war veteran, declared at the podium. "His friends died at his side. But he vanquished his fear and fought not for glory, but for a cause larger than himself—the cause of liberty." Among the officials gathered in the East Room of the White House shortly after three o'clock on that April afternoon were Secretary of Defense Dick Cheney, chairman of the Joint Chiefs of Staff General Colin L. Powell, and Mickey Leland and Joseph DioGuardi, the two former congressmen who had introduced the bill to confer the Medal of Honor on Corporal Stowers.[2]

Freddie Stowers's wife and daughter never learned of his heroic acts, but his younger sisters, Georgiana Palmer and Mary Bowens, eighty-eight and seventy-seven years old respectively, traveled to Washington to attend the ceremony. Wearing pink dresses and hats, they sat in the East Room next to first lady Barbara Bush. Behind them an honor guard stood at attention. Georgiana had been fourteen years old when her brother, one of six children, left their rural South Carolina home to enlist in the army in October 1917. She remembered working in the cotton fields alongside Freddie. Her brother had been "a nice boy. He never gave his father any trouble."[3]

Stowers's great-grandnephew, Staff Sergeant Douglass Warren of the 101st Airborne, had flown from Saudi Arabia to join his family members at the White House. The president joked that the Operation Desert Storm veteran appeared jet-lagged. "I want to welcome you home," President Bush told Warren before recounting the actions for which Corporal Freddie Stowers was finally receiving the nation's highest military award for valor.

> It's been said that the ultimate measure of a man is not where he stands in moments of comfort and convenience but where he stands at times of challenge. On September 28th, 1918, Corporal Freddie Stowers stood poised on the edge of such a challenge and summoned his mettle and courage.
>
> He and the men of Company C, 371st Infantry Regiment, began their attack on Hill 188 in the Champagne Marne sector of France. Only a few minutes after the fighting began, the enemy stopped firing and enemy troops climbed out of their trenches onto the parapets of the trench, held up their arms and seemed to surrender.

Stowers's Medal of Honor citation notes the South Carolina native's "conspicuous gallantry, extraordinary heroism and supreme devotion to his men . . . reflect[ing] the utmost credit on him and the United States Army."

In his remarks at Corporal Stowers's Medal of Honor presentation, President Bush did not mention that the young hero had served in a segregated army. The squad Stowers led, the company to which it belonged, and its larger regiment and division consisted of African Americans commanded mostly by white officers.

DURING WORLD WAR I more than 90 percent of black combat soldiers were assigned to one of two divisions.[4] This was not an arrangement that coincidentally comported with the way of life throughout much of America in 1918. Rather, the United States segregated its army and navy because its military and civilian leaders firmly believed that because black people were inferior to whites, black soldiers and sailors were likewise inferior. One major general's memorandum to the army chief of staff suggested that black men be excluded from "the Field Artillery as the number of men of that race who have the mental qualifications to come up to standards of efficiency of the Field Artillery officers is so small that the few isolated cases might be better handled in other branches."[5] The navy permitted black sailors to work only as cooks or stewards, and the marine corps altogether excluded African Americans from its ranks.

Not all white commanders adhered to the military's systematic subjugation of African American soldiers. Indeed, it was Corporal Stowers's white commanding officer who first petitioned for him to receive the Medal of Honor. Such exceptions aside, however, the American military during World War I made official the discriminatory practices that had been largely unofficial policy since the founding of the republic. The way the military and public treated black servicemen during and after the war ignited a righteous anger among African Americans. That they had fought for freedom abroad only to be denied it anew at home awakened African Americans to the fact that only a collective, nationwide effort would secure their basic constitutional rights. In time this effort would come to be known as the civil rights movement, but it began with the struggle to desegregate America's military.

FROM THE ADVENT of the Revolutionary War until the end of the Korean War, the complexity of black people's collective life in America was mirrored by their service in defense of country. In March 1770 a middle-aged half-Indian, half-black sailor who had been born into slavery but escaped to a life of danger and drudgery on the high seas became the first casualty in what would become the American Revolution. Believing that British guards were being attacked by hoodlums, Crispus Attucks dashed from a Boston tavern with several other colonists intent on defending the soldiers. The men arrived on the scene to witness the guards abusing local adolescents who were throwing snowballs. The colonists turned on the guards and Crispus Attucks struck the first blow. The British opened fire with their muskets, killing Attucks and four other colonists.

Five years later, in October 1775, the Continental Congress voted overwhelmingly to exclude African Americans, slave or free, from serving in the military. The newly formed Continental Army, led by a slave-owning French and Indian War veteran named George Washington, would accept only white enlistees. South Carolina's delegates sought to have all African Americans currently serving in the armed forces summarily dismissed, but northern colonists forced the compromise that allowed those soldiers and sailors to complete their enlistments.

As a slave-owning Virginian, George Washington understood South Carolinians' uneasiness with the prospect of training a large number of black men in the use of firearms. During the 1760s Virginia experienced fierce slave rebellions in Frederick, Loudon, Fairfax, and Stafford counties. Virginia's slave owners remained nervous in the mid-1770s, and Washington was no exception. Providing military training to freed black men could lead to an armed slave insurrection.

In Virginia members of the landholding class were more united than in any other colony; the Commonwealth would produce three of the first four presidents of the United States. By the time of the Revolution, the institution of slavery had come to define Virginia's governing men. Slaves accounted for half of Virginia's population. They were extraordinarily valuable property. Thomas Jefferson, who inherited dozens of slaves and thousands of acres from his father, noted that "a child raised every 2 years is of more profit than the crop of the best laboring man."[6] That is, the value of a child born in slavery increases more each year than the most productive crop. Jefferson's calculation elucidates how slavery concentrated wealth throughout the South. Slaves increased in value much more quickly than the land on which they worked.

Wealthy plantation owners bought slaves to grow their crops and hired overseers to drive their slaves, thereby freeing themselves to engage in more noble pursuits, such as politics and revolution. As one economist has noted, the average landed gentleman in the South in 1774 possessed almost exactly twice as much wealth as his counterpart in New England. This was despite the fact that "per capita wealth—land, livestock, producer and consumer goods—was almost exactly the same in 1774 in every region of the country. White southerners had more wealth than white northerners only because black southerners had none."[7]

The vast majority of Virginia's slave owners possessed just one or two slaves. These minor slaveholders often defended slavery more ardently than wealthy plantation owners, because slave ownership was their only realistic means of escaping a life of hard labor for themselves and their children. Owning slaves provided their families with upward mobility. First, there was the significant growth in value as each slave matured and learned new skills. Second, and more important for these smaller land-owners, owning slaves permitted them to send their children to school rather than putting them to work on the farm.

ONE MONTH AFTER the Continental Congress closed the military to African Americans, a Scotland-born soldier turned politician named John Murray, the fourth Earl of Dunmore and governor general of the Colony and Dominion of Virginia, proclaimed that all slaves who took up arms against their colonial masters to fight for the British were free men. Dunmore had lived in Virginia's capital, Williamsburg, for more than three years. He knew the agrarian colony would be brought to its knees by the sudden loss of its slave labor force—if the slaves answered his call. Twice before, Dunmore had threatened to "declare freedom to the slaves and reduce the City of Williamsburg to ashes."[8] When the Continental Congress announced its refusal to accept black enlistees, Dunmore shocked both enslaved and free Virginians by making good on his threats: "And I do hereby further declare all indented servants, Negroes, or others (appertaining to the rebels), free, that are able and willing to bear arms, they joining his Majesty's troops, as soon as may be, for the more speedily reducing this colony to a proper sense of their duty to his Majesty's crown and dignity."[9]

Virginia's slaves leaped at the chance to earn their freedom, even if doing so carried the risk of receiving any of the severe punishments mandated by the laws the Commonwealth enacted in the wake of Dunmore's declaration. More than eight hundred African Americans escaped to join what became known as Lord Dunmore's Ethiopian Regiment. He housed them on ships in the Rappahannock River. Despite his stipulation that any freed slave must be able to wage battle, many of the escaped slaves whom Dunmore sheltered were women and children.

In December 1775, Dunmore took his freedmen into battle at Great Bridge. There they suffered a devastating defeat at the hands of the colonists, and Norfolk burned. Shortly thereafter, a smallpox infestation all but wiped out Dunmore's Ethiopian Regiment. One month before the colonies formally declared independence, Lord Dunmore surrendered his forces to the colonists on the Rappahannock.

Although largely forgotten among stories of the American Revolution, Dunmore's proclamation was an important moment in the history of African Americans' military service. By freeing only those escaped slaves who agreed to fight for the British monarchy, Dunmore for the first time connected African Americans' military service with their liberation. In the following decades African American leaders, soldiers, and veterans repeatedly sought to link the two, but never again would the connection be expressed by a government official with the authority to act on the issue.[10]

Another reason Dunmore's emancipation experiment is significant is that it convinced Virginia's slaveholders that rebellion was the most viable way to defend their economic interests. They knew that King George III, like his faithful servant Lord Dunmore, would free all slaves in the colonies if doing so would allow him to maintain rule over those colonies. Conversely, the king would maintain slavery if doing so would quell a colonial revolt. President Abraham Lincoln would profess identical moral ambivalence in a famous letter to Horace Greeley ninety years later, and in neither case would wealthy slaveholding Virginians accept their leader's irresolution. In both cases, first against their king and later against their president, Virginia's ruling class chose rebellion.

WHEN ENTHUSIASM FOR THE ONGOING revolution began to erode throughout the colonies, both the Continental Congress and the citizenry lessened their opposition to black enlistees. Congress, less than three months after Dunmore's proclamation, announced: "The free Negroes who have served faithfully in the army at Cambridge, may be re-enlisted, but no others."[11] From January 17, 1776, until the end of the Revolutionary War, enslaved and free African Americans fought and died in the new nation's integrated military. Slaves often enlisted as substitutes for their owners, whose opposition to arming them was weaker than their desire to avoid combat duty.

In September 1776, Congress ordered all member states to raise eighty-eight battalions of infantry soldiers for the Continental Army. This proved a difficult proposition, because even many state militia veterans were loath to join the army, which, unlike the militias, required long periods of service, possibly on faraway battlefronts. A Virginian serving in the army might fight and die in New York while the British seized his farm and land at home. Enlistments of white men became insufficient as the war raged on, and this allowed for an increase in the number of African Americans serving. Runaway slaves posing as freemen were so readily accepted by the army that the Virginia Assembly in 1777 forbade "any recruiting officers within this Commonwealth to enlist any negro or mulatto into the service of this, or either of the United States, until such negro shall produce a certificate . . . that he is a freeman."[12]

The overwhelming majority of black soldiers served in integrated units. One Hessian officer, serving alongside the British, observed: "The Negro can take the field instead of his master, and therefore no regiment is to be seen in which there are not Negroes in abundance, and among them are able-bodied and strong fellows."[13] The Continental Army so badly needed soldiers that, in the end, more than five thousand African Americans fought for America during the Revolutionary War. Many who survived, such as James Roberts of Maryland's Eastern Shore, would forever remember those awful days when "human blood ran down in torrents, till the waters of the river were as red as crimson."[14]

THE FIRST DRAFT of the Articles of Confederation was prepared in the summer of 1776 by Pennsylvania's wealthiest man, a slaveholding lawyer named John Dickinson. Upon presentation the draft caused much consternation among Southern delegates, because it mandated that regulation of states' internal affairs be subject to approval by a central government. South Carolina's John Rutledge, the future chief justice of the United States, declared that the Articles of Confederation as written would lead to "nothing less than ruin to some colonies . . . The idea of destroying all provincial distinctions and making every thing of the most minute kind bend to what they call the good of the whole, is in other terms to say these colonies must be subject to the government of the eastern provinces." The "provincial distinction" to which Rutledge referred was slavery. "I am resolved to vest the Congress with no more power than what is absolutely necessary."[15]

Southern delegates joined Rutledge's protest, and the Articles of Confederation were modified to reflect their concerns. As adopted in November 1777, the Articles provided: "Each state retains its sovereignty, freedom and independence, and every power, jurisdiction and right which is not by this confederation expressly delegated to the United States, in Congress assembled."[16] With this language, the newly formed federal government forfeited the power to regulate slavery within states.

When the federal government sought to strengthen its authority by replacing the Articles of Confederation with the Constitution ten years later, slavery was left untouched. The Constitution adopted the "three-fifths compromise," which had been narrowly defeated during debate over the Articles of Confederation. According to the compromise, the government counted each slave as three fifths of a person for purposes of determining a state's congressional representation and taxation. Southern congressional delegates had hoped to count each slave as a full person, but Northern representatives, such as Connecticut's Roger Sherman, argued that only free men should count as persons. The delegates finally agreed on the three-fifths accounting measure.

2

The First to Come and the Last to Leave

In 1792, with the Revolutionary War won and the newly formed United States of America stabilizing, Congress expunged African American soldiers from the army. Congress had no intention of admitting freed black men into the army to fight in the unpopular War of 1812. Louisiana's governor made a direct appeal to President James Madison asking that his state's free black men be permitted to fight. In the face of an anticipated British invasion of Louisiana and in desperate need of soldiers, Madison relented. Hundreds of black soldiers fought valiantly under General Andrew Jackson in the Battle of New Orleans.

African Americans' efforts in Jackson's legendary stand, which took place at the end of the war, did little to influence those in command of federal defense policy. During the War of 1812, then, nearly all African Americans who wore uniforms served as sailors, not soldiers. The United States Navy consisted of a mere twenty ships at the war's beginning, but African Americans served in integrated crews on those ships. Black sailors also served on merchant marine vessels. By the middle of the war, one sixth of all Americans at sea were black. The British employed a significant number of black sailors as well, more than a few of whom had been impressed into serving the crown after their merchant marine vessels were defeated by British Navy ships.

The primary reason for the prevalence of African Americans at sea was that the work was unattractive to most white men. It was terribly arduous and dangerous to serve aboard square-rigged vessels powered by the wind. Sailors were required to go aloft to trim sails during heavy winds or seas. Food rations were at the subsistence level; disease and malnutrition were constant threats. Because conditions aboard sailing vessels were so abysmal, the navy and merchant marine captains did not have the luxury of turning away men deemed less desirable by employers on land. Alcoholics, petty criminals, and men who arrived on docks professing no history at all were among those who found themselves scaling ratlines and trading deferred pay for grog. African Americans, particularly former slaves like Crispus Attucks, found themselves welcomed aboard.

Unlike the navy, the U.S. Army remained all white. In 1820 the federal government affirmed its stance on military service when it announced, "No Negro or mulatto will be received as a recruit to the Army."[1] Yet even twenty years later, the American navy still employed so many black sailors that some seafaring Europeans believed that "all Americans were black."[2]

UNLIKE THE WAR OF 1812, the nature of the Civil War demanded that President Abraham Lincoln confront the issue of whether the United States would accept black citizens into its army. As Frederick Douglass wrote, "A war undertaken and brazenly carried on for the perpetual enslavement of colored men calls logically and loudly for colored men to help suppress it."[3] Three decades before Lincoln's first inauguration, Great Britain already had abolished slavery both in England and in the West Indies. France abolished slavery in its colonies in 1848. Conversely, one out of every seven Americans was a slave.

South Carolina seceded from the Union in December 1860. Within three months Alabama, Arkansas, Florida, Georgia, Louisiana, Mississippi, North Carolina, Tennessee, Texas, and Virginia had joined South Carolina in establishing the Confederate States of America. Their president was Mississippian Jefferson Davis and their vice president was Georgian Alexander H. Stephens, who proclaimed in his "Cornerstone Speech" that the Confederate States of America's "corner-stone rests upon the great truth that the negro is not equal to the white man; that slavery—subordination to the superior race—is his natural and normal condition. This, our new government, is the first, in the history of the world, based upon this great physical, philosophical, and moral truth."[4]

Preserving slavery was the reason the South seceded from the Union. The sociologist James W. Loewen notes that "the North did not go to war to end slavery, it went to war to hold the country together and only gradually did it become anti-slavery—but slavery is why the South seceded."[5] President Lincoln himself acknowledged "that slavery is the root of the rebellion, or at least its *sine qua non*. The ambition of politicians may have instigated them to act, but they would have been impotent without slavery as their instrument."[6]

Due in part to his spiritual devotion to the Union and in part to the political necessities of raising an army from a population of skeptical immigrants and citizens of slaveholding border states, Lincoln insisted that the war was being waged not to end slavery but solely to preserve the Union. In an 1862 letter to the abolitionist editor of the *New York Tribune*, Horace Greeley, the president wrote, "I would save the Union. I would save it the shortest way under the Constitution." Even as he considered emancipating all slaves owned in the South, Lincoln emphasized his own ambivalence toward abolition. "If I could save the Union without freeing *any* slave I would do it, and if I could save it by freeing *all* the slaves I would do it; and if I could save it by freeing some and leaving others alone I would also do that." He insisted, "What I do about slavery, and the colored race, I do because I believe it helps the Union."[7]

THE UNION ARMY INITIALLY REFUSED to employ African Americans. Beginning in the summer of 1861, Lincoln permitted African Americans to work as laborers, blacksmiths, scouts, and spies. The president refused to allow black men to become soldiers because he feared doing so would turn the border states against the Union. Lincoln also thought little of African Americans' fighting ability and feared that arming African Americans would hinder more than help the Union's military cause. "I am not so sure we could do much with the blacks," he remarked frankly. "If we were to arm them, I fear that in a few weeks the arms would be in the hands of the rebels; and indeed thus far we have not had arms enough to equip our white troops."[8] He remained concerned about the "fifty thousand bayonets in the Union armies from the Border Slave States" that likely would "go over to the rebels" if the Union Army employed black soldiers to kill white rebels in the South.[9] "Unless some new and more pressing emergency arises," the president professed no desire to arm African Americans in the war to save the nation.[10]

That emergency arose in the form of the unanticipated talent and tenacity of the Confederate Army. White Northerners, who outnumbered white Southerners nineteen million to eight million, expected to make quick work of the rebellion. Southerners rich and poor alike rallied to the Confederacy's cause and proved to be fearsome warriors. Many prominent Southerners' loyalty was not to their newly formed nation but to the states of their birth and fortune. General Robert E. Lee, whose expansive Virginia estate one day would become Arlington National Cemetery, lamented, "If I owned the four million slaves of the South I would sacrifice them all to the Union. But how could I draw my sword against Virginia?"[11] The United States Army suffered a series of surprising and devastating losses. President Lincoln, his generals, and Congress reexamined their opposition to employing black troops.

On January 1, 1863, shortly after General Lee's army invaded the North at Antietam, Maryland, President Lincoln signed the Emancipation Proclamation. There were four million slaves in the South. With so many white men away from their hometowns to fight the war, the Confederate government had to guard against the realistic possibility of a massive and bloody slave rebellion. In the proclamation the president stated: "I further declare and make known that such persons of suitable condition will be received into the armed service of the United States to garrison forts, positions, stations, and other places, and to man vessels of all sorts, in said service."

The Emancipation Proclamation had a much greater effect on the American military than it had on slavery, because it freed only those slaves owned in the Confederacy. The slave owners subject to the proclamation ignored it, because, from their perspective, it was issued by the leader of a foreign country. Union Army officials, however, enacted the new policy of recruiting African Americans. One year after Lincoln issued the Emancipation Proclamation, fifty thousand ex-slaves were fighting in the Union Army.

President Lincoln's concern for how white border state residents would react to armed African American Union soldiers proved well founded. One of Lincoln's former colleagues in Congress tried to persuade him not to allow black Union troops in Maryland. "The advent of troops of that complexion will necessarily stir up deep feeling," John W. Crisfield wrote in a letter to Lincoln, "and no one can tell to what result it may lead." White Marylanders might be compelled to express their "disgust . . . which may produce serious consequences."[12] General Ambrose Burnside objected to the War Department's plan to recruit black soldiers in Kentucky. When the War Department ignored Burnside and established a recruiting station in Paducah, Kentucky's governor, Thomas E. Bramlette, personally visited the White House to register his protest against the presence of black Union soldiers in his state.

Black men joined America's armed forces despite this resistance. Frederick Douglass used his considerable influence to swell the ranks of black volunteers. He encouraged African Americans by prophesying a time "when the war is over, the country saved, peace established and the black man's rights are secured."[13] So many African Americans sought to enlist that, just five months after the Emancipation Proclamation, the War Department established the Bureau of Colored Troops to manage "all matters relating to the organization of Colored Troops."[14]

The army chose Captain Thomas Wentworth Higginson of the Fifty-first Massachusetts Militia to command the first regiment of black soldiers. Higginson was a prominent Boston abolitionist who had helped fund John Brown's raid at Harpers Ferry. His regiment, the First South Carolina Volunteers, was based in Beaufort, South Carolina, a place quite foreign to a Boston Brahmin. Higginson also served as a Unitarian minister and reveled in the fact that, as he described it, "the whole Southern coast at this moment trembles at . . . the camp of a regiment of freed slaves."[15] Higginson was promoted to colonel upon taking command of the hundreds of soldiers who comprised the First South Carolina Volunteers. The new commander recorded in his journal, "Already I am growing used to the experience, at first so novel, of living among five hundred men, and scarce a white face to be seen—of seeing them go through all their daily processes, eating frolicking, talking, just as if they were white."[16]

Black men served admirably after the federal government permitted them to bear arms and fight for their country, albeit segregated into units such as the Massachusetts Fifty-fourth Regiment, commanded by Colonel Robert Gould Shaw. More than 179,000 African Americans joined the Union Army and Navy. Black soldiers and sailors accounted for 20 percent of the Union's casualties.[17] One in twelve Union soldiers was an African American. When the Union defeated the Confederacy, forty thousand black soldiers lay dead; tens of thousands more were wounded.

As Reconstruction commenced in the defeated Southern states, America's black citizens, so many of whom had fought to save the Union, looked forward to living in a nation made better by their sacrifice. White abolitionists likewise celebrated African Americans' wartime service. Reflecting on the war, Colonel Higginson asserted, "Till the blacks were armed, there was no guaranty of their freedom. It was their demeanor under arms that shamed the nation into recognizing them as men."[18]

SENATOR HENRY WILSON of Massachusetts served as chairman of the Senate's Committee on Military Affairs during and after the Civil War. From his chair in the center of the dais, the abolitionist Bostonian, who had spent his childhood as an indentured servant and as an old man would die just steps from the Senate floor, wielded considerable influence in favor of the African American soldiers and veterans. This was but an extension of what Wilson viewed as his life's work: to abolish slavery in the United States. In no small part because of his extraordinarily difficult childhood as a cobbler's apprentice, the portly, unpretentious senator enjoyed a reputation for honesty and moral conviction. Almost immediately after the Civil War, Wilson began working to pass legislation that would establish in the army permanent infantry, artillery, and cavalry regiments for black soldiers. These units would be segregated from white regiments and, in most cases, commanded by white officers.

Senior army officials lobbied against the bill, contending that black men were not intelligent enough to work in artillery units. But Senator Wilson and his Republican colleagues defeated this opposition and in 1866 established four black infantry regiments and two black cavalry

regiments. Three years later, when the army was reorganized, it collapsed the four infantry regiments into two, the twenty-fourth Infantry
(Colored) and the twenty-fifth Infantry (Colored). The two cavalry
regiments remained intact.

THE MEN OF THE NINTH and Tenth Cavalries spent years waging
horseback warfare against the Cheyenne, Apache, and members of other
American Indian tribes in the Southwest. Commanded by white officers, the soldiers faced hostile acts of racism at posts near cities and com-
mercial centers across the country. For example, in 1867 the commander
of Fort Leavenworth ordered that no member of the Tenth Cavalry
could come within ten feet of a white soldier. Invariably the black soldiers were ordered to leave these better-equipped camps and reassigned
to the Southwest frontier. By the early 1870s 20 percent of the nation's
cavalry soldiers in Texas and the Indian Territories were black men.

The men's blessing and curse was that they were stationed at posts in
the distant Southwest, far from the basic comforts of more populated
forts but also far from the violent oppression that African Americans
faced in more populated regions. Cavalry soldiers fought on the front
lines of America's westward expansion. Many of them became sick from
constant exposure to the elements. Thirst was a relentless threat to their
lives in the desert. Their rations were of dangerously poor quality, with
such basic victuals as flour being reserved for the officers.

The Ninth and Tenth Cavalries sometimes fought alongside white
soldiers. That the army tended to treat African American soldiers more
like the enemy Indians than like their fellow white soldiers did not escape the men. One private stationed near Wounded Knee in the South
Dakota Badlands wrote what became a popular verse, memorized by his
fellow soldiers:

> *The rest have gone home, To meet the blizzard's wintry blast.*
> *The Ninth, the willing Ninth, Is camped here till the last.*
> *We were the first to come, Will be the last to leave.*
> *Why are we compelled to stay, Why this reward receive?*
> *In warm barracks, Our recent comrades take their ease,*
> *While we poor devils, And the Sioux, are left to freeze.*[19]

Terrible though the conditions of their service were, the Ninth and Tenth Cavalry soldiers remained largely insulated from the racial violence that had taken hold of the nation by the turn of the century. The black troops were subject to racial injustice, particularly when local law enforcement authorities became involved in disputes with locals, but by and large the men enjoyed a certain dignity in the West. Although members of the Ninth and Tenth Cavalries were issued worn-out horses to ride, their missions were largely indistinguishable from those of white mounted troops. "I had three horses in the cavalry," recalled the Tenth Cavalry soldier Madison Bruin, who served in Texas in the 1870s. "The first one played out, the next one was shot down on campaign and one was condemned."[20]

On account of their woolly hair and tough mien, their Indian adversaries called them buffalo soldiers. One white officer's wife, living with her husband in the Indian Territory, remarked after seeing the men in action, "These 'Buffalo Soldiers' are active, intelligent, and resolute men; are perfectly willing to fight the Indians, whenever they may be called upon to do so, and appear to me to be rather superior to the average of white men recruited in time of peace."[21]

WHILE THE BUFFALO SOLDIERS fought on the frontier, African Americans serving in the United States Navy stood on the front lines of America's descent into rigid segregation. During the late nineteenth and early twentieth centuries, whites united across ethnic and religious lines to make America a Jim Crow nation. African Americans were stripped of the political and economic gains for which they had fought during and after the Civil War. In contrast to the navy's earlier practice of having sailors work and live in integrated quarters aboard ships, a new breed of naval officers began segregating sailors near the end of the nineteenth century.

The navy had never accepted black officers. In the 1890s its senior officials began to fear, perhaps justifiably as states across the Union enacted segregation laws, that lower-ranking white sailors would not take orders from black senior enlisted men. The navy subsequently began withholding promotions from black sailors. Within a few years, African American sailors were relegated to the navy's lowest ranks with no prospect of promotion.

The dawn of the twentieth century ushered in steam as the navy's primary means of moving ships. No longer would ships arrive days late into port on account of poor winds. Since the 1830s steam had been used as auxiliary power aboard sailing vessels, but the navy's acceptance of steam as its preferred means of power changed both the military branch and the type of man it sought to recruit. With coal- and fire-powered steam machinery powering the ships, a recruit's seafaring experience mattered little. Knowing how to go aloft, trim sails, or tar wood became irrelevant. The early twentieth century's new white recruits, who came of age during the years after the Supreme Court's *Plessy v. Ferguson* decision declared segregation to be constitutional, shared a virulent disdain for the notion of working alongside black Americans. They had grown up in a harshly segregated nation.

On December 16, 1907, President Theodore Roosevelt sent sixteen battleships to circumnavigate the globe as a display of America's seapower. The ships were painted white and christened the Great White Fleet. They would travel forty-three thousand miles in fourteen months, making port calls on six continents.

Among the fourteen thousand sailors aboard were African American enlisted men, who, regardless of their rank or specialty, were reassigned to mess and steward duty. They were permitted only to cook and serve food for white sailors. Ten years before America's entry into World War I, this was the U.S. Navy. It now resembled the army that had segregated black servicemen since the Revolutionary War.

3

THE ONLY REAL NEUTRAL

IN THE YEARS BEFORE America entered the Great War, the battles in Europe concerned African Americans much less than the violent repression they suffered at home. Lynching had been a national scourge since the Civil War, and the horrid murders increased in number and violence in the new century. From 1914 through 1916, white mobs lynched 126 black Americans, often in spectacularly gruesome fashion. The influential writer and activist James Weldon Johnson, who later became a national leader of the NAACP, proclaimed in 1915 that America was "a nation of hypocrites" whose citizens bemoaned the wartime destruction of "old churches in Europe" while ignoring rampant lynching in Southern states.[1] Johnson was far from alone in decrying the disparate amounts of attention paid to atrocities committed by German troops in Europe and those committed by mobs in the American South. The editorial board of the *Chicago Defender* wrote that black Americans in the South had more legitimate reason to take up arms against their domestic oppressors than against Europeans. "Truly not as much provocation have they as we who, without rhyme or reason, are lynched and mutilated in the most barbaric way, simply because we differ in color from our persecutors, who are in the majority." The editors anticipated the day "when the colored people do come to their senses, and in holding their ground find it necessary to mow down with the shotgun these defiers of law and order."[2]

Charged as its language was, the *Defender* made a crucial point in noting the lynch mobs' open defiance of the constitutional court system. By 1914, lynching was so common across the South that it directly challenged the criminal justice systems of ten Southern states. The practice had morphed from an extrajudicial act of barbarism into an entirely separate system of judgment, both of the accused criminal and of the justice system that the mob believed unfit or unwilling to deal rightly with him. Groups of armed white men routinely "stormed" Southern jailhouses to seize the prisoners they sought. A law-enforcement official sometimes claimed that he tried to protect the prisoner but was overpowered by the mob. This specious defense often belied the fact that the officers were sympathetic to the mob's aims. In February 1915, an officer in Vicksburg, Mississippi, offered what one writer called "the same old story" of having been "overpowered" by a group of armed men intent on seizing his prisoner. The prisoner, an African American man accused of stealing a cow, was lynched the same day that a white boy was released after having stabbed to death a black boy.[3]

A few months later, during the summer of 1915, twelve miles outside Dekalb, Mississippi, a black farmhand was charged with stealing cottonseed; he was kidnapped, beaten, and lynched.[4] Two weeks later, two black men were lynched near Hawkinsville, Georgia.[5] In Forrest City, Arkansas, an enraged group of white men "stormed the county jail" and, according to the *Washington Post*, seized a black man named William Patrick. They hanged him from a telephone pole.[6] A mob in Henderson, Kentucky, kidnapped twenty-three-year-old Ellis Buckner from his jail cell on a cold December Saturday night. Buckner was accused of assault. The mob dragged him into town and lynched him.[7]

Lynching had become a public and, among Southern whites, socially accepted form of punishment. Lynchings sometimes resembled official, state-performed executions. On August 7, 1915, exactly three months after Germany's attack on the *Lusitania*, nine African American men were hanged across the South. Seven were hanged by their governments and two were lynched. Alabama executed four men as a squadron of armed state militiamen held back a crowd screaming for the convicts to be burned instead of hanged. After the men had been hanged, the crowd unsuccessfully demanded that their bodies be turned over for burning.[8]

In Fresno, Mississippi, women and children mixed in the crowd of five thousand gathered to watch two of the three hangings scheduled to take place that day in the state. Spectators traveled from nearby towns to witness the executions. When the executioner sprung open the trap doors beneath the bound feet of Peter Bolen and Jim Scales, the crowd began singing the religious hymn "There Is a Land of Pure Delight." In Oklahoma and Florida, two black men were lynched by whites whom witnesses described as being "armed to the teeth."[9] Journalists reported that the Shawnee, Oklahoma, lynching of Ed Berry was "one of the most orderly lynchings in the history of the state."[10] Finally, the *Washington Post* reported that, as of evening press time, "a mob of 500 men were closing in on a colored man near Liberty, Mo." The man was accused of attacking a farmer's wife, and "a lynching is almost certain there."[11]

IN THIS ATMOSPHERE of near lawlessness, African Americans paid little attention to the war raging in Europe. They were largely unconcerned with the state of freedom and democracy in foreign countries while their own government denied them their rights as citizens. Of all Americans, it was perhaps easiest for black citizens to comply with the request made by President Wilson in his 1914 declaration of neutrality. Wilson asked all Americans to "act and speak in the true spirit of neutrality, which is the spirit of impartiality and fairness and friendliness to all concerned."[12] Most white Americans could trace their lineage or heritage back to a European nation that, in some direct way, was affected by the ongoing war. President Wilson acknowledged in his declaration, "The people of the United States are drawn from many nations, and chiefly from the nations now at war. It is natural and inevitable that there should be the utmost variety of sympathy and desire among them with regard to the issues and circumstances of the conflict. Some will wish one nation, others another, to succeed in the momentous struggle. It will be easy to excite passion and difficult to allay it."[13] Many white Americans ignored the president's admonition. Among white American immigrants and their descendants, tempers flared in the months before America entered the war.

Black Americans' battles lay at home, in a nation that seemed increasingly hostile to their very presence. As millions of black Southerners migrated to Northern cities, the North became, in the words of one black Minnesotan, "just as prejudiced as the South, only not so frank and open with its vituperations."[14] While the Wilson administration exchanged increasingly tense messages with the German imperial government, it was rather easy for African Americans to adhere to the president's request to remain "neutral in fact as well as in name."

Members of the *Baltimore Sun*'s editorial board wrote, "The Afro-American is the only hyphenate, we believe, who has not been suspected of divided allegiance."[15] The Washington attorney Thomas L. Jones summarized the popular thinking best when he remarked to a judge and reporter in his office, "The only real neutral in this country is the colored man."[16]

REPORT TO GOD THE REASON WHY

O N APRIL 2, 1917, after Germany announced unrestricted submarine warfare against any and all vessels approaching ports in Great
Britain, Ireland, western Europe, and many ports in the Mediterranean
Sea, President Wilson stood before a joint session of Congress to request
a declaration of war against the German government. "The present German submarine warfare against commerce," the president declared, "is a
warfare against mankind. It is a war against all nations. American ships
have been sunk, American lives taken . . ." Wilson conceded that "armed
neutrality, it now appears, is impracticable."[1] He asked Congress to declare war against Germany. After a swift vote in both houses, Congress
issued a joint resolution stating "that the state of war between the United
States and the Imperial German Government which has been thrust upon
the United States is hereby formally declared."[2]

No doubt in part because of Wilson's repeated appeals for neutrality,
Americans widely believed that Germany had forced them into joining
the war. America's quarrel, as articulated by President Wilson, was not
with the German people, but rather with the German imperial government. The typically staid editorial board of the *Washington Post* proclaimed, "No more astounding and stupefying blow has fallen upon
Germany than the drawing of the sword by America. It is the word of
doom." The *Post* concluded, "The manhood of this country is ready.

The materials are at hand . . . The rapidity with which this nation puts on its armor and fashions its war-gear will astonish the world."[3]

ACROSS THE NATION, African Americans publicly affirmed their loyalty to the United States. The Baltimore County Colored Teachers' Association unanimously passed a resolution professing "loyalty to every effort being made by President Wilson in the war with Germany."[4] That same day in Annapolis, Maryland, African American residents unanimously adopted a resolution pledging their support to the nation's war effort.[5] In Indianapolis, black men demanded the right to fight for their country, and in Minneapolis and St. Paul, more than one hundred men joined a military company established by veterans of the Spanish-American War. Three hundred African American residents of Norfolk, Virginia, attended a meeting to swear their loyalty to the flag. African American citizens in Louisiana, Mississippi, and Georgia likewise swore their allegiance to the country of their birth. Black St. Louis residents observed "Loyalty Day," and more than 2,500 African Americans in Tampa attended a mass meeting to declare their fidelity to the Stars and Stripes.[6] The leader of the Colored Patriots' Defense League asserted that "nothing must be preached but undiluted Americanism" as he called on black Americans to "redeclare allegiance to the United States."[7] The dean of Morgan College in Baltimore proclaimed at an NAACP rally that "America's least privileged and most persecuted class proves to be in a critical time its most dependable citizenship."[8]

Expressions of loyalty soon gave way to more direct appeals to the government to raise companies of black soldiers. At a rally in Kingston, North Carolina, a prominent black businessman claimed that black men were telling the president, "Call us, arm us, give us a place at the front and we will make America feel proud of her colored citizens or report to God the reason why." Men in churches from New Bedford, Massachusetts, to Atlanta, Georgia, demanded the right to fight.[9] More than one hundred men gathered at the Colored YMCA on Twelfth Street in Washington, D.C., to offer their services to help the Wilson administration mobilize black soldiers.[10]

The governor of Virginia told Secretary of War Newton Baker how Benjamin Braxton, a black Norfolk resident, had committed himself to raising an entire regiment of black men to fight against the Germans. Braxton declared that his people "never have and never will be traitors to Old Glory."[11] Braxton began recruiting soldiers for the regiment after hearing a rumor that was gaining traction nationwide: German undercover agents had invaded the Southern states and were attempting to incite Southern black citizens to commit acts of disloyalty. Newspapers published reports of these German "evil counselors" preying upon African Americans' "bitterness."[12] The future executive director of the NAACP, Walter White, explained that the kaiser's master plan in the South, according to the "wild rumors," was to incite black men's anger over lynching and state-sponsored racism and, once enough white sons of the South had shipped out to war, lead the men to "rise up and massacre white people in their beds." The stories gained enough credence that white army recruitment officers began refusing to enlist black men who were light-skinned enough to be mistaken for white, because the officers believed that the kaiser's agents would use the white-appearing black men to lead the uprisings.[13]

Such fanciful stories sparked African Americans to redouble their public claims of undivided loyalty and to call more forcefully for black men to be granted the right to fight against the German enemies. Black leaders encouraged families to hang the American flag over their doors and to teach their children "to love and respect that flag."[14] The pastor of a prominent Baptist parish in Washington, D.C., offered the church as a recruiting station for African American soldiers, rousing his congregation with a spirited review of black soldiers' heroism in American wars dating back to the Revolution.[15] The city of Atlanta for the first time permitted African Americans to hold a meeting in the city auditorium, and local leaders there worked an enthusiastic crowd into patriotic cheers. In Boston, the National Equal Rights League issued a statement proclaiming its members' patriotism: "Deep is the resentment against enforced segregation by city, state or the federal government whether in the civil or military service. But we have no thought of taking up arms against this our country."[16] The most prominent endorsement of African Americans' allegiance in the wake of reports about Germans allegedly inciting disloyalty came from former president William Howard Taft, who, at the all-black Hampton Institute's 1917 commencement exercises, called any questioning of black Americans' loyalty "a joke" because "loyalty . . . has always characterized" their relationship to the country.[17]

In July 1918, W.E.B. DuBois, editor of the NAACP's widely read magazine the *Crisis*, issued perhaps the most eloquent call to African Americans' collective sense of patriotism. About the Great War, DuBois wrote:

> We the colored race have no ordinary interest in the outcome. That which the German power represents today spells death to the aspirations of Negroes and all darker races for equality, freedom and democracy. Let us not hesitate. Let us, while this war lasts, forget our special grievances and close our ranks shoulder to shoulder with our white fellow citizens and the allied nations that are fighting for democracy. We make no ordinary sacrifice, but we make it gladly and willingly, with our eyes lifted to the hills.[18]

Historians at times have exaggerated the influence of DuBois's spirited call. As the previous examples indicate, by the summer of 1918, when DuBois published his "Close Ranks" article, African Americans already had expressed strong support for the nation's war effort. Angry as they were with the Wilson administration's indifference to their plight, African Americans had communally decided to stand with their fellow citizens when Congress declared war on Germany. More than a year before DuBois urged African Americans to "close our ranks shoulder to shoulder with our white fellow citizens," Hampton Institute had sent a letter to its alumni stating, "We are all Americans together and must stand shoulder to shoulder in this crisis."[19]

By the summer of 1918, African Americans were fully immersed in the domestic wartime atmosphere. Black Chicagoans flocked to the Pickford Theater to see a show offered for the "First Time on the South Side, Direct from The Loop." For twenty cents (children only ten cents), adults enjoyed *The Kaiser, the Beast of Berlin*, a propagandistic production exploring "the dastardly deviltry of the Kaiser's hosts."[20] Colonel Roscoe Conkling Simmons, a political powerbroker who was as influential among the black working class as he was in the national Republican

Party, wrote, "Behind Woodrow Wilson is an undivided and indivisible nation, all races one, all colors blended, all hopes beating in one time . . ."[21]

Within weeks of Congress's declaring war against Germany, black men across the nation resolved to join the military. Whether and to what extent the military would accept African American volunteers was a question the War Department soon had to answer. Commenting on white Americans' aversion to seeing black Americans in military uniforms while being quite accustomed to seeing them in other uniforms, Langston Hughes wrote, "We are elevator boys, janitors, red caps, maids—a race in uniform."[22]

THE SELECTIVE SERVICE ACT became effective on May 18, 1917. Every able-bodied man between the ages of twenty-one and thirty-one was required to register for the draft.[23] The law made no reference to race, meaning that African American soldiers would not be limited by law to serving in menial labor positions. They would be trained and called upon to fight. Congressman Julius Kahn, a California Republican, made no secret that this was an express purpose of the law. Black soldiers would "be trained in separate units," he explained to reporters, "but they would be called to arms exactly the same as would white citizens. There is no reason why they should not be called to service. Nobody questions that they make good soldiers."[24] A retired army lieutenant colonel, a Southerner, agreed, writing in a Virginia newspaper, "The colored soldier is not a menace. He is an asset. He has won golden opinions in many communities."[25]

Southern congressmen opposed the law, but not primarily because they believed that African Americans made poor soldiers. Rather, Southern members opposed what the race-neutral law necessitated: the training of thousands of Southern black men in the art of warfare. Segregationists' concerns were almost identical to those expressed by slaveholders generations earlier. One South Carolina congressman spoke on behalf of the Southern delegation when he avowed, "We of the South cannot stand for inclusion of Negroes in the [draft]. It would bring down upon the districts where Negroes far exceed the whites in number a danger far greater than any foreign foe . . . This would accomplish the very thing which the South has always fought against: the placing of arms in the hands of a large number of Negroes and the training of them to work together in organized units."[26]

The military's highest-ranking officers accepted Southern politicians' intransigence on the issue, even as they acknowledged that it stymied their ability to raise a larger fighting force. A few months before he was promoted to serve as the army chief of staff, Major General Tasker H. Bliss accurately summarized the predicament: "At this moment at the snap of a finger we could recruit all of our colored regiments to war strength and plenty more." The army could do so, however, only with agreement from the Southern congressional delegation, which was loath to agree to a plan whereby, by the end of the war, most black men in the South "will have been trained to arms."[27]

Although they did not train as many black recruits as they could have absent Southern opposition, War Department officials did disregard Southern resistance to black enlistees training at camps in the South. The department announced that black recruits would report to each one of the sixteen training camps located in states from Massachusetts to Georgia. Southern politicians urged that black men from Northern states, who would be foreign to the ways of the rigidly segregated South and therefore might cause trouble there, should be trained at camps in Northern states, but War Department officials decided at an August 1917 meeting that granting such a request was impracticable.[28] Black recruits would train at all American camps. The War Department also decided that proper training during the winter months could best be obtained in the Southern states, whose congressional representatives relented, stating that black soldiers "will be welcomed if they are well disciplined."[29]

Any gratification African Americans might have felt with the War Department's decision was tempered swiftly by the announcement that "every effort will be made" by the army to keep white and black recruits from training together at the camps.[30] An integrated delegation of college educators met with Secretary of War Baker to register their protest against the decision, but the secretary told them that the training camps would remain segregated. He then issued an official statement: "The rule of the regular Army in the matter of training of colored troops, which is that they be trained in separate organizations, will be adhered to."[31] In order to make the policy most effective, the War Department issued the following edict to all district draft boards: "Hereafter the notation 'white' or 'colored' will be made opposite the name of any person certified [for military service]."[32]

Ignoring Southern opposition, African American men registered and prepared to serve in the armed forces. Because the marines refused to accept black registrants and the navy restricted black sailors to mess duty, most African Americans registered for the army. They stood in lines to sign the war registry. In all, two million black men registered for the draft. Of those, 367,410 served in uniform, accounting for 13 percent of all American draftees.[33]

Race-based selectivity pervaded some draft boards in the South. Despite Southern opposition to African Americans serving in any combat capacity, the leaders of many communities viewed the draft as a means to decrease significantly the number of young black men in their counties. Draft boards in these communities typically required African American registrants to tear off a corner of their registration forms so they could be identified easily during selection rounds.[34] The large-scale result was that black men were drafted into the military in disproportionately high numbers. Those with legitimate claims to exemption were drafted into army labor battalions. South Carolina's draft rolls perplexed War Department officials because, although whites outnumbered black citizens in the state, six thousand more blacks than whites registered. The War Department dismissed the draft board members in Fulton County, Georgia, for meting out "unwarranted exemptions and discharges." Out of 815 white men reviewed by the board, 526 were exempted. The same board exempted just 6 of the 202 black registrants.[35]

These anomalies aside, the total number of men who registered in just a few weeks greatly pleased Secretary of War Newton Baker, who called it "a spectacular demonstration" of national unity.[36] About black registrants' answering the call of duty, one army general wrote, "His race furnished its quota, and uncomplainingly, yes, cheerfully. History, indeed, will be unable to record the fullness of his spirit in the war, for the reason that opportunities were not opened to him to the same extent as to the whites. But enough can be gathered from the records to show that he was filled with the same feeling of patriotism, the same martial spirit that fired his white fellow citizen in the cause for world freedom."[37]

Of course, not everyone joined in praise of the swelling draft rolls. In Washington, D.C., a thirty-year-old black man named Reuben Burke was enjoying a morning stroll through the city when he happened upon a long line of African Americans waiting to register for the draft. Burke appeared disgusted. "Go on ahead, you slaves!" he yelled, and promptly was arrested. Within a half hour, Burke was in Judge Mullowney's court-room. "I was only funning," Burke explained. "I'm for my country and I'm going to enlist." The judge fined Burke one dollar per word and, upon learning that Burke did not have five dollars, sent the morning stroller to jail.[38]

Tragedy and Triumph:
Houston and Des Moines

Southern politicians' unease with African Americans from Northern states being sent to training camps in the South proved well founded. The self-assured manner in which many urban black men carried themselves conflicted with the mores of the harshly segregated South. On July 28, 1917, 654 members of the Third Battalion of the Twenty-fourth Infantry arrived at Camp Logan in Houston, Texas. The Twenty-fourth Infantry had undergone a radical transformation in the weeks before it was ordered to Camp Logan. Most of the unit's senior noncommissioned officers had been selected to attend the Colored Officer's Training Camp at Fort Des Moines, Iowa. Less experienced NCOs now led the men of the Twenty-fourth, whose junior enlisted ranks were teeming with green recruits.[1] The few weeks when the men were stationed at Camp Logan would affect the military for decades to come.

In Houston, the soldiers were forced to sit in the rear of streetcars and buses and to drink from water fountains marked by COLORED signs, and were barred from entering some public facilities. They endured verbal assaults from white residents who resented the soldiers' presence at Camp Logan. Houston's white population was infuriated by the troops' ill-concealed disdain for segregation. Whenever they left Camp Logan, the men said they were "treated like dogs." The soldiers chafed at the racism to which they were subjected. Some of them brazenly ignored the COLORED signs on streetcars and sat in the front seats, prompting at least one police officer to announce to all passengers that he might "have to kill" a soldier on the car. One white salesman diplomatically remarked of the recruits, "They sure have things their own way."[2]

Most significant, soldiers of the Twenty-fourth Infantry were repeatedly brutalized by Houston's police officers. Soldiers complained to their white commanding officer, Major Kneeland Snow, that nearly every encounter with police officers resulted in getting "their heads beat up."[3] The men's sense of helplessness soon hardened to rage.

Early in the afternoon of August 23, 1917, a policeman with a reputation for viciousness, Lee Sparks, arrested a black housewife and mother of five who had complained about police habitually using excessive force against suspects in her neighborhood. "You all goddamn nigger bitches," Sparks yelled at the woman as he and his partner dragged her down the street; "since these goddamn sons of bitches nigger soldiers came here, you are trying to take the town!" An African American soldier intervened and offered to pay whatever fine the woman owed if the officers agreed to release her. Sparks severely beat the soldier with his gun before arresting him and hauling both him and the woman to jail. "I wasn't going to wrestle with a big nigger like that," Sparks later explained. "I hit him until he got his heart right."[4]

Corporal Charles Baltimore went to the jail to inquire about the incident. Sparks struck Baltimore on the head, fired his gun into the air, and arrested Baltimore as well. By the time news of the arrests reached Camp Logan at around three P.M, the story had been embellished such that most soldiers believed Sparks had killed Baltimore—until Baltimore was released from jail and returned to post. Still, the men talked loudly of revenge, of reclaiming their manhood.[5] They urged one another, "Let's go get the man that shot Baltimore."[6]

Major Snow realized that his men had reached the breaking point. He ordered all troops to remain on post until morning, and, knowing that some of the most irate soldiers might be tempted to disobey this order, he also ordered all the men to surrender their weapons. Two companies complied immediately, but the men of two other companies balked at the order. "Major, what are we going to do," one soldier asked Snow, "when they . . . beat us up like this?"[7]

Between six and eight o'clock in the evening, Snow and his officers demanded compliance with the order, but any hope of full compliance vanished shortly after eight, when some soldiers mistakenly reported that a white mob was approaching Camp Logan. A tall soldier named Frank Johnson went running through camp yelling, "Get your rifles, boys!"

Men who had surrendered their weapons retrieved them from the supply station and raided the ammunition depot. The group of more than one hundred low-ranking enlisted men fell in behind Sergeant Vida Henry, the widely respected acting first sergeant of Company I.[8]

The men marched four abreast out of Camp Logan and into Houston's Fourth Ward. As they made their way down the long road into town, they happened upon a white man driving his car. Sergeant Henry motioned for the man to stop the car. The man complied. Henry instructed him to get out of the car. The man refused. Every soldier standing in front of the car opened fire. They shot the man more than fifty times. He could be heard groaning as the soldiers marched past his car. The man died minutes later.[9]

Henry placed the corporals he trusted most at the front and rear of the formation. He ordered them to shoot dead any man who broke ranks. The marching men, by now in full mutiny, hollered, "We have a job to do; let's do it!" and "Stick by your race!"[10] They were disciplined, focused, and bloodthirsty. One soldier shot and killed a white woman's dog because it barked at the men as they passed by.[11] White residents later commented on how the men marched through the city "as orderly as they could be." The soldiers shot residents sitting on their porches, stabbed bystanders with bayonets, and shot at every police officer they saw. "On to victory!" they cried as they shot a man three times in the head.

With their organization and ruthless pursuit of revenge, the mob of black soldiers embodied Southern white Americans' worst fears. In two hours of mutiny, the soldiers killed fifteen whites and critically wounded twelve others. Among the wounded were a city detective shot in the knee and a young girl shot in her stomach.[12] An injured policeman later died.[13] Police officers returned fire, wounding several soldiers. Much of Houston resembled a war zone.

The mutineers began to disband shortly after ten o'clock. Some scattered into the woods and others dove into ditches and ravines. Some returned to Camp Logan. A few were welcomed to hide in the homes of black Houstonians. By then a mob of more than 250 armed white men was marching on Camp Logan to exact revenge on the Twenty-fourth Infantry—albeit on the soldiers who had opted to remain on post rather than join the mutiny. An Illinois National Guard unit of African American soldiers stationed in Houston succeeded in turning back the horde.

The day after the melee, district attorney John Crocker filed murder charges against thirty-four members of the Twenty-fourth Infantry. The army ordered the Twenty-fourth to vacate Camp Logan immediately and report to Columbus, New Mexico. The unit's six hundred soldiers were relieved of their weapons and placed under guard. Despite these unprecedented security precautions, many in the neighborhood nearest the camp fled their homes.

Hours later two children found the body of Sergeant Vida Henry near the railroad tracks. He apparently had shot himself through the head.[14] Several months later, after courts-martial, thirteen mutineers were executed and dozens of Twenty-fourth Infantry soldiers, some who took no part in the melee, were sentenced to long terms in military prisons.

Many Southern whites still seethed even after this harsh repudiation of the mutineers. They had warned the army not to send Northern African Americans to train at camps in Southern states. After the massacre, these Southerners made no distinction between Northern and Southern black soldiers. One Texas newspaper editorialized:

> It is not a time to talk about "fairness" to Negro troops that have caused no trouble. It is not a time to make observations to the effect that if these troops cannot be safely sent to the south, then the south is to blame. It is not time, in short, to go into subtleties of the race question. The COLD FACT IS THAT NEGRO TROOPS CANNOT SAFELY BE QUARTERED IN A SOUTHERN COMMUNITY. The War Department was wrong. Why not prevent further trouble by withdrawing all Negro troops from the south immediately?[15]

In the wake of the Houston mutiny, white Southerners were not alone in calling for black troops to be trained henceforth at camps in Northern states. The *New York Times* recommended this remedy, urging the government to show "no sign of leniency" toward the mutineers.[16] Members of the upper house of the Texas legislature introduced a resolution declaring that black soldiers in Texas cities had become "a serious menace to the safety and welfare of white citizens" and charging the state's congressional delegation to persuade the War Department to move the soldiers to another state. The governor of South Carolina registered his formal protest with the secretary of war regarding National Guard or army units of black soldiers being sent to train in his state.[17]

African Americans professed mixed emotions about the mutiny. "It is difficult for one of Negro blood," W.E.B. DuBois wrote, "to write of Houston."[18] The *Chicago Defender* noted that the Twenty-fourth Infantry's stellar reputation inspired many African Americans to extend to the soldiers the benefit of the doubt. "That they were goaded to the point of mutiny . . . by the taunts and insults of the prejudiced whites," the *Defender* editorialized, "is a fact admitted by those familiar with the conditions. That they were in the wrong, even under these conditions, to take the law in their own hands is also admitted. But we are all human."[19] The African American newspaper the *New York Age* contended that "quartering Negro troops in the South is equivalent to sending them into the enemy's country with the difference that they are forbidden to exercise the right of self-protection."[20]

While black editors studiously avoided voicing strong support for the Houston mutiny, the reaction among African Americans nationwide tended to be less measured. A woman in Iowa praised the "disciplined men" who "had stood the insults of these ruffian police and other Southern huns until they said 'That is enough.'"[21] Most famously, the Texan teacher Clara Threadgill-Dennis wrote a letter to the mutineers published in the November 24, 1917, edition of the *San Antonio Inquirer.* Threadgill-Dennis, the wife of a school principal, harkened back to the immediate genesis of the violence: a soldier had defended a black woman being attacked by a white policeman. She told the men of the Twenty-fourth Infantry to "rest assured that every [Negro] woman in all this land of ours . . . reveres you, she honors you." After expressing "regret that you mutinied," she wrote: "It is far better that you be shot for having tried to protect a Negro woman, than to have you die a natural death in the trenches of Europe, fighting to make the world safe for a democracy that you can't enjoy." For publishing Threadgill-Dennis's letter, G. W. Bouldin, the editor of the *San Antonio Inquirer*, was tried and convicted of violating the Espionage Act. Bouldin was sentenced to two years in the Leavenworth federal penitentiary for making "an unlawful attempt to cause insubordination."[22]

When the Eighth Illinois National Guard arrived in Houston for five months of training, the men took note of how white Houstonians, including police officers, appeared to fear them. The men of the Eighth Illinois appreciated what they believed the Twenty-fourth Infantry had done for them. Some of the National Guard troops, like the Twenty-fourth before them, refused to sit in the COLORED rear section of Houston's streetcars. The men newly stationed at Camp Logan enjoyed a measure of dignity. War Department officials, fearful of another outbreak of violence, transferred the unit out of Houston.[23]

JOEL E. SPINGARN was the thin, erudite son of a Jewish immigrant tobacco merchant. In 1911 he resigned his position as a comparative literature professor at Columbia University to devote his time and considerable inheritance full time to the two-year-old National Association for the Advancement of Colored People. From 1913 through 1919, Spingarn served as chairman of the executive committee of the NAACP.

Before America entered World War I, Spingarn joined the army as an intelligence officer. Ever the progressive Republican, he thought it undemocratic that the army provided fourteen officers' training camps for white officer candidates but none for black officer candidates. The Wilson administration's War Department excluded African Americans from attending the training camps. The inevitable result was the wholesale absence of black officers from the military. As chairman of the NAACP's board of directors, Spingarn was committed to eliminating segregation from American life. He spent a good deal of his life and money fighting against segregation and inequality.

Like most executives of the integrated NAACP, however, Spingarn also was a realist. He knew that the army would not allow black men to attend officers' training camp with whites. So, as the War Department official Emmett J. Scott recalled, "the next best thing seemed to be a separate camp."[24] Spingarn consulted Major General Leonard Wood, a former army chief of staff and future Republican presidential candidate, about the prospect of establishing a training camp for black officer candidates. Wood assured Spingarn that he would support such a camp if Spingarn could provide two hundred college-educated black men who wanted to become officers. With this assurance, Spingarn embarked on an extensive letter-writing, speaking, and lobbying campaign to persuade eligible candidates to commit to attending an officers' training camp created just for them.

Nothing Joel Spingarn did for the rest of his life wrought as much controversy or stoked as much anger as his effort to establish a training camp for black officer candidates. Even in the burst of patriotism that followed Congress's war declaration, Spingarn's proposal met widespread condemnation from African American leaders and editors. They were disappointed because Spingarn appeared to be compromising his long-held opposition to segregation.

"No one denies that we sorely need efficient military training for officers, privates and every citizen," the *Chicago Defender* editorialized, "but we do not want it, nor will we take it in a 'Jim Crow' way, if we never get it." Noting that a movement to raise exclusively Jewish regiments had been defeated by Jewish protests, the editors concluded, "If we are good enough to fight, we are good enough to receive the same preparatory training our white brothers receive. When a separate training camp is established for the Irish, German, Italian, Swede, and all other hyphenated Americans, then, and not till then, will we consider it our duty to support such an organization."[25]

"The camp is intended to fight segregation, not to encourage it," Spingarn insisted. "Colored men in a camp by themselves would all get a fair chance for promotion."[26] He traveled to universities and encouraged any college man interested in the camp to write him at 70 Fifth Avenue in New York City. "Colored men would make a serious mistake," he believed, "if they did not take advantage of ANY opportunity to serve as commissioned officers in the army during this great war."[27]

At Howard University in Washington, D.C., Spingarn found his most receptive audience. Howard's students, faculty, and administration swiftly rallied behind the prospect of a training camp for black officer candidates. They worked to gather support from their peers. By May 1, 1917, Howard students and their professors had raised enough money to dispatch a team of delegates to lobby students at other colleges. The young men correctly presumed that their tour would be more successful than Spingarn's. Before long the students organized themselves as the Central Committee of Negro College Men. Coordinating their efforts from an office in the basement of Howard's chapel, the committee obtained the signatures of more than fifteen hundred black college students committed to attending an officers' training camp.[28]

Spingarn excitedly presented the Howard petition to General Wood, who then helped Spingarn procure an audience with the secretary of war. Along with several professors who worked with the Central Committee of Negro College Men, Spingarn met in Washington with Secretary of War Baker.

Spingarn first asked Baker to open the existing officers' training camps to black candidates, well knowing his likely answer. Baker replied that that was simply out of the question. Spingarn and the professors then presented their proposal for a separate training camp for black officer candidates. The secretary was more amenable to this idea and agreed to introduce the idea to the General Staff. The Central Committee representatives then told Secretary Baker that if this were the only way to train a sizable number of black officer candidates, they could agree to the army's establishing a segregated part of one of the existing camps. Baker agreed to present that proposal to the General Staff as well. Before the men left, the secretary of war assured them that he personally opposed separating the races for military training but that, in his position, he could not seek to solve the race problem.

Spingarn left the meeting discouraged. He doubted that the War Department would act unless the White House or Congress compelled it to act. Woodrow Wilson's administration not only tolerated segregation; it encouraged and often mandated segregation throughout the federal government and in Washington, D.C. Spingarn and the Central Committee of Negro College Men turned to Congress.[29]

A group of committee students took the streetcar down Seventh Street and marched east to the Capitol, where they presented a small group of lawmakers with the signed petitions. The congressmen told the students that they were unaware African Americans were barred from officers' training camps.[30] In every congressman's office, the students left a card that read:

TRAINING CAMP FOR NEGRO OFFICERS

Our country faces the greatest crisis in its history; the Negro, as ever, loyal and patriotic, is anxious to do his full share in the defense and support of his country in its fight for democracy. The Negro welcomes the opportunity of contributing his full quota to the Federal army now being organized. He feels very strongly that these Negro troops should be officered by their own men. The following statement presents the facts upon which we base our request for an officers' reserve training camp for Negroes.

1   (a) Fourteen officers' training camps are to be opened on May 14, 1917, to provide officers for the new Federal Army.

(b) No officers are to be commissioned unless they receive training in one of these fourteen training camps;

(c) The War Department has stated that it is impracticable to admit Negroes to the fourteen established camps;

2   (a) The Negro is able to furnish his proportionate quota in this army.

(b) It seems just that the competent and intelligent Negroes should have the opportunity to lead these troops;

(c) One thousand Negro college students and graduates have already pledged themselves to enter such a training camp immediately;

(d) In addition, men in the medical profession desire to qualify for service in the Medical Corps, and there are other competent men ready to qualify for other specialized corps provided for;

(e) Record of Negro officers and troops warrant the provision for Negro officers to lead Negro troops.

decreed at a rally, "and return home to fight it out also in Tennessee, in Georgia and in every other southern state, then the 'Jim Crow' camp will not have been tolerated in vain."[40]

To those who denigrated the "Jim Crow camp," the Central Committee of Negro College Men retorted, "Let them talk. This camp is no more 'Jim Crow' than our newspapers, our churches, our schools. In fact, it is less 'Jim Crow' than our other institutions, for here the Government has assured us of exactly the same recognition, treatment, instruction and pay as men in any other camp get." The committee members dryly added that "no one who was not in the fight knows what a struggle we had to obtain the camp."[41]

On the Howard campus, one student recalled, "The news was heralded far and wide." Faculty, administrators, and students joyously shook hands and cheered in a celebration that made the entire campus "seem like an old-fashioned Methodist prayer meeting."[42] Through press releases and pamphlets, committee members immediately began rallying even more possible recruits. "Let us not mince matters; the race is on trial," their leaflets announced.[43]

The committee's continued publicity campaign swiftly reaped benefits. More professional men between the ages of twenty-five and forty— the army's preferred ages for officers at the time—committed to joining the camp. If accepted into training, they would be paid $75 per month; once commissioned, they would earn at least $145 per month. As June 15, 1917, the training start date, approached, the Central Committee of Negro College Men implored their brethren in the fervent language of salesmen-prophets. They charged all men who had come to be trained to commit to graduating successfully from the camp: "If we fail, our enemies will dub us COWARDS for all time; and we can never win our rightful place. But if we succeed—then eternal success; a mighty and far-reaching step forward; 1250 Colored Army officers leading Negro troops. Look to the future, brother, the vision is glorious!"[44]

ON OCTOBER 14, 1917, after four months of rigorous training, the United States Army commissioned 639 black officers. Witnesses reported that their commanding officer, as he delivered words of farewell, "showed visible signs of emotion."[45] With their heads shaved clean and their right hands raised, 106 captains, 329 first lieutenants, and 204 second lieutenants took the officers' oath administered by the War Department's chief of the division of training camps. Chosen mostly from the African American elite, the newly commissioned officers believed that their impending fight for freedom abroad was intrinsically connected to black Americans' struggle for full citizenship rights at home. Before boarding a ship bound for France, one captain poignantly acknowledged, "I am leaving today a wife and three children. As great as the sacrifice is, I shall be satisfied never to see America again, if my wife and children will share greater opportunities and enjoy more liberty than I now enjoy."[46]

6

THE TRAVELS OF EMMETT J. SCOTT
AND THE TRAVAILS OF
COLONEL CHARLES YOUNG

ALTHOUGH THEY OCCURRED less than two months apart in 1917, black soldiers' violent mutiny at Camp Logan in Texas in August and their triumph at the Fort Des Moines officers' training camp in Iowa in October were the bookends of what it meant for black servicemen to train during the Great War. Each group of servicemen sought to seize what they perceived to be a measure of manhood, a salve of dignity in an army that seemed determined to strip them of both. One soldier working seven days a week in a Virginia labor battalion noted that black recruits' "manpower was wanted but not their manhood."[1]

Neither Fort Des Moines's new officers nor Camp Logan's mutineers attained the respect they sought. The officers quickly learned that the army had no intention of treating them like commissioned officers. Lieutenant William Dyer, a medical officer traveling to the European battlefront aboard a converted passenger vessel, recalled, "Among the first orders issued were those barring Colored officers from the same toilets" and other facilities as white soldiers.[2] Further insults and physical harm at the hands of white American soldiers awaited the new officers overseas.

THE MAN CHARGED WITH BRIDGING the divide between black Americans' somber empathy for the Houston mutineers and their pride in Fort Des Moines's commissioned officers was Emmett J. Scott, a special assistant to the secretary of war. The mild-mannered, bespectacled Scott began his career as a journalist at the *Houston Post* in his home state of Texas. When the renowned educator and civil rights leader Booker T. Washington visited Houston in 1897 to give a speech on his work, Scott orchestrated the event. Washington was so impressed with how professionally the affair was conducted, with every last detail accounted for, that he persuaded Scott to come work for him at Tuskegee Institute. For the next eighteen years Emmett Scott worked selflessly as Washington's "confidential secretary." He advised the civil rights leader on policy and strategy while ministering to the growth and expansion of Tuskegee, which was swiftly becoming a premier bastion of higher education for African Americans. After Washington's death in 1915 but well before Scott obtained an office in the Department of War, at least one observer recognized Scott as "the most influential man in the race today."[3]

Woodrow Wilson was not the first president to call on the man widely known in black communities for being "painstaking and thorough, tactful and discreet, patient and well-poised."[4] Scott took a leave of absence in 1909 both from Booker T. Washington's employ and from his duties as an officer in the National Negro Business League when President William Howard Taft asked him to become one of three commissioners to travel to Liberia on behalf of the White House. President Taft charged Scott with documenting Liberia's financial, industrial, and agricultural resources.

On October 5, 1917, Secretary of War Newton Baker hired Scott away from his job as a senior administrator at Tuskegee Institute. Scott served as a special assistant to the secretary, advising Newton on the department's proposed initiatives most directly affecting black Americans. He described his role as that of a "confidential advisor in matters affecting the 10,000,000 Negroes of the United States and the part they are to play in connection with the present war."[5] Black leaders across the nation lauded the appointment. The *New York Age* editorial board contended that the newly created position and the exceptional man chosen for it were evidence of "a more liberal and sympathetic policy on the part of the national administration toward its twelve million loyal Negro citizens."[6] For twenty-one months the black Texan reported directly to the secretary of war and held the highest federal government appointment ever yet attained by an African American.

To millions of African Americans, Scott became the face of the War Department. At meetings and press conferences he explained the department's positions to them and then returned to the department to explain the people's views to department officials. He traveled extensively with Secretary Baker to inspect training camps, paying particular attention to the black soldiers' barracks at Camp Sheridan in Montgomery, Alabama, and at Camp Gordon in Atlanta, Georgia.[7] When a black soldier was buried at sea en route to Europe, a physician submitted to Scott a detailed report of the serviceman's death and burial ceremony, in which the flags of all the fleet's ships were flown at half mast, their engines checked, and taps sounded as the soldier's American flag–wrapped body was gently laid astern.[8]

To be sure, Scott was in many ways a talisman, a symbol adopted to deflect criticism from the Wilson administration, which consistently refused to use federal power to protect Southern black Americans from lynch mobs. Scott unsuccessfully sought to end numerous racist military practices, such as the army's stated reluctance to promote black men beyond the rank of captain.[9]

Emmett Scott knew that the government had hired him to assist in maintaining "an opinion and sentiment among colored people that will be behind the national government in its prosecution of the war," but he used his perch in the Wilson administration for much more.[10] He rallied the faithful at churches and delivered ceremonial speeches at hospital openings. He challenged African Americans to better themselves through education and to guard their good health by "maintain[ing] high standards in civilian life."[11]

At what reporters described as "a monster patriotic meeting at Carnegie Hall" sponsored by the Circle of Negro War Relief, Emmett Scott argued passionately against any war-ending truce that would return to Germany its colonies in Africa. "In truth, the hour has come, in my opinion," Scott told the huge crowd, "when the world should declare that not only are these colonies not to be turned back to Germany, but to no other nation as well." He grouped Germany's colonies with "other oppressed peoples" who should not be forced to live "under the iron heel of malignant oppressors." All present realized that this was not the typical wartime message delivered by a Wilson administration official. Whipping the New York City crowd into fevered applause, Scott asked his audience, "May not we, brothers by racial ties and blood sympathy of these African peoples, speak for them and call for their freedom, for their liberties, for the self-determination of their destiny?"[12]

With this speech Scott became one of the first American leaders to proclaim Pan-Africanism: Black Americans were not alone in their struggle against racist oppression, but rather were connected—were bonded "by racial ties and blood sympathy"—to the millions of Africans who suffered beneath similar government-sanctioned injustice. Surely most audience members knew that not all the "malignant oppressors" of which Scott spoke lived overseas.

By the middle of America's involvement in the war, there was no doubt that, as the *Baltimore Afro-American* reported, Scott "enjoyed the full measure of trust and confidence of the majority of colored Americans."[13] Black voters urged the administration to name Scott as an assistant secretary of war. Such a move, one Maryland man wrote, "would go a long way toward dispelling some of the doubts that the colored people have regarding the Wilson Administration."[14]

Scott's title remained special assistant to the secretary of war, however. War Department officials tellingly chose not to list him in the United States Blue Book and Official Register as a special assistant. Rather, the man who met regularly with the secretary of war and whose advice often reached the desk of the president of the United States was listed in the register as a "clerk."[15]

EMMETT SCOTT LOGGED THOUSANDS OF MILES traveling across the country to investigate reported instances of racial strife at military bases. He quickly learned that conditions for black servicemen varied widely. The most important factor in determining whether black soldiers on a base would be physically and verbally abused or treated humanely was the stance taken by the camp's commanding officer.

The commanding officer at Camp Upton in New York, General F. Franklin Bell, took it upon himself to quell an escalating dispute between a group of black soldiers and a regiment of white Southern servicemen who had attempted to remove the black soldiers from a recreational facility. General Bell dismissed all the soldiers except the Southern white officers. "Now, gentlemen," he said to them, "I am not what you would call 'a Negro lover.' I have seen service in Texas and elsewhere in the South." The fact was, however, that the Southern whites had "started this trouble. I don't want any explanation. These colored men did not start it. It doesn't matter how your men feel about these colored men. They are United States soldiers. They must and shall be treated as such. If you can't take care of your men, I can take care of you." If the Southerners instigated another racial incident, Bell assured them, "you will be tried, not by a Texas jury but by General Bell, and not one of you will leave this camp for overseas."[16] After Bell delivered this message to the white officers on his base, Camp Upton quickly developed what one contemporary historian called "the finest atmosphere surrounding Negro soldiers in America," which was due primarily to "the high stand and impartial attitude taken by the late Gen. Franklin Bell, commander."[17]

THE ARMY'S SEVERAL HUNDRED African American officers became frequent targets for white soldiers' resentment. After completing training at Fort Des Moines, the men were scattered to camps nationwide. White officers raised numerous logistical questions as the black officers arrived at the front gates: Where would the black officers live? Officers as a matter of custom and regulation eat, sleep, and enjoy recreation in facilities separate from enlisted servicemen. Black officers, however, were quartered apart from white officers. They could not work or eat with the white officers. After a few days in camp, they sometimes learned that they would be given no responsibilities at all.

According to military observers at the time, "one matter that constantly arose" was that many white enlisted men and officers refused to salute black officers.[18] When black officers arrived at Camp Funston in Kansas, less than 10 percent of the white soldiers saluted them.[19] White soldiers at Camp Grant in Illinois did not know if they were expected to salute black officers.[20] The resolution of such issues of racial strife depended largely on the base's commanding officer. At Camp Meade in Maryland, Major General Charles Ballou told black officers under his command that they should not be "hypersensitive" if white servicemen failed to salute them.[21] When General Adelbert Cronkhite, commanding officer of Camp Lee in Virginia, witnessed such insolence taking place on his base, he quickly ended it. "I met some junior officers," he told a local newspaper reporter, "who said they were not keen on saluting Negro officers. They would not feel that way if they understood the spirit of the salute."[22]

Importantly, the War Department established an unofficial policy that allowed black officers to command only black soldiers. This practice contributed to the widespread perception among white soldiers that the black officers were not truly officers. White officers who found themselves outranked by black officers requested and usually received transfers.[23]

THE WAR DEPARTMENT'S CALAMITOUS MISHANDLING of Lieutenant Colonel Charles Young's career showed the lengths to which the department would go to keep white officers from falling under a black officer's command. Young was born to freed slaves in a Kentucky log cabin. His father had fought for the Union in the Civil War. He was a gifted student and in 1889 became the third African American to graduate from West Point. One of his white classmates wrote of "our colored classmate Charles Young, whom we esteem highly for his patient perseverance in the face of discouraging conditions."[24] By the time America entered the Great War, Charles Young was the highest-ranking African American officer ever in the United States armed forces. Young was as urbane as he was tough and spoke French fluently.

As American troops prepared to enter the Great War, it was a young white officer who contributed to Young's unseemly removal from the army. A lieutenant in the Tenth Cavalry filed an official complaint with the War Department, stating that, as a Southern man, he found it "distasteful to take orders from a black superior."[25] Secretary of War Newton Baker ordered the junior officer to "either do his duty or resign," because there was "nothing else we can do about it."[26] Mississippi senator John Bell Williams alerted the White House to the soldier's objections and Baker's response. President Woodrow Wilson deemed the matter important enough to intervene personally. He overruled his secretary of war's decision and the lieutenant was transferred from Young's command.

Most white officers in the Tenth Cavalry immediately filed similar complaints with their senators and the War Department.[27] Secretary Newton considered transferring Lieutenant Colonel Young to Fort Des Moines to command officers of his own race, but knew this would not solve the larger problem. Even if Young were to command solely black combat troops in Europe, he almost certainly would cross the threshold of performance, experience, and command at which the army promoted its finest colonels to the rank of brigadier general. Once Charles Young became America's first black general, there would be no way to avoid assigning him to command white officers.

For this reason, Secretary Newton decided that the lieutenant colonel would not see combat in the Great War. Instead, the army declared Young medically unfit for active duty and forcibly retired him. Young was incredulous. Americans of all races were shocked. As one newspaper reported, "people all over the country felt that an effort was being made by the Southerners in the War Department to side-track a man who was in line very shortly to become a Brigadier General."[28] W.E.B. DuBois, a friend of Young's, astutely noted that the army refused to allow the decorated colonel to fight in the Great War because "if he had gone to Europe he could not have been denied the stars of a General."[29]

African American newspapers widely publicized Young's story and the War Department was besieged with letters protesting his retirement. Secretary Baker assured the public that he personally had reviewed the medical board's report indicating that Young suffered from hypertension. "I want to be able to give the assurance to all who inquire," Baker told reporters, "that I have given my own personal thought and attention to this case, in which so many are interested."[30]

But Baker's assurance did little to quell the controversy. At a time when the federal government was drafting black men to work almost exclusively as laborers in a foreign war while lynchings continued unabated in the men's hometowns and Congress continued to refuse to make lynching a federal crime, Charles Young's forced retirement was the final insult. The outcry against the War Department's action was strident enough that President Wilson felt compelled to respond personally to an inquiry sent to the White House by Robert Moten, who succeeded Booker T. Washington as president of Tuskegee Institute. By letter,

Wilson told Moten, "You may be sure that I am no less deeply interested than yourself in the matter to which you call my attention and I think that you are laboring under a misapprehension as to the case of Lieut. Col. Charles Young." Wilson acknowledged the concern over Young's retirement but denied that race was a factor in the War Department's decision. "There is no possible ground in [Young's] case for the fear that he is in any way being discriminated against and you may be sure that he will be treated as any other officer would be in similar circumstances."[31]

In an effort to prove his physical fitness, Young mounted his best horse and rode it from Ohio to Washington, D.C. His ride received widespread press coverage and the War Department faced even more criticism. The department responded by promoting him to full colonel, but did not change its order that he be forcibly retired. Charles Young would receive a larger pension but would serve no longer in the active military.[32]

Despite Young's lengthy ordeal, African American civilians and servicemen alike remained optimistic that one of their own would attain the rank of general officer. The editors of one black newspaper confidently wrote, "The European War is going to see to it that we have several colonels before it is over, and even a general or two is not improbable."[33] These editors underestimated the depth of the military's opposition to promoting black officers.

FRANCE BY WAY OF CAROLINA

DURING THE GREAT WAR no camp commander vexed black Americans like Major General Charles Ballou, the former commander of the celebrated officers' training camp at Fort Des Moines. Ballou imposed exceptionally stringent restrictions on the black soldiers under his command at Camp Funston, Kansas.[1] In March 1918, an African American sergeant in the Ninety-second Division's medical department stationed at Camp Funston left base and met his wife to view a film in the town of Manhattan, Kansas. He purchased two tickets for balcony seats. The theater's manager refused to admit the soldier, who was in uniform, because he feared that his white patrons would object.[2] The soldier exchanged bitter words with the manager but relented. His wife returned home and he returned to base, where he reported the incident to his superiors.

Word of the incident crawled up the chain of command to reach Major General Ballou, who responded on March 28, 1918, by issuing Bulletin No. 35, which was read to every soldier in the Ninety-second Division. "It should be well known to all colored officers and men," Ballou began, "that no useful purpose is served by such acts as will cause the 'color question' to be raised." The bulletin's first sentence made clear where Ballou believed fault lay for the verbal incident at the theater. Unlike commanders in the South, however, he could not take refuge behind a state law mandating segregated theaters. "It is not a question of legal rights," he explained in the bulletin. There was no doubt that the sergeant "had a legal right" to enter the Manhattan theater. "He is strictly within his legal rights in this matter, and the theater manager is legally wrong."[3]

Despite their legal right to do so, Major General Ballou ordered his troops to "refrain from going where their presence will be resented." He contended that the sergeant under his command was "guilty of the GREATER wrong in doing ANYTHING, NO MATTER HOW LEGALLY CORRECT, that will provoke race animosity." In a line that would haunt him as well as the Ninety-second Division, Ballou wrote, "White men made the Division, and they can break it just as easily if it becomes a trouble maker."[4] He closed by ordering his men: "Don't go where your presence is not wanted."

Bulletin No. 35 held that the sergeant had done nothing wrong, and yet, in his commanding officer's eyes, he was at fault. That the rebuke was issued by the army general who had worked more closely with African Americans than any other offered a painful disillusionment for African Americans. Bulletin No. 35 was read at community gatherings across the nation, and African Americans' responses to it in black communities and newspapers ranged from disbelief to fury. Editors at the *Baltimore Afro-American* initially gave the benefit of the doubt to a commander long trusted by black servicemen and their families: "A statement is being awaited to clear up this bulletin from a well-meaning commander."[5] But the response in Cleveland's *Advocate* better represented the prevailing sentiment. "We expected better than this of Major General Ballou," the editorial board wrote, "in this day of bitter warfare when the President is calling upon all America—white and black, we presume—to rally to the Flag and help to crush 'the foe of humanity.'"[6] The general's refusal to stand by the law and his men, the *Advocate* argued, sowed the very sorts of divisions all Americans sought to avoid during this time of war. The *Chicago Defender* caustically demanded, "General Ballou may be a fighter, but is he a soldier? . . . Are slaveholders fit to lead freemen to fight slavery?"[7]

The secretary of war's special assistant Emmett Scott requested a formal explanation from Ballou. Responding at length, the general first informed Scott that, even as he issued the controversial bulletin to his troops, he had pushed the local U.S. attorney's office to prosecute the theater manager. That this fact was not shared with the general public "was a malicious attempt to stir up race feeling by misrepresentation." Second, the instructions set forth in the bulletin were merely "advice." Contrary to published news reports, the bulletin "had nothing to do with any policy of segregation . . . Its purpose was to prevent race friction, with the attendant prejudice to good order and military discipline."[8]

The major general pointedly contrasted the record of his troops at Fort Des Moines with the violent mutiny launched in Houston: "In the midst of all the feeling and excitement caused by the . . . Houston troubles, the colored officers' training camp at Fort Des Moines won golden approbation all over the United States, made thousands of friends for the colored race and achieved a glorious success." Ballou unapologetically linked the officer candidates' success to the very modus operandi for which he now received so much criticism. The officer candidates had attained local respect and national renown "by following precisely the advice that was repeated to the 92d Division in Bulletin No. 35." Despite his attempts to publicize his efforts to prosecute the theater manager for discriminating against the sergeant, Ballou never regained a high standing among uniformed or civilian black Americans.[9]

THE CONTROVERSY OVER BULLETIN NO. 35 did nothing to slow the rate at which both black and white army units prepared to travel to camps in the South to continue training as the winter of 1917–18 approached. The impending moves worried army field commanders, white Southerners, and black soldiers. Of particular concern was the looming prospect that black soldiers from Northern states would be stationed at camps in the South and experience the vehemence of Southern racism for the first time. Indeed, this had proved combustible at Camp Logan in Houston.

The New York Fifteenth Regiment was that state's only National Guard regiment for black soldiers and was one of just six African American National Guard regiments in the nation.[10] They were a proud, highly educated lot whose ranks included black officers who remained even after white officers were assigned to the regiment in preparation for deployment. Paul Robeson's brother Benjamin served as a lieutenant in the New York Fifteenth, and Napoleon Bonaparte Marshall, a Harvard-educated lawyer, was a captain. The orchestra conductor and composer James Reese Europe was a household name when he joined the New York Fifteenth as a lieutenant.[11]

The New Yorkers' commanding officer was a white colonel named William Hayward, a dapper attorney and former secretary of the Republican National Committee. Although he had been appointed colonel by New York's governor, Hayward enthusiastically took to his wartime duty. He acted as both an advocate and a protector of his soldiers, persistently lobbying War Department officials for proper accommodations and training facilities for the regiment. Hayward was well respected by his soldiers. What the federal government denied his men he sought to obtain by other means; he once resorted to forging dozens of letters on behalf of nonexistent civilian shooting clubs in order to procure one thousand rifles for his regiment.[12]

Shortly after Hayward took command of the Fifteenth Regiment, the soldiers were ordered to report to Camp Upton on Long Island, where they performed most of the guard duty on post.[13] As winter approached, the unit received orders to report to Camp Wadsworth, just outside the rigidly segregated town of Spartanburg, South Carolina. Through the press and their elected politicians, white residents vented their fury at the prospect of Northern black men training near their town.

Before the Fifteenth Regiment departed for South Carolina, reporters asked Colonel Hayward to comment on the reaction of Spartanburg's white residents to news of his soldiers' imminent arrival. "I have heard of the story that Negro troops are not wanted at Spartanburg," Hayward said. "All I can say is that my men pray for only two places: France or Heaven." That is, his men wanted to fight for their country abroad, not fight their fellow Americans at home.[14]

Privately, however, the colonel expressed misgivings about his men being transferred to a base in the South. They were New Yorkers, and, while they certainly were not strangers to racial discrimination, Hayward worried that they would not fare well in South Carolina. As much as he appreciated the benefits of training in Southern camps, including "working all winter and saving months of time they probably would lose in the North," the colonel did not "believe in sending colored troops from the North to Southern training camps."[15]

The men arrived on October 9, 1917, to an atmosphere that was so violently hostile that on October 22, Colonel Hayward traveled to Washington, D.C., to meet personally with senior War Department officials about improving the environment in which his men were forced to train. At best, the racist epithets and insults hurled by white Spartanburg residents were embittering distractions to the Fifteenth Regiment; at worst, the camp and the town were reeling toward a bloody confrontation reminiscent of Houston. The New York National Guard soldiers quickly tired of suffering physical and verbal abuse. Talk was spreading in the regiment that the only way to tame the town was to "shoot it up" the way the Twenty-fourth Infantry had "shot up" Houston.[16] Hayward maintained control of his men, but the situation, as one department official described it, was growing "more and more intense."[17]

The War Department dispatched Emmett Scott to Camp Wadsworth. Upon arriving at the base, Scott "easily observed" that "the atmosphere . . . was surcharged." The colonel asked Scott to address the Fifteenth Regiment's noncommissioned officers, senior enlisted men who were "the backbone of the regiment." Hayward and all officers then left the room. Scott and the sergeants were, as he recalled, "left alone to discuss the delicate situation face to face and in the frankest way possible."[18]

The men were frustrated and angry. Several could not help but break into bitter tears as they recounted the things the white townspeople had said and done to them. The soldiers did not know if they could restrain themselves much longer. Scott commiserated with them, understood their pain and frustration, but asked them to bear it for the greater good. He made what he later called "an appeal and admonition to do nothing that would bring dishonor or stain to the regiment or to the race." He understood why they wanted "to visit violence upon the community" that had visited violence upon them, but the fact was that they had to exercise restraint "for the sake of the Negro race and for all that was at stake for it and the country during the war." Asking this of the soldiers pained Scott.[19]

The noncommissioned officers accepted his call for forbearance. After adjourning the meeting, Scott met again with Colonel Hayward before returning to Washington. Upon arriving in D.C., Scott explained to the War Department's senior leadership that the situation in Spartanburg was untenable. Within weeks the New York Fifteenth Regiment of the National Guard received orders to report to France, where it would be reborn as the 369th Infantry, the first black combat unit in the Great War. In battle the men of the 369th would become legend.

8

THE LOST CHILDREN

SHORTLY BEFORE THEY DEPARTED for France, an army colonel ad-dressed a regiment of freshly drafted young black men. Figuring that the new soldiers might be apprehensive about going to war, fighting, and possibly dying in a faraway land, the colonel wanted to raise morale. He explained to them that they need not worry about fighting or dying in combat. "Men, we are going overseas in two weeks. We are going to see the country and have some fun. You'll probably never hear a gun fired." The men did not bother to hide their disappointment. They wanted to fight, but the colonel made it clear that they would be fortu-nate to be promoted from laborer to cook. This was because, he ex-plained, "it takes a damned good man to be a cook."[1] One stevedore spoke for many others when he said, "I don't want to stagger under heavy boxes. I want a gun on my shoulder and a chance to go to the front."[2]

ALMOST IMMEDIATELY AFTER the Houston mutiny, the War Depart-ment eliminated plans to establish sixteen black combat infantry regi-ments. The overwhelming majority of black recruits and draftees were restricted to the Service of Supply (SoS) corps. They could serve only as laborers, drivers, or cooks.[3] Some 380,000 black soldiers served in the army during the Great War, and of these only 42,000 were members of combat units.[4] Of the 200,000 black soldiers deployed to France, 160,000 served as stevedores in the SoS corps. Their war experiences differed greatly from those of most other soldiers.

By appearance, duty, and the treatment they received from their officers, it often scarcely appeared that the stevedores were in the military at all. Labor battalions of black men were systematically last to receive housing, rations, uniforms, or any other items the army supplied to its troops.[5] The men received very little military training, and some units did not even have uniforms to wear. One stevedore recalled, "Our drilling consisted in marching to and from work with hoes, shovels and picks on our shoulders."[6] The men were drafted from the lowest rungs of American society and placed in the lowest rungs of the army. They would not be promoted and certainly would not be issued arms.

Stevedores typically worked sixteen hours a day. They loaded and unloaded ships at docks, shoveled coal onto ships, and built and repaired docks and piers. They constructed roads, railroads, bridges, and even a water-filtering plant. They dug nearly every American grave, and, when the fallen soldiers could be removed to safer ground, they exhumed the bodies, carried them to their new resting place, and reburied them.[7] Many stevedores rarely saw their camps in daylight, because they worked from dark in the morning until dark at night, reminiscent of the American slaves' day of working "can't to can't."[8]

Leaders in black communities across the country expressed concern about the highly disproportionate number of black men ordered into army labor battalions. Filling the ranks of the military's most menial jobs was not what community leaders had envisioned when they had encouraged black men to join the military and lobbied the War Department to include blacks in the war effort.

It quickly became clear that the army intended to employ nearly all its black soldiers as laborers. The common refrain from the army and white observers was that this was the work to which the men were best suited. The *Washington Post* expressed this very point in a November 1917 report: "There has been considerable speculation since the arrival of colored troops as to how the War Department planned to use them—whether as workmen behind the lines or as fighting men. With very little training,

virtually all of these men, most of whom were recruited from the laboring class, would make excellent trench diggers and stevedores."[9]

Contrary to the *Post*'s reporting, a significant number of stevedores
held college degrees. They had hoped to serve in combat units with, as
DuBois wrote, their "eyes lifted to the hills." Instead they found themselves assigned to labor battalions in the Service of Supply command.[10]
Members of all-black Service of Supply units were among the first Americans to arrive in Europe. The War Department planned to deploy three
to four million soldiers, and each one of these soldiers would need to be
fed, clothed, and sheltered as best as possible. When America entered the
war, senior army officers estimated that labor battalions in France would
unload 250,000 tons of beef and 30.5 million gallons of coffee for the
troops, and two million tons of hay to feed the army's five hundred thousand horses, for each of which the stevedores would make and attach
horseshoes.[11] The task set before the SoS soldiers was formidable.

Army generals and African American leaders alike stressed both the
difficulty and the importance of the work placed before the Service of
Supply units. The ports and docks in France were, as one reporter stated,
"choked with American ships" carrying munitions, food, and other supplies needed by the American Expeditionary Forces (AEF).[12] During
one month at the height of the war, American stevedores at French ports
unloaded 25,588 tons each day.[13] There was no denying that, as the *Baltimore Afro-American* reported, "the work of the colored stevedores may
be menial and laborious, but it is as essential as the manning of guns at
the front."[14]

The white writer George Rothwell Brown visited the American ports
in France and reported that the "regiments of hard-working Southern
negroes from the seaport towns of Dixie form one of the most pictureque
elements in the entire army in France." The soldiers, whom Brown called
"negro roustabouts [wearing] toil-stained khaki," were commanded by
"Southern men" who "know how to handle negroes." Consequently,
Brown reported, "this corps has been efficiently organized, is being efficiently managed and is doing the good work of the hard, grim kind
that wins no glory."[15] Stevedore companies were commanded by white
sergeants who invariably were bitter at having been assigned not just to
a black unit, but to a black Service of Supply unit.[16]

As crucial as their work was to the American Expeditionary Forces' success, the black labor units consistently were ridiculed by their fellow soldiers in Europe and white civilians back home. Their accents, alleged superstitions, and even the relatively good spirit in which they worked became fodder for accounts portraying the soldiers as minstrels. Officers and senior enlisted men traded apochryphal stories about the laborers like baseball cards. The white press published accounts such as the one where Secretary of War Baker, visiting with army enlisted men in France, expressed satisfaction with the troops' high morale:

> Only one complaint was made. It came from a negro in one of the stevedore regiments serving at an improvised shipyard.
> "How do you like the cooking?" the Secretary asked.
> "Well, I gets only one piece of bread," the man replied.
> "Is it good bread?" asked Mr. Baker.
> "Oh, it's good boss, but when I asks for another piece, I wants it."[17]

In an anecdote published in the *Chicago Daily News*, an African American stevedore from Georgia fell to his knees for fear that the steamship carrying him and hundreds of other soldiers across the Atlantic would capsize. "Lord the ocean is getting worse and worse," the stevedore is said to have prayed. "I am a scared niggah. I need your help right away at this minute. Come right away, Lord, don't wait. And Lord, if by any reason you can't come in pusson, I want you to send your fastest messenger!"[18]

Stevedores were caricatured in a manner that reinforced the worst stereotypes of African Americans. If black Americans planned to use their loyal military service in the Great War as a catalyst for attaining their civil rights after the war, then they would need more than stevedores and cooks. They would need heroes who had killed Germans.

BEFORE THEY COULD DEPART for Europe, the men of New York's Fifteenth Regiment, like one quarter of all war-bound American soldiers, first had to pass through the organized chaos that was Camp Merritt, outside of Hoboken, New Jersey. Thousands of the army's black laborers glistened with sweat despite the cold as they loaded ocean liners bound for the war zone. After standing in an array of long lines for medical and equipment evaluations, the Fifteenth Regiment's soldiers at last boarded a confiscated German ocean liner renamed *Pocahontas* by her new owner, the United States government. Their trip across the Atlantic was eventful; *Pocahontas* needed significant repairs to her hull after encountering fearsome winter gales.

Twenty-four tumultuous days after leaving New Jersey, the men stepped onto the docks at the sprawling port at Saint-Nazaire. Twenty-eight miles of warehouses stretched farther than their eyes could see. But for the fact that it was considerably larger, the port was similar to Camp Merritt back home. Black stevedores bent and lifted cargo from the ships to the docks. More than fifty thousand of them were stationed at Saint-Nazaire. They worked from early morning until after sunset. "The spirit of Saint-Nazaire," remarked one white officer who commanded black SoS soldiers at the port, "is the spirit of the South."[19]

The men of the 369th were as shocked as Colonel Hayward when they received orders to labor alongside the stevedores. The "Fighting Fifteenth," as the men had taken to calling themselves, was ordered to work constructing a railroad yard, paving roads, and unloading ships. The soldiers could not believe their orders. They wanted—and had trained for—frontline duty. "While stevedoring may be all right," one soldier complained, "it is not war." Worried that the army intended to convert them into a stevedore unit, they began asking their officers, "When do we fight?"[20] One officer confronted Colonel Hayward and told him, "You are without a doubt the best fixer in the world; and if you can get to General Pershing, face to face, we'll get into the trenches within a week."[21]

Colonel Hayward agreed that his men had trained too hard to be confined to service in a labor battalion. He drafted a letter to AEF commander General John J. Pershing respectfully requesting that the men of the New York Fifteenth be assigned to duties more befitting their training. Pershing responded by reassigning the Fifteenth to serve alongside French soldiers. The French Army desperately needed troops. If Hayward's men were so anxious to fight, they could exchange their American-issued weapons for French ones and fight under French commanders.[22]

Hayward and his soldiers reported to Givry-en-Argonne, where they were taught to use French grenades, rifles, and machine guns. The New Yorkers also learned sufficient French in short order. The French high command renamed the Fighting Fifteenth *le 369 ième Régiment d'Infanterie États Unis.*[23] "We are now a combat unit," Hayward excitedly wrote, "one of the regiments of a French Division in the French Army, assigned to a sector of trenches."[24] Because the black soldiers seemingly had been abandoned by their own army, the French called them *les enfants perdus*— the lost children.

THE 369TH JOINED THREE OTHER black infantry regiments—the 370th, 371st, and 372nd—to form the United States Ninety-third Combat Division. General Pershing assigned all four regiments to serve with the French Army for the duration of the war. Although similarly ordered to fight under French command, the American regiments served separately. Colonel Hayward wrote to a friend about the sudden new arrangement:

> There are no American troops anywhere near us, that I can find out, and we are *"les enfants perdus,"* and glad of it. Our great American general simply put the black orphan in a basket, set it on the doorstep of the French, pulled the bell, and went away. I said this to a French colonel . . . and he said, "Weelcome leetle black babbie." The French are wonderful—wonderful—wonderful.[25]

A few months after abandoning the black combat troops to French commanders, Pershing issued a directive to the French military, instructing them to treat black soldiers as white Americans did:

TO THE FRENCH MILITARY MISSION STATIONED WITH THE AMERICAN ARMY—Secret Information Concerning Black American Troops: It is important for French officers who have been called upon to exercise command over black American troops, or to live in close contact with them, to have an exact idea of the position occupied by Negroes in the United States . . . Although a citizen of the United States, the black man is regarded by the white American as an inferior being with whom relations of business or service only are possible. The black is constantly being censured for his want of intelligence and discretion . . . The vices of the Negro are a constant menace to the American who has to repress them sternly.

We must prevent the rise of any pronounced degree of intimacy between French officers and black officers . . . We must not eat with them, must not shake hands or seek to talk or meet with them outside the requirements of military service. We must not commend too highly the black American troops, particularly in the presence of Americans.[26]

French soldiers who served alongside black Americans all but ignored Pershing's directive. The Frenchmen saluted African American officers and shook hands with black enlisted personnel.[27] "A new equality was tasted at this time by these American colored men," one contemporary historian wrote, "while their officers moved with perfect ease among the highest officials of the French Army."[28] When they were warned, "*Qu'elles ne gâtent pas les nègres*," or "Don't spoil the Negroes," French soldiers dismissed it as a crude American request that had nothing to do with winning the war. As one white American officer explained, "The French people could not grasp the idea of social discrimination on account of color. They said the colored men were soldiers, wearing the American uniform, and fighting in the common cause."[29] Conversely, America's commanding general in his directive had drawn a contrast between "the Negro" and "the American."

The primary reason why French soldiers treated their black American comrades so fairly was that their help was desperately needed. The French had been fighting for three and a half years. Morale was waning and some generals worried that soldiers might begin to refuse orders. Four regiments of black American soldiers were welcome news to the French soldiers fighting under General Henri Gouraud. The general already had lost his right arm in the war. French troops across the front called him the Lion of France, and his mere presence caused them to burst into cheers.[30] General Gouraud now prepared his men—both French and American—for what promised to be their most trying battles yet. The successful Bolshevik Revolution effectively ended Germany's

war with Russia, and, through the winter of 1917–18, Germany transferred more than five hundred thousand troops from the Russian front
into France, bringing the kaiser's total number of soldiers on the Western Front to 1.5 million.

The German reinforcements and the American troops alike arrived in
a country that had been bombarded and battered nearly to the point of
collapse. Artillery fire had reduced whole villages to remnants and splin-
tered beams. German soldiers were determined to crush France before
the American Expeditionary Forces could stop the bloodletting, and
the French people knew this. "When we landed in France," an officer
in the 369th wrote in his diary, "she was so sick of body and heart that
the common people of the towns and the soldiers of the ranks not only
sensed defeat but admitted it."[31] Another soldier recalled, "Our first
words of welcome from the population of the humble classes were words
of protest at our coming. Why had we come? We could do nothing now
but prolong the suffering of the nation! Germany was too strong . . . If
we had come sooner—perhaps; but now, it was too late."[32]

After several weeks of training, on April 8, 1918, General Gouraud
moved the men of the 369th to the front lines alongside French soldiers.
Colonel Hayward commanded several French units as well as his own
men, and they conducted patrols and raids every night. The men held a
fifty-mile front between Rheims and the Argonne.[33] German artillery
fire rained down day and night.

The prospect of close combat fraught with danger excited the Americans. In the distance they could hear German cannons' thunderlike fire.
Around them shells exploded. In this mayhem, to the consternation of
their French officers, the 369th soldiers, as one officer recalled, "laughed
and screamed in gleeful excitement." Having fought so long for the right
to fight, "the men were never really scared." Instead, they kept "looking
at the big flashes in the north and saying 'goddamn, let's go!' "[34]

FOR ALL THE BLACK SOLDIERS' enthusiasm, there was no escaping the
fact that life in the trenches was miserable. The men slept in dugouts
when they were not on patrol, on a raid, or manning the trench. Dugouts were thatch-roofed underground shelters. The farther from the
front lines a dugout was located, the nicer it was. Several miles behind

the front, dugouts were furnished with beds, rugs, tables, chairs, and even oil lamps—whatever soldiers could loot from nearby deserted homes. Time spent in a dugout was precious, because its makeshift roof provided some protection against the seemingly incessant rain. From standing so long in muddy puddles in the trenches, many soldiers developed a condition known as trench foot, whereby their feet developed blisters and alternated between aching with pain and going numb.

And then there were the rats. The war zone teemed with rats feasting on scraps of food, unburied corpses, and soldiers' boots. Like the water and the mud, they seemed omnipresent. Perhaps worse than the rats were the body lice. The bloodsucking parasites attached themselves to soldiers in their armpits, on their stomachs, and at the groin. The trenches and dugouts were infested, and the men were cold from the rain and itchy from lice.

THE 369TH RECEIVED ORDERS to establish communication as soon as possible with the French Twenty-seventh Infantry, which held a position more than three kilometers away from the New York regiment. In order to do this, the regiment's officers immediately realized, they would have to send a relay of runners across the entire three-kilometer stretch, all of which fell under enemy fire. "Let's go!" had become the regiment's unofficial motto, and the relay runners embraced their assignment accordingly. The runners accomplished their mission so efficiently and with such apparent disregard for the constant barrage of enemy fire that the division commander issued a commendation to the 369th Infantry.[35]

One soldier stood out among the brave message carriers. Private Elmer McCowin of Company K was one of the relay runners. "On September 26th the Captain asked me to carry dispatches," McCowin recounted. "The Germans pumped machine gun bullets at me all the way. But I made the trip and back safely.

"Then I was sent out again. As I started with the message the Captain yelled to bring him back a can of coffee. He was joking, but I didn't know it at the time." Private McCowin dashed back out of the trenches and immediately drew enemy machine-gun fire. For three kilometers he scampered through thick mud, dodging death all the while. "Being a foot messenger," he recalled with wry humor, "I had some time ducking those German bullets. Those bullets seemed very sociable, but I didn't care to meet up with them, so I kept right on traveling on high gear. None touched my skin, though some skinned pretty close."

McCowin made it to the French soldiers' encampment and delivered his message. He had run nine kilometers through a hail of bullets. He did not pause to reflect on the fact that he had to run three final kilometers back to his company's trench. Instead he asked for a can of coffee for his captain. Then he bid the men of the French Twenty-seventh farewell and dashed back out into the thick muck.

"On the way back, it seemed the whole war was turned on me. One bullet passed through my trousers and it made me hop, step and jump pretty lively." The gunfire was becoming too intense. McCowin knew he had to take cover. "I saw a shell hole six feet deep. Take it from me, I dented another six feet when I plunged into it hard. In my fist I held the Captain's can of coffee." When he emerged from the shell hole, so many bullets came flying at him that it was all he could do to get to the next shell hole and dive again. He figured that the can of coffee might be bringing him good luck, as the Germans had managed to shoot several holes in the can but none in him. After this second treacherous round trip, McCowin at last "got back safely. And what do you think? When I got back into our own trenches I stumbled and spilled the coffee!"[36]

Elmer McCowin's fantastic story was confirmed independently by his superior officers. Lieutenant George Miller told War Department officials, "When that soldier came back with the coffee, his clothes were riddled with bullets."[37]

About a half hour after his safe arrival, the daring private learned that several of his fellow soldiers of the 369th lay wounded in the mire back in no-man's-land. McCowin gathered his gear and again climbed out of the trench into the torrent of German fire. He carried back wounded soldier after wounded soldier. It seemed as if the bullets could not hit him. Finally, he was severely gassed, but he still refused to fall back. Instead he crawled out again and carried back another wounded soldier. For his awe-inspiring bravery, Private McCowin was awarded the Croix de Guerre. In relaying the private's story, one of his commanding officers stressed that McCowin did "all this under fire. That's the reason he got the Distinguished Service Cross," one of the army's highest honors.[38]

JUST AS THE AMERICAN and French troops raided German encampments to kill and capture enemy personnel, German infantrymen conducted raids on Allied outposts and trenches. Late on the night of August 12, 1918, German soldiers raided an American trench in the Champagne district, taking the doughboys by surprise. It was, as one newspaper reported, "a perfect surprise raid of the sort the Yanks themselves like to pull off."[39] With their short trench knives and clubs, the Germans killed as many soldiers as they could before deciding to take four privates and Lieutenant G. R. Jones as hostages.

Jones felt thick hands seize his throat. "*Silenz!*" the German hissed into his ear. "*Silenz!*" The steel nose of a pistol jammed against the small of his back. The white officer surrendered and his black soldiers followed suit. The Germans pulled them out of the trenches and began to march them toward no-man's-land. They were marched so that any Allied bullets shot their way in a rescue attempt would hit the doughboys.

Jones could not believe his misfortune. How could he not have heard the Huns coming? There had been gas in the air. He should have heard them. This was the second time he had been taken captive. The previous time, the men of his regiment had rescued him. Of course, they were white men, soldiers he described as "fighting men."[40]

After his first rescue, Jones was assigned to be an officer in the 370th Infantry. The white man from Alabama suddenly found himself in command of a regiment of black troops from New York City. Neither he nor his men were happy with the assignment, but the rigors of warfare had forced them to bridge their differences. Though he still hoped to return to his former regiment, Lieutenant Jones and his men had come to respect each other. As he marched with four of his most junior soldiers with an enemy gun jammed against his back, Jones wondered whether he would be rescued again.

Somewhere in the dark a doughboy shot a green flare into the night. The Germans and their American captives were illuminated for a few moments.

Sergeant William Butler was a Pullman porter back home in New

York City, but tonight he lay still as a corpse in a shell hole. His face and uniform were caked with mud, his index finger poised just aside the trigger of his rifle. The flare's green light allowed the wiry, thin-faced Butler to see his five fellow soldiers. He discerned that the Germans and their captives would have to march close to his shell hole on the way back to their lines. Butler waited, waited, and then leaped from his hole. He charged at seventeen Germans. "Look out for me, you bush Germans," he screamed, "I'm coming!"[41]

Sergeant Butler fired his rifle into the night with amazing accuracy. Ten German soldiers fell dead, and Butler took after those remaining with his knife. The American captives crawled to safety as the German soldiers, including one whose arm Butler had hacked off, retreated into no-man's-land.[42] Sergeant Butler made a prisoner of a severely wounded German lieutenant. The six Americans, with their prisoner, returned to camp.

A few hours later daylight revealed yards of mire and barbed wire littered with the body parts of German soldiers. It looked as if Sergeant William Butler had conducted his own war against the enemy—and won. The lieutenant he had captured later died of his wounds. The truth was, as the war correspondent Herbert Corey reported, "nobody knows how many Germans he killed."[43] Butler later explained, "I must have run amuck."[44] For no small reason did the German soldiers call the men of the 369th Infantry "Hellfighters."

General Pershing awarded Sergeant Butler the Distinguished Service Cross "for extraordinary heroism in action near maison de Champagne, France, August 18, 1918."[45] Butler and his "Look out for me, you bush Germans" line became famous. After the war, in 1919, some members of the NAACP mentioned William Butler's name along with the likes of Emmett J. Scott and W.E.B. DuBois as a possible nominee for the organization's prestigious Spingarn Medal.[46]

THE NINETY-THIRD DIVISION included three black regiments in addition to the 369th Infantry. The 370th Infantry had been known as the Eighth Illinois Regiment before the war. Like the former "Fighting Fifteenth" of New York City, the Eighth Illinois boasted a storied tradition. Unlike any of the other black National Guard units that had survived

Reconstruction, the Old Eighth Illinois was commanded exclusively by black officers. Its commander was the Texas-born former assistant city prosecutor of Chicago, Colonel Franklin Denison. "We men didn't let our officers down," one of Denison's soldiers declared. During a time when War Department officials and senior military personnel believed that black soldiers performed best under the command of white Southern officers, Denison's men declared, "We were out to show the whites that not only were we as good in everything as they, but better."[47]

The Eighth Illinois arrived in France on April 16, 1918. Just as he had done with the New York Fifteenth, Pershing ordered the Eighth Illinois to serve as an auxiliary unit in the French Army. The unit was renamed the 370th Infantry and served with distinction: Sixty-eight members earned the Croix de Guerre while twenty-one received America's second-highest honor, the Distinguished Service Cross. Nearly half the soldiers in the 370th died in battle.[48]

THE 371ST INFANTRY REGIMENT, composed mostly of poor African Americans drafted from Georgia, Alabama, and the Carolinas, was the first unit of black draftees to serve in the trenches. Senior army officers expected little from this regiment. Acquiescing to local demands, the army had postponed drafting these men so that the cotton harvest could be completed. Soldiers of the 371st were commanded by white Southern officers who army officials believed "knew how to handle Negroes," but these officers soon answered to French commanders.[49]

Along with the 372nd Infantry Regiment, the 371st was assigned to France's famous Fifteenth French Army—a unit that so relished hand-to-hand combat that everyone called it the Red Hand. Both American regiments performed heroically in battle. The black Americans' French commanding general told a white American, "You must be proud of your officers and men, and I consider it an honor to have had them under my command."[50]

The Ninety-third Division's four infantry regiments of African American soldiers performed exceptionally well in the French Army. Answering to commanding officers who considered a soldier's race less important than his ability and willingness to fight, the African American soldiers excelled under fire. The black press back home extolled their bravery and discipline. As one columnist wrote, the men had fought "not only for America but for their Race." The soldiers and their families believed that their having fought so valiantly for their country would "do a lot toward diminishing race prejudice."[51] African American veterans and their families would soon learn how wrong they were.

DISILLUSIONED BY ARMISTICE

THAT BLACK AMERICANS WERE FIGHTING and dying "to make the world safe for democracy" when most of them could not vote in their own country was a bitter irony that did not escape the enemy. Woodrow Wilson's administration remained indifferent to the violent oppression African Americans faced, particularly in the Southern states, and African American soldiers on the Western Front were relentlessly barraged with propaganda materials stressing the paradox of their bravery in battle. One German pamphlet printed in September 1918 read in part:

> To the Colored Soldiers of the U.S. Army,
>
> Hello, boys, what are you doing over there? Fighting the Germans? Why? Have they ever done you any harm? . . . Do you enjoy the same rights as the white people do in America, the land of freedom and democracy? Or aren't you rather rated over there as second class citizens? Can you go to a restaurant where white people dine, can you get a seat in a theatre where white people sit? . . . And how about the law? Is lynching and the most horrible cruelties connected there with a lawful proceeding in a democratic country?
>
> Now all of this is entirely different in Germany, where they do like colored people, where they do treat them as gentlemen and not as second class citizens . . .

To carry the gun in [America's] defense is not an honor but a shame. Throw it away and come over to the German lines. You will find friends who will help you along.[1]

The soldiers who received this particular pamphlet did not deny what truth it contained. African American soldiers from the South could not vote at home, and those from the North, such as the men of the 369th Infantry, could not live in most neighborhoods or dine in most restaurants. When their officers questioned the men and collected copies of the pamphlet, one soldier summarized the pervading sentiment. "We know what they say is true, but don't worry; we're not going over."[2]

Back in Washington, federal government officials nervously read copies of the German propaganda materials. They worried not just about the effect of such pamphlets on black soldiers serving overseas but also about their effect on black Americans' feelings on the home front. They reached out to editors of black-owned and -operated newspapers, hoping that the black press would shape public opinion "along helpful lines rather than along lines that make for discontentment and unrest."[3]

In response, the editors of America's most prominent African American newspapers released a collective statement addressing Germany's propaganda efforts. "German propaganda among us is powerless," the editors wrote, "but the apparent indifference of our own Government may be dangerous." African Americans believed that, by fighting to make the world safe for democracy, they would finally enjoy their democratic rights at home.[4]

As lynchings continued in the South and racial tensions and violence increased in the North, Wilson decided to address the worsening situation. He issued a written statement on lynching. He did not mention the South specifically. On July 26, 1918, nearly every major newspaper in the country published Wilson's statement.

We are at this very moment fighting lawless passion. Germany has outlawed herself among the nations because she has disregarded the sacred obligations of law and has made lynchers of her armies. Lynchers emulate her disgraceful example . . .

By directly comparing Germany's use of submarine warfare against civilian vessels to lynch mobs' sadistic attacks against black Americans, Wilson adopted a metaphor that had been used in black newspapers since before America entered the war. The president continued:

> We proudly claim to be the champions of democracy. If we really are, in deed and in truth, let us see to it that we do not discredit our own. I say plainly that every American who takes part in the action of a mob or gives it any sort of countenance is no true son of this great Democracy, but its betrayer . . . [5]

In the wake of Wilson's statement, many white-owned newspapers began to devote more articles and editorials to violent attacks against black Americans. The editorial board of a Florida newspaper that previously had defended lynching reversed itself and condemned the practice.

For all its rhetorical value, however, the president's statement did nothing to quell the violence. Wilson continued to oppose a federal law against lynching. The gruesome killings continued through 1919. The violence at home outlasted the war overseas.

THE CELEBRATED NINETY-THIRD DIVISION was not the only division of African American soldiers during World War I. On November 29, 1917, the United States Army raised another division, the Ninety-second, which boasted 26,000 men. Unlike *les enfants perdus* of the Ninety-third, however, the Ninety-second functioned as an American army unit and not a French auxiliary one.

The army attempted to rouse African Americans' enthusiasm for the all-black unit by calling it the Buffalo Soldier Division. Major General Charles Ballou served as its commanding officer. African American officers commanded enlisted men in the Ninety-second Division. In fact, most black army officers were assigned to the Buffalo Division, and, in this respect, the division embodied the dream envisioned by many African Americans—black officers were poised to lead black troops into battle.

In contrast to the educated men who served as officers in the Ninety-second, the overwhelming majority of the division's enlisted men were impoverished draftees from Southern states. There was a substantial chasm between their prewar civilian lives and those of their mostly middle-class cadre of officers. Back home the black officers had their alumni associations, fraternities, and literary and social clubs, while many of the poor Southern men they commanded were barely literate. Even in segregated cities such as Washington, D.C., middle-class African Americans enjoyed shows at the Howard Theatre and dined on U Street—a lifestyle utterly foreign to impoverished African Americans from the rural deep South. The senior officers of the Ninety-second Division were almost all white Southerners, most of whom openly resented being assigned to command the division of black draftees.

Because the army sought to avoid training a large number of black combat troops on one base after the Houston mutiny, the men of the Ninety-second were dispersed among seven camps for training. The division's headquarters were at Camp Funston in Kansas, but its four infantry regiments trained at Camps Grant, Dodge, Upton, and Meade. Its three machine-gun battalions were stationed at Camps Funston, Grant, and Upton.

The soldiers' morale ran high despite their dispersal during training. Many approached military service as an opportunity to better themselves. In basic training army instructors taught the men not only marksmanship, hand-to-hand fighting, and grenade launching, but also how to carry themselves in a more refined manner. Over five to seven months of training, the draftees, whom one contemporary writer called "undeveloped young men from the farms and cotton-fields of the South," became so sharp in their appearance and demeanor that the army proudly included them in parades.[6] In 1918 the 367th Infantry marched in New York City on George Washington's birthday and the 368th was reviewed by President Wilson in Baltimore. The soldiers' crisp appearance belied the fact that their combat training had been woefully inadequate.

ON AUGUST 25, 1918, the Ninety-second Division relieved the Army's Sixth Infantry Division and assumed responsibility for France's Saint-Die sector. Almost immediately after the Ninety-second's arrival, German troops attacked the French village of Frapelle, catching the Americans off guard. Major General Ballou's soldiers performed poorly. One month later, during the Meuse-Argonne offensive from September 26 to October 5, the men were beaten again. They ceded ground and became so ineffective and disorganized that Ballou ordered a retreat from the line. The army court-martialed thirty African American lieutenants and captains for desertion. Four were convicted and sentenced to death, but their punishments later were reduced to long prison sentences.[7]

In time the Ninety-second Division essentially divided itself into two groups: The 367th and 368th Regiments fought valiantly against German attacks. French officials awarded the First Battalion of the 367th the Croix de Guerre. The 365th and 366th Regiments, in contrast, never developed the necessary fighting acumen and soon were relegated to service assignments. For years to come some senior military officials would use the experiences of the 365th and 366th to justify their assertions that black soldiers simply were not brave or intelligent enough for combat.[8]

The American Expeditionary Forces' commanding general was willing to recognize that the most unfortunate hours of the Ninety-second Division's service did not result from the inadequacy of the unit's African American junior officers. The Ninety-second's "officers are on the average with the officers of the A.E.F."[9] The problem appeared to stem from higher up the chain of command. Ballou's superiors removed him from command. Preparations were made to reorganize the Ninety-second Division.

Before the transfer could take place, however, Germany surrendered. On the eleventh hour of the eleventh day of the eleventh month of 1918, the war ended. "At exactly 11 o'clock," Colonel Hayward, commander of the Harlem Hellfighters, recalled, "we came out into a clearing and as we did, a rocket went up from the heights behind us. We did not know it at that moment but this was a signal that the war had ended." The most advanced and awful war the world had ever known, replete with nerve gas attacks, machine-gun fire, and torpedo explosions, at last had ended. Within minutes the reality dawned on the men and they were smoking cigarettes and shaking hands all in full view of the men who moments ago had been their mortal enemies.[10] The 369th Regiment marched all the way to the Rhine River in western Germany and found that the country's citizens were ecstatic about the peace. Festively dressed German women waved at the Americans.[11]

AMERICA'S BLACK SERVICEMEN soon discovered that victory in Europe did not earn them equality at home—it did not even earn them equality in Europe. The United States Army ordered its African American soldiers to rebury fallen Americans who had been buried hastily in shallow graves. One black soldier remembered it as a "gruesome, repulsive and unhealthy task." When units of black soldiers finally received orders to return home, U.S. Navy officers sometimes denied them a place aboard American ships.[12] Senior army officials ordered soldiers not to salute any officers—white or black—who commanded African American units. W.E.B. DuBois summarized black soldiers' postwar experience when he declared, "With the Armistice came disillusion."[13]

It is difficult to overstate how completely the American government disregarded the contributions of black soldiers to the Allies' victory. Emmett Scott wrote that "the Negroes did their full share in the great struggle to make the world safe for democracy," but their own government remained intent on keeping from them their rights as citizens.[14] In Southern states black Americans could not vote; in Northern states they suffered racial violence at the hands of union members and recent immigrants.

In July 1919, France hosted a Bastille Day victory parade in Paris. The United States was the only Allied nation to forbid its black soldiers from marching in the parade. African American veterans were enraged at being excluded. "Every nation had all the races that fought in the war," one lamented, "except the United States."[15] Despite African Americans' wartime service, the American military was more segregated than ever.

AFRICAN AMERICAN VETERANS OFTEN FACED violent hostility from white civilians.

Although the War Department permitted veterans to wear their uniforms for three months after being discharged, white Southerners warned African Americans returning home to do so in civilian clothes. But, in part because uniforms were the only clothes owned by many impoverished black veterans, African Americans, like white veterans, wore their uniforms when they returned home. The educator and activist Carter G. Woodson, one of the first African Americans to earn a Ph.D. from Harvard, wrote, "To the reactionary, the uniform on a Negro man was like a red flag flown in the face of a bull."[16]

White civilians began gathering at railroad stations throughout the South. They accosted black veterans, beat them, and ripped off their uniforms. Southern politicians abetted their constituents' antipathy toward African American veterans. Mississippi senator James K. Vardaman urged "the best and bravest white men in the community" to "pick out these suspicious characters—those military, French-women-ruined negro soldiers and let them understand that they are under surveillance."[17]

The Great War veteran Daniel Mack was twenty-two years old when he arrived back home in Worth County, Georgia, in the spring of 1919. He had served with the 365th Infantry Regiment in Europe and returned to his job as a sharecropper. On Saturday, April 5, he made plans to go to the nearby town of Sylvester. He planned to meet up with some old friends he had not seen since before the war. Mack donned his army uniform, complete with the medals he had earned for meritorious service.[18]

Sylvester was bustling. The sidewalks teemed with shoppers, diners, and families enjoying the afternoon sunshine. A white pedestrian named Samuel Hannan bumped into Mack. When Mack refused to apologize for violating the long-standing Southern custom that African Americans yield to whites on the sidewalk, Hannan struck Mack hard enough to knock him off the sidewalk. Hannan's friends leaped onto Mack, and the veteran began fighting them all. Soon the police arrived. They asked no questions before arresting Mack. They handcuffed him and dragged him down the crowded street. In the dust and sunlight he yelled that this was no way to treat a veteran.[19]

For two days Mack languished in a jail cell. Finally he was called for arraignment, where he pled guilty to disturbing the peace but not guilty to assault. "I fought for you in France to make the world safe for democracy," the uniformed veteran announced to the courtroom. "I don't think you treated me right in putting me in jail and keeping me there, because I've got as much right as anybody else to walk on the sidewalk."[20]

Astonished by Mack's statement, the judge admonished him that "this is a white man's country and you don't want to forget it." He sentenced Mack to thirty days of hard labor on a chain gang. Bailiffs led Mack back to his cell in shackles.[21]

The NAACP, joined by local African American churches and business leaders, vigorously protested both Mack's sentence and, more urgently, his detention in the county's jailhouse. They feared that the young veteran might not live to serve his sentence. In open court Mack had given voice to the sentiments of tens of thousands of African American veterans. Black men in Georgia had been killed for far less.

Nine days after his arrest, on the night of April 14, a mob of white townspeople gathered outside the jailhouse. The attendant guard suddenly became ill and the police chief who relieved him let the crowd into the jail and into Daniel Mack's cell. With rifle butts and ax handles they beat Mack unconscious even before dragging him from his cell. Both his wrists and ankles remained shackled. The vigilantes beat him with wooden rods while they carried him to a waiting car. For two and a half miles they drove, beating him all the while.

At last he stopped reacting to their blows. Satisfied, the men dumped his body on the side of the road. Still shackled, Mack was also still wearing his army uniform. Daniel Mack miraculously survived his ordeal. The chief of police blamed the assault on "a very bitter feeling against colored soldiers because of the supposed friendly treatment shown to them by the French people while in Europe." No one was ever charged for the attack.[22]

THE YEAR AFTER THE WAR ENDED, white mobs lynched eleven black veterans. Seventy-eight African Americans were lynched in 1919, including fourteen who were burned alive. Race riots erupted in twenty-eight cities across the nation. In July 1919, fires raged in American cities during a time so bloody it became known as the Red Summer. DuBois captured black people's angry exasperation: "They cheat us and mock us; they kill us and slay us; they deride our misery," he wrote. "When we plead for the naked protection of the law . . . they tell us to 'GO TO HELL!' "[23]

Eventually there would be another war and America would need all its citizens to rally to freedom's cause. This next time, however, African

Americans would not be content to fight for freedom abroad while ignoring their own plight at home. This next time, whenever it might be, African Americans in uniform would fight for victory abroad *and* for victory at home. Their postwar experience taught them that they could not achieve this victory at home by serving in an unjust military. Widespread military service had changed black Americans, and black Americans now would seek to change military service.

10

Old Draft in a New Day

A YEAR BEFORE THE POLLS OPENED, black voters excitedly anticipated the November 1940 elections. In the twenty years since the Great War's end, they had become a national political force. Candidates and incumbents from both parties ignored black voters' collective concerns at their peril. What mattered to African Americans mattered to white politicians more than it ever had: Because millions of them had migrated to Northern states where they could vote, they were now poised to play a possibly decisive role in the 1940 presidential and congressional elections. After war erupted in Europe on September 1, 1939, few issues mattered more to millions of black voters in 1940 than abolishing segregation and race-based inequality in the armed forces.[1]

African Americans of voting age had grown from being an occasionally potent bloc in a few Northern states to being a national political power by moving by the millions from Southern towns to Northern cities. Southern state and local governments employed poll taxes and other means effectively to prohibit their black citizens from voting. When these official measures failed, white residents used economic and violent coercion to intimidate African Americans. Political parties in Southern states routinely enjoined African Americans from voting in their primaries until NAACP Legal Defense and Education Fund chief counsel Thurgood Marshall convinced the Supreme Court in the 1944 landmark case *Smith v. Allwright* that such coercion violated the federal

Constitution. In states such as Texas, where Marshall filed *Smith*, the Democratic primary invariably determined the winner of the general election, so being prohibited from voting in the primary on account of one's race amounted to being stripped of the right to vote. By migrating north, African Americans largely escaped such disenfranchisement. The political concerns they held now mattered, because in Northern states, they, like white Americans, could vote.

It is important to note that millions of black mothers and fathers loaded their children and precious few belongings onto northbound trains for reasons more economic than political. The migration wreaked havoc on the economy of the rural South, which had grown dependent on plentiful and inexpensive black labor. In 1939 the Works Progress Administration released a study showing the migration's unprecedented scope and duration. From 1920 to 1930, the study noted, "it was largely whole families that migrated," resulting in "the mass depopulation of some rural districts." Black families "moved from Southern farm areas to large Northern cities—not retiring but seeking work and a better livelihood."[2]

Along with better jobs, African Americans gained political power in the North. "On approach of the 1940 presidential election," one political observer wrote, "both of the outstanding political parties are becoming concerned about the alignment of the Negro vote. This vote is strategically distributed along the free voting states of the North and West [and] may throw the wavering balance of the election to one side or the other." The Republican Party appointed former War Department official Emmett Scott to lead its effort "to stem the revolt of the Negro vote and head it back to the Republican fold."[3] Within the Democratic Party, white Southerners resented black voters' new power. One Democratic delegate from South Carolina lamented, "Our national party is being led around by the negroism of the North. I am mortally afraid of the negro in our national party." Virginia's segregationist Democratic senator Carter Glass warned his fellow Southerners to "have spirit and courage enough to face the new Reconstruction era that Northern so-called Democrats are menacing us with."[4]

Competition for African Americans' political support was fierce in Northern states. There were enough black voters in some states to turn them into swing states. A poll conducted in February 1940 by the Institute of Public Opinion found that 66 percent of black voters nationwide supported Roosevelt's reelection, but that Republicans' 34 percent showing was stronger than during any presidential election since the 1920s. Citing this poll, the *Washington Post* reported, "Obviously there has been a substantial movement on the part of Negro voters toward the GOP in the last three years, as shown by the number who now say they would like to see the Republican candidate elected in November." This was because "the colored voter today is voting far more in terms of his income status than in terms of his traditional party lines." Democrats still enjoyed the support of a convincing majority of black voters. Many of the likely Republican African American voters lived in New York, Pennsylvania, Ohio, Michigan, and Indiana. The *Post* averred that this strategic disbursement of voters meant that "whatever the trend of the colored man's political sentiments should be, he is likely to be an important factor in the election."[5]

On account of the continuing Great Migration, increased access to high school and college, and their experiences during and after the Great War, African Americans perceived themselves and their place in the nation differently. Having survived Southern segregation, millions of newly arrived black Northerners refused to suffer racist insults quietly. The new Northerners, as Walter White wrote, had "fled from lynching, disfranchisement, inferior schools, confinement to menial and lower-paid employment, and all the other evils from which they had suffered in the South."[6] In Boston, what one newspaper called "a group of irate colored women" protested the American Legion Auxiliary's production of a play replete with racial epithets. Calling the show "generally disgusting and nauseating," the women lodged a formal protest with the Suffolk County Council against the Jordan Theater's presenting such "a ridiculous, unfair disgrace."[7] This small but forceful protest exemplifies African Americans' middle-class militancy in the wake of the Great War and Great Migration.

Black Americans were now less separated by geography and class. They lived in both Northern and Southern states, and more of them were working in better-paying urban jobs. But in most Northern cities, racially restrictive covenants confined black professionals to overcrowded, segregated neighborhoods. One Chicago newspaper reported that the city's "Black Belt" was "pinned in on three sides by restrictive covenants, balked in the north by factories." Legal agreements among white property owners forbade black Chicagoans from "owning or renting property" across a large swath of the city.[8] Until the NAACP lawyer Charles Hamilton Houston won a Supreme Court case declaring unconstitutional the judicial enforcement of racially restrictive covenants, the contracts served to segregate housing across the entire northern half of the United States. When Houston argued the case before the nation's highest court, three justices recused themselves because their own homes were bound by racially restrictive covenants. Restrictive covenants bound many white homeowners from selling their homes to the first or highest bidder, but they also bound together black families of varying means and levels of education. In this predicament lay political power.

African Americans in Northern states held the power to sway elections, and this new political power infused black communities with a sense of responsibility: If they mobilized their votes for progressive candidates, they could help improve the lot of all African Americans, including the millions still living in Southern states that effectively prohibited them from voting. Mary McLeod Bethune, the renowned educator and federal government adviser, captured African Americans' sense of urgency when she addressed the congregation at Moore Street Baptist Church in Richmond, Virginia, on a Christmastime 1939 Sunday afternoon. Bethune, one of seventeen children born to two former slaves in South Carolina, was in her mid-sixties and near the height of her influence. She stood at the pulpit and announced that the "Negro must keep awake!" The time had come, she preached, "when black faces must be seen in high places."[9]

Black political power in Northern states helped elect more progressive candidates who were willing to speak directly to black voters' concerns. New York congresswoman Caroline O'Day declared in a speech at Columbia University, "Americans who are rightly concerned with the loss of democratic rights in many countries abroad will have to overcome their apathy toward the denial of equal citizenship rights for the Negro minority in this country if democracy is to be kept alive in the United States." O'Day was a liberal Democrat who counted first lady Eleanor

Roosevelt among her friends. "Unless the fight is made to pass a federal anti-lynching bill," O'Day continued, "and to open up to the Negro opportunities for education and cultural advancement on a plane of equality with every other citizen, respect for democratic rights and democracy itself will wither."[10] Her words could have been spoken just as easily by NAACP executive secretary Walter White—who also was among O'Day's friends.

IN 1939 AFRICAN AMERICANS did not uniformly support America's entering the war. Like all Americans, they were wary of fighting another bloody and costly battle to save European countries. Some black voters, however, opposed entering the war for reasons born in racial identity. They did not want black men again drafted to sacrifice and die for democracy abroad while they continued to be denied democracy at home. They wanted no part of a war fought on behalf of America's European allies who were fighting to save their African colonies as much as to save their own nations.

Speaking for thousands of workaday citizens who claimed not to have forgotten what he called "the raw deal of 1919" was the prominent trade union leader Revels Cayton, who used his position as secretary of the Maritime Federation of the Pacific to rally black labor opposition to fighting in another world war. "Negro maritime workers especially," Cayton asserted, "have joined in our declaration that 'The Yanks Are Not Coming' to help Britain and France keep their colonies or save Hitler from the wrath of the German people." Lofty calls to defend democracy only reminded Cayton of black soldiers' Promethean struggles in Woodrow Wilson's war to make the world safe for democracy. "Every Negro who faced the guns at Metz to 'save democracy' in the last war will remember how much 'democracy' he got when he came back home. Why, they lynched Race soldiers in the South and beat them up in race riots in the North."

The internationally acclaimed actor and singer Paul Robeson espoused a more Pan-Africanist reason why black Americans should oppose their nation's entering the war. In a November 1939 interview at a friend's home in New York City, Robeson told a reporter that the war raging in Europe was an "imperialist war in which the Negro people

have nothing to gain no matter which side wins." The renowned bari-
tone had recently returned from visiting several African nations. "The
terrible irony of it all is that there are about one million black Senegalese
troops being used by [French prime minister Édouard] Daladier now to
help make French imperialism richer and more ruthless against the colonies." It was clear to Robeson that "the Negro people in America have
every stake in keeping America out of this conflict and in battling
against the war hysteria which now seriously threatens civil rights."[11]

Some activists concluded that direct protest was necessary. The multiracial organization American Peace Mobilization declared "all-out war"
on a potential new military draft. Thousands of demonstrators, encouraged by celebrity activists like Robeson, traveled to Washington to protest
the draft. They marched from the Supreme Court to the steps of the
Capitol, where police ordered them away after they sang "God Bless
America." Demonstrators picketed the Mayflower Hotel because Speaker
of the House William Bankhead lived there.[12] Police arrested several
American Peace Mobilization members who distributed leaflets lambasting the new draft law. The activists, represented by Charles Hamilton Houston, in turn filed suit against the city of Washington and its
police department.[13]

BUT EVEN AFRICAN AMERICANS who were sympathetic to the progressive or Pan-Africanist arguments against America's involvement in
the war had to accept that America soon would enter it. In the summer
of 1940, President Roosevelt ordered the largest rearmament in American history. The fact that France had fallen to Nazi Germany persuaded
many isolationists in Congress to support the order.

By summer's end, members of Congress were debating yet another
Selective Service Act. The charismatic labor and civil rights leader Asa
Philip Randolph declared in August 1940, "Universal compulsory conscription is unnecessary in a time of peace. If enacted by Congress, the
draft bill will sound the death knell of American democracy. It is the
essence of totalitarianism. It means regimentation of our social, economic
and political life."[14] The Buffalo, New York, chapter of the NAACP
strongly opposed the draft and America's potential involvement in the
war overseas.[15]

There was no denying, however, that war again was coming to America. After the Great War, the War Department had dramatically reduced its number of African Americans in uniform. When House members and senators commenced debate over the Selective Service Act, there were fewer than five thousand African Americans in the 230,000-member army. Black people comprised 10 percent of the nation's population but less than 3 percent of the army. The only black officers in the army shared the same name: Colonel Benjamin O. Davis, Sr., and his son, Captain Benjamin O. Davis, Jr.

African American leaders launched an intense lobbying campaign to persuade Congress to include language in the Selective Service Act that would outlaw racial discrimination in the armed forces. Howard University professor and former army lieutenant Rayford W. Logan testified before Congress to demand that African Americans "be given equal opportunity to participate in the national-defense program, civil as well as military . . . [and] to serve in the naval and military services of this country in proportion to their numerical strength in the whole population."[16] Charles Hamilton Houston, testifying forcefully on behalf of the NAACP, told a congressional committee, "Negroes want some of the democracy they fought for in 1917 this time, and the sooner the better."[17]

In both houses of Congress, legislators were moved to act. New York's senior senator, Robert F. Wagner, proposed an amendment to the draft bill that would outlaw race-based discrimination in any of the military branches. Senator Tom Connally of Texas fought Wagner's amendment with noteworthy virulence. According to Connally, Wagner wanted black army volunteers to "serve in the same companies, sleep in the same rooms and eat at the same tables as white soldiers."[18] He argued that passing the Wagner amendment would mean surrendering to the bourgeois sort of black Americans "who want continually to agitate, disturb, stir up discussion, and raise the devil about what they speak of as their political and social rights."[19]

Despite Connally's exhortations, the Senate adopted Senator Wagner's amendment by a vote of 53 to 21. The House, led by Congressman Hamilton Fish of New York, enacted similar language in what was widely hailed in African American–owned newspapers as a substantive victory for the NAACP.[20] On September 14, 1940, President Roosevelt signed the peacetime draft bill into law.

In its entirety, the Wagner Amendment to the peacetime draft law provided "that any person between the ages of 18 and 35, regardless of race or color, shall be afforded an opportunity voluntarily to enlist and be inducted into the land or naval forces (including aviation units) of the United States for the training and service prescribed . . . , if he is acceptable to the land or naval forces for such training or service."[21]

Activists such as Houston, Logan, and Walter White foresaw trouble in that dangling clause: "if he is acceptable to the land or naval forces for such training or service." The army also managed to insert into the Selective Service Act a provision that no man would be admitted into the army unless he was "acceptable" and "adequate provision" had been made for his "shelter, sanitary facilities, medical care and hospital accommodations."[22] This meant the army would accept black men as neither draftees nor volunteers until it possessed facilities sufficient to segregate them all. The military's largest branch was determined to remain segregated.

THE BURKE-WADSWORTH SELECTIVE SERVICE ACT, as signed into law by President Roosevelt, called for 16.5 million men ages twenty-one to thirty-five to register with the federal government to make themselves available for military service. Aside from the contentious debate in Congress over the racial aspects of the legislation, the bill swiftly passed both houses in September. By November seventy-five thousand men were expected to be mustered in training. By January 1941, this number would grow to four hundred thousand troops. These men were to be drafted by lottery and serve twelve-month tours. Drafted soldiers were to receive $21 per month for their first four months of duty and $30 for each subsequent month.[23]

As during the draft for the Great War, some men would qualify for exemptions or deferments. Specifically, ministers, theological students, men with dependents, designated government officials, and the physically incapable and unfit would not be called in for military service. Conscientious objectors could be drafted for noncombat duty. Local registration boards could reject a registrant's request for an exemption or deferment, but he then could appeal to an appellate board.

Senior army officials expected approximately four hundred thousand black men to "be affected by the first call" of the draft law.[24] No matter how many black men would be drafted under the Burke-Wadsworth Selective Service Act, the future servicemen could take little solace in the law's watered-down ban on racial discrimination in the military. Black men lined up at recruiting stations, only to be rejected because the army had too few colored-only facilities to absorb them.[25]

Days after the law became effective, state governments and members of draft boards across the nation made clear that, for them, little had changed since the draft for the last world war. Fourteen states established all-white local draft boards.[26] South Carolina established an all-white state draft board. Governor Homer A. Holt of West Virginia told the NAACP only that he would give "careful consideration" to appointing a black person to his state's draft board.[27]

Tennessee's governor, Prentice Cooper, was less interested in using such polite euphemisms. When a local group of African American pastors asked him to appoint black people to the state's draft boards, he retorted, "This is a white man's country." Cooper explained, "America was settled by English, Scotch and Irish settlers who came here and shed their blood for it. White men cut down the trees, plowed the fields and developed America. The Negro had nothing to do with the settling of America.

"You fellows ought to feel proud that you are in a great country like America. It is the best place for you and your people." About the draft, the governor told the ministers, "You preachers ought to tell your boys to go to the stations and register for military service because if they don't they will be fined $10,000 or put in prison until they work it out."[28]

Politics Unusual

D URING JUST THE FIRST weeks after the Burke-Wadsworth Selective Service Act went into effect, African American leaders realized the extent of its shortcomings. Despite the law's purporting to ban racial discrimination, the military and most draft boards operated just as they had during World War I. The difference now was that Franklin Roosevelt, and not Woodrow Wilson, was president—or, perhaps more pertinently, the difference now was that the president was married to Eleanor Roosevelt.

Walter White had enlisted the first lady's help in trying to convince the president to support federal antilynching legislation. She was unsuccessful in that effort because her husband refused to risk alienating Southern members of his own party, whose support he needed to enact and sustain his ambitious New Deal agenda. As America prepared to enter another war with a segregated military, White, Mary McLeod Bethune, and other prominent African Americans sought Mrs. Roosevelt's assistance.[1] They knew her heart was with them and hoped she could counsel the president to act forcefully to improve the lot of black Americans in uniform.

The first lady wrote a letter to her husband. "There is a growing feeling amongst the colored people [that] they should be allowed to participate in any training that is going on in the aviation, army or navy," she told him. Perhaps remembering the political reasons why he refused to endorse federal antilynching legislation, she reminded him that he was facing reelection in just a few weeks. "This is going to be very bad politically," she predicted, "besides being intrinsically wrong and I think you should ask that a meeting be held."[2] Less than one week later, the president, along with Assistant Secretary of War Robert P. Patterson and Secretary of the Navy Frank Knox, met at the White House with Walter White, T. Arnold Hill, and A. Philip Randolph.

In advance of their visit, the leaders submitted a memorandum to the president delineating the changes they contended were necessary. Their primary demand was that "existing units of the army and units to be established should be required to accept and select officers and enlisted personnel without regard to race."[3] The men insisted that the War Department assign black volunteers and draftees to units in all branches of the military without regard to their race. Service members' qualifications and abilities alone should determine their rank and station. Plainly put, White, Hill, and Randolph were asking the War Department to desegregate the army.

At the meeting President Roosevelt appeared at once sympathetic and impervious to their demands. He assured them that he intended to lessen racial discrimination in the military and announced, as if granting a concession, that units of black soldiers henceforth would be organized in all segments of the army. The War Department would activate black officers in the army reserves at an undetermined future date.

The visitors pressed the president to agree that African American professionals, such as doctors, lawyers, and dentists, upon being inducted into military service, should be commissioned as officers just as their civilian white colleagues were. Roosevelt refused. Instead he told them that his administration planned to assign only white officers to command black draftees.[4] Black officers, after being called up from the reserves, would be permitted to command only black units already under the command of black officers. Black officers therefore could serve only in one of two National Guard regiments.[5] White, Randolph, and Hill were stunned. This was a blatant step backward.

The secretary of the navy spoke next. Frank Knox, who refused to allow African American reporters in the room to cover his press conferences, told the men that the navy would make no concessions or changes in its policy. He declared that the racial quandary was "insoluble" in the navy because sailors served aboard ships. The navy could not, Knox explained, establish "Northern" desegregated ships and "Southern" segregated ones. The only rational solution was to maintain the status quo; black sailors would continue to serve exclusively as stewards and cooks.[6]

The White House's corresponding press release made clear that President Roosevelt had officially sanctioned segregation in the armed forces. The White House's statement addressed the issue clearly:

> The policy of the War Department is not to intermingle colored and white enlisted personnel in the same regimental organizations. This policy has proven satisfactory over a long period of years, and to make changes would produce situations destructive to morale and detrimental to the preparation for national defense. For similar reasons the department does not contemplate assigning colored reserve officers other than those of the Medical Corps and chaplains to existing Negro combat units of the Regular Army.[7]

War Department officials began referring to "the President's policy of segregation of the races."

The announcement surprised many observers because it appeared to contradict the conscription bill Roosevelt had signed into law just weeks before. The White House's statement was consistent, however, with advice the administration received from the War Department's General Staff, which stated in a memo that "every effort should be made by the War Department to maintain in the Army the social and racial conditions which exist in civil life in order that normal customs of white and colored personnel now in the Army may not be suddenly disrupted."[8] In so many words, the president's highest-ranking military advisers had asked him to keep the military segregated.

Just as he sought an unprecedented third term in office, Roosevelt had seriously damaged his standing among African American voters. Civil rights leaders joined the black press in condemning his announcement. "White House Blesses Jim Crow," trumped the headline in the *Crisis*.[9] In black neighborhoods in Northern cities, outrage poured from preachers' pulpits and from lecterns at fraternal and community gatherings. Many black middle-class voters already had grown disenchanted with the president because of his steadfast refusal to support federal antilynching legislation, the passage of which had been for years the NAACP's foremost lobbying cause. (Conventional wisdom among political observers, as expressed by the *Baltimore Afro-American*, was that "a nod from [Roosevelt] would have caused Congress to make [the bill] a law.")[10] Now he officially opposed desegregating the armed forces—the very cause that was supplanting antilynching legislation as the NAACP's signature effort. "In ordinary times," Roy Wilkins wrote in his popular newspaper column, "Negroes would have no defense against a statement from the White House. But this is election time and Mr. Roosevelt is asking for votes. Someone has blundered badly."[11]

Some white political observers who otherwise were indifferent to the substance of Roosevelt's announcement nonetheless expressed consternation at its timing. The election was little more than one month away. To win, Roosevelt would need the support of African American voters in Northern states. Black political pundits were flatly declaring that the black vote would determine who won the presidency in November.[12] With war raging overseas and civil rights becoming a prominent political and judicial issue at home, one commentator wrote that the 1940 election was the most significant for "the Negro and other minority groups and underprivileged classes in this country than at any time since the campaign that elected Abraham Lincoln."[13]

FRANKLIN ROOSEVELT'S REPUBLICAN opponent, Wendell Willkie, was an Indiana-born corporate lawyer and businessman who was earning an annual salary of $75,000 when he ran for his first elective office, the presidency of the United States. Dark hair crowned Willkie's burly six-foot-one-inch frame. Despite favorable press coverage about his having "married a small-town girl," Willkie was an unapologetic philanderer whose own wife did not deny his notorious exploits. He once held a press conference in his mistress's apartment.[14] Despite such reckless behavior, in the summer of 1940 Wendell Willkie beat better-known and better-funded candidates such as Thomas E. Dewey to secure the Republican nomination.

Willkie's primary campaign themes were attacking President Roosevelt on issues of foreign policy and for seeking a third term as president. Unlike the incumbent, Willkie spoke forcefully in favor of civil rights. He vowed to roll back the institutionalized racism in the federal government that, set firmly into place by Woodrow Wilson, seemed to some black workers to have become more entrenched during Roosevelt's years in office. "I say to you," Willkie told black reporters, "that under my administration, if elected, there will be no discrimination between people because of race, creed or color in the appointments to federal positions . . . Colored citizens [will be] appointed to any branch of the Civil Service to which they are qualified."[15]

The Republican Party wasted no time in capitalizing on Roosevelt's announcement favoring continued segregation in the armed forces. In Harlem Willkie excoriated the president's policy in an address to more than five thousand New Yorkers.[16] His wife toured the storied Manhattan neighborhood as well, visiting the new state-of-the-art Harlem Boys Center and extolling it as a "practical . . . way to build good American boys."[17]

At a Chicago meeting of more than one hundred prominent African Americans, speakers blasted the president for opposing antilynching legislation and supporting segregation in the military. Francis Rivers, an African American attorney and Republican Party official, declared after attending the meeting, "Wendell L. Willkie will be the next president of the United States." Thanks in no small part to the president's granting official sanction to a segregated military, the Republican believed that "victory was in the air."[18] Republican pollsters reported strong black support for Willkie in states from Connecticut and Rhode Island to West Virginia.[19]

The White House's tacit support of military segregation reminded many African American voters of why they had initially greeted Franklin Roosevelt's candidacy with skepticism. Walter White did not vote for Roosevelt in 1932.[20] When Roosevelt first ran for president, NAACP officials remarked in the *Crisis*: "FDR has spent six months out of every twelve as Governor of New York and the rest swimming in a Georgia mudhole. If he is elected president, we shall have to move the White House to Warm Springs, [Georgia,] and use Washington for his occasional vacations."

The New York patrician had never hidden his affinity for the South. He vacationed at his second home in Warm Springs and was embraced by Georgians. Georgia's powerful senator Richard Russell, a strident segregationist, called Roosevelt the man "who is most beloved by Georgians of any man in the life of our state." Governor Eurith Rivers called the New Yorker one of Georgia's "very own" and a "fellow Georgian." Roosevelt in turn spoke fondly of the harshly segregated state, "because for many long years I have regarded Georgia as my 'other state.' "[21]

Roosevelt's sudden support for maintaining segregation in the armed forces confirmed African Americans' fears about him. The president appeared unwilling to do anything to ameliorate the scourge of Jim Crow. Charles Hamilton Houston quipped to Walter White, "All along I've been telling you that your President had no real courage and that he would chisel in a pinch."[22]

Wendell Willkie's prospects with African American voters appeared quite good after Roosevelt expressed support for continuing to segregate members of the armed forces. Roy Wilkins summarized black Americans' frustration when he wrote, "Mr. Roosevelt has failed to do many things he might have done for Negroes. He could have passed the Anti-Lynching Bill. But this announcement of his endorsement of Jim Crow [in the armed forces] is a greater blow than all his failures."[23]

Influential speakers urged black voters to reconsider their support for the president. Heavyweight boxing champion Joe Louis told those gathered at a crowded rally in St. Louis to vote for Willkie, "because he will do what the President has failed to accomplish." The Brown Bomber continued, "I am just Joe Louis. I am a fighter, not a politician. This country has been good to me and . . . I am for Willkie because I think he will help my people."[24] Charles Edward Russell, a white civil rights activist who helped found the NAACP, urged African Americans not to vote for Roosevelt, citing the "gross discriminations practiced in both the army and navy" about which the president "has responded only with evasions and polite notes of acknowledgement."[25] In his column "As the Crow Flies," W.E.B. DuBois flatly declared, "Roosevelt has depended and must depend on the solid, lynching, reactionary South for reelection."[26] The *Baltimore Afro-American* editorialized, "After sixteen years of campaigning for Democratic and Progressive nominees, this newspaper today announces its support of Wendell Willkie, a Republican, for the Presidency of the United States."[27]

Franklin Roosevelt at last realized the political cost of his announcement. He personally wrote a letter to White, Randolph, and Hill, expressing regret that his statement on the military had been misinterpreted in the press. "You may rest assured," the president wrote, "that further developments of policy will be forthcoming to insure that Negroes are given fair treatment on a non-discriminatory basis."[28]

Privately, White House advisers Harry Hopkins and Will Alexander told Roosevelt that, based on Alexander's meetings with prominent black leaders, the nation's restive black citizens had four immediate demands: First, they wanted segregation abolished in all branches of the military. Second, Colonel Benjamin O. Davis, Sr., who, with his son, accounted for all the black men in the officer corps of the United States Army, should be promoted to brigadier general. Third, to ensure greater equality in administration of the draft, Major Campbell C. Johnson should be appointed assistant to the selective service director. Last, William H. Hastie, the highly respected former federal judge and current dean of Howard Law School, should be appointed assistant secretary of war.[29] African Americans were still disturbed by how the army had forced Colonel Charles Young to retire rather than promote him to the rank of brigadier general and desired some confirmation that their most accomplished citizens could advance under Roosevelt's leadership. The president considered these demands while his campaign directors, with growing consternation, watched Willkie's support rise in African American communities.

Days before the election, the White House announced that the president was granting three of the leaders' four demands. First, he promoted sixty-two-year-old Colonel Benjamin O. Davis, Sr., commander of the 369th Coast Artillery Regiment of the New York National Guard, to the army rank of brigadier general. Davis became the first black soldier to be promoted to the rank of general. Roosevelt had promoted dozens of white colonels to the brigadier general rank just two weeks earlier and now claimed merely to have "overlooked" Davis. It appeared impossible for an officer to hold the rank of general without commanding both white and black soldiers. When asked about his future assignments, the diplomatic Davis replied, "Well, generals don't command regiments, you know, but I really can't say what orders I will receive."[30]

Second, Roosevelt named Major Campbell Johnson to be the executive assistant to the director of Selective Service. After serving as an army captain in the Great War, Johnson had returned to his native Washington, D.C., where he taught military science and established an ROTC unit at Howard University. Johnson was the consummate soldier-activist who, according to the *Washington Post*, served as "a board member of almost every large community welfare organization in Washington." He was a formidable advocate, whom the White House hired to "assist in the fair and effective utilization of the colored in all branches of the armed forces."[31]

William H. Hastie's appointment as a civilian aide to the secretary of war proved to be the most controversial, because Hastie, a brilliant attorney and former member of the *Harvard Law Review*, possessed a different understanding from that of the president on how he could best aid the War Department. Roosevelt expected Hastie's position to be similar to that held by Emmett J. Scott during the Great War, but Hastie balked at such a comparison. A fervent believer in Booker T. Washington's more patient approach to activism, Scott in the decades after the war had come to be viewed by many of his fellow middle-class African Americans as a leader too willing to accommodate institutionalized racism and segregation. Hastie had no intention of suffering Scott's fate. More important, times had changed a great deal since the Wilson administration.

By the time Roosevelt asked Hastie to join the War Department, the push to integrate every branch of the armed forces had become the single most important issue to NAACP members. The National Urban League had unanimously adopted a resolution stating that it was "unalterably opposed to the policy and practice of racial discrimination and segregation in the Army, Navy, Air Force and Marine Corps of the United States."[32] Gone were the days when African American college men marched on Howard University's campus to demand a segregated officers' training camp. African American Great War veterans were among those most ardently opposed to military segregation.

BORN INTO A MIDDLE-CLASS Tennessee family, William Hastie graduated with honors from both Amherst College and Harvard Law School. He had served as an assistant solicitor in the Department of the Interior and later as a federal judge for the United States District Court in the Virgin Islands. He left the bench to become the dean of Howard Law School, which he, along with Charles Hamilton Houston, turned into a veritable West Point for civil rights legal advocacy. Recent Howard Law School graduates such as Thurgood Marshall and Oliver Hill were beginning to win landmark desegregation cases in courtrooms across the country. They had learned the law under Hastie's demanding tutelage and, as practicing attorneys, still consulted him on their most difficult cases.

Now, as he considered whether to accept the War Department post, it was Hastie's turn to ask Thurgood Marshall for advice. If he accepted the position, Hastie intended to push the administration to provide the equal military service opportunities that the president claimed to support. The question, as Marshall aptly framed it, was whether Hastie's appointment would be seen "as (a) a victory for Negroes in their fight for full integration into the armed forces without discrimination or segregation or (b) as an act of appeasement, as an effort to fool the Negroes and to use a Negro leader for this purpose." Marshall, then a young attorney already nationally known for his landmark victories in civil rights litigation, was nothing if not a realist. "At this stage of the fight," he wrote to Hastie, "the odds are that such an appointment will be considered as an act toward appeasement on the part of the War Department without them actually giving up anything."[33] Despite this unfortunate reality, Marshall thought Hastie should accept the position but, in doing so, issue a statement vowing to continue the fight to desegregate the military.

William Hastie accepted the official title of civilian aide to the secretary of war. When War Department officials refused to list desegregation policy development as one of his duties, Hastie followed Marshall's advice and took the extraordinary step of issuing his own statement. "I have always been consistently opposed," Hastie announced upon accepting his appointment, "to any policy of discrimination and segregation in the armed forces of this country." Lest the president or his fellow War

Department officials mistake his intentions, he explained, "I am assuming this post in the hope that I will be able to work toward the integration of the colored man into the army and to facilitate his placement, training and promotion."[34]

Hastie's declaration placed him on a political collision course with Secretary of War Henry L. Stimson, his new boss, who believed that the military should remain segregated so long as segregation existed in American life. Stimson made clear that official War Department policy would not change: "The Army would not be used as a sociological laboratory for effecting social change within the military establishment."[35]

POLITICAL CONSIDERATIONS obviously weighed heavily on the president's mind when he decided, days before the election, to promote Colonel Davis and to appoint Major Johnson and Dean Hastie. Republican congressman Thomas Reed, Jr., of Maine, charged the president with making pandering gestures to African Americans because "he knew their votes held the balance of power in some states."[36] Rather than scorn the blatantly political moves, however, African American leaders such as Roy Wilkins embraced the gestures as a realpolitik nod to African Americans' new and undeniable power in national politics. "Of course it was political," Wilkins remarked about Hastie's appointment. "Of course it was hammered out under pressure. All concessions in government are the result of pressure. Through Hastie we can fight toward the objective we want."[37]

Secretary of War Stimson deplored the Roosevelt administration's sudden sensitivity to the civil rights lobby. He wrote in his diary that African American leaders were "taking advantage of the last weeks of the campaign in order to force the Army and Navy into doing things for their race which would not otherwise be done and which are certainly not in the interest of sound national defense." The president's decision to promote Colonel Davis to brigadier general struck Stimson as a somewhat amusing act of political appeasement. He joked with Secretary of the Navy Frank Knox "over the necessity that [Knox] was facing the possibility of appointing a colored Admiral and a battle fleet full of colored sailors according to a Resolution passed by the Colored Federal

Employees Association and I told him that when I called next time at the Navy Department with my colored Brigadier General I expected to be met with the colored Admiral."[38]

IN NOVEMBER 1940, President Franklin Roosevelt won reelection. Willkie carried just ten states, none with a substantial population of African American voters. Roosevelt garnered 449 electoral votes to Willkie's 82. The incumbent president won the popular vote with 27.2 million votes to Willkie's 22.3 million votes. In Midwestern and Western states, Willkie received nearly 50 percent of the black vote, but in the Northeastern states, African Americans' support for Roosevelt remained strong.

Upper-middle-class black voters who were willing to support the Republican candidate were outnumbered by working-class and middle-class voters who believed that the president's New Deal programs were working. As one Baltimore housewife told a reporter, "Only rich people want Willkie." A domestic worker remarked, "I am not even worried about Willkie. I can't forget that working people had no rights before Mr. Roosevelt."[39] In endorsing Roosevelt's second reelection, the *New York Amsterdam News* editorial board lamented the president's failure "to speak out against the recently announced jim crow army policy" and his refusal to support antilynching legislation, but could not deny "the advantages that have come to the Negro through President Roosevelt's social legislation." Under the New Deal, the editors claimed, African Americans had made more progress "than under any other administration."[40]

Roosevelt's administration ensured that African Americans were hired both by the New Deal agencies and by government contractors. The Work Projects Administration employed 350,000 African American workers, who accounted for 15 percent of the WPA's workforce. African Americans comprised more than 10 percent of the National Youth Administration and the Civilian Conservation Corps, and the Public Works Administration issued contracts only to companies that agreed to hire a certain number of African American workers.[41]

Also in Roosevelt's favor was the fact that many African Americans simply did not trust Willkie, if elected president, to back his pro–civil rights rhetoric with action. The columnist Ralph Matthews expressed many working-class voters' views when he wrote that "anybody who deludes himself into thinking that either Mr. Willkie or anyone associated with him has a consuming desire to get into power just so he can abolish discrimination, give colored people jobs or get the anti-lynch bill passed is too naïve to be trusted with the ballot." The Republican nominee was a businessman above all, and for his campaign, African Americans' quest for equality was "an annoyance that must be reckoned with just as a large firm has to reckon with the custodial staff."[42] One Ohio bishop explained, "We know [Roosevelt] and we do not know Willkie. Roosevelt has started on a work which he has not completed."[43] Another African American editorial board noted, "There is nothing in Mr. Willkie's record to indicate that his interest in Negroes would lead him to do any more for them than was done by Harding, Coolidge or Hoover."[44]

After helping him win reelection, Roosevelt's African American supporters demanded anew that he stand up to the senators and congressmen they called "undemocratic Southern oligarchs." They wanted him to take a more direct interest in African Americans' collective plight. "Negroes must not now be misled," declared one black attorney in Pittsburgh who voted for Roosevelt. "For although they have benefited greatly from the laws enacted by the New Deal, they still have ahead the fight against discrimination in public offices, [for] the right to participate equally in monies appropriated for public use, [and against] segregation of all descriptions." He now hoped that the president, whom he doubted would seek a fourth term in office, would feel free to "now see through the anti-lynching bill."[45]

These supporters in time would learn that Franklin Roosevelt had no intention of using his office or his political capital to push forcefully for African Americans' constitutional rights. As his biographer Frank Freidel noted, Roosevelt's "was a position of benevolent neutrality."[46] The president was loath to actively oppose or support civil rights for African Americans. Whether Roosevelt's posture could amount to anything more than a clever oxymoron when held by the president of the United States in 1940 was a riddle African Americans would have to decipher by experience.

———————

THE THIRD-TERM PRESIDENT was not the only man in Washington
who owed his 1940 reelection in part to support from African American
voters. More so than the president, the junior senator from Missouri, a
bespectacled Great War veteran with a high school education, owed his
return to Washington to the support he received from African American
voters. More than 130,000 black Missourians cast ballots in the extraordinarily close Democratic Senate primary in which Harry S. Truman
narrowly defeated Governor Lloyd C. Stark. Truman defeated the primary challenge by five thousand votes, the closest Missouri Senate race
since 1822. Nearly every black voter's ballot was cast for Truman.[47]

Despite being born into a self-professed "unreconstructed" Southern
family, Truman consistently had earned African American voters' support since winning election to local office in 1926. As a county politician, Harry Truman had courted the powerful Kansas City chapter of
the NAACP and fought back rumors that he once had belonged to the
Ku Klux Klan. More important, Truman made sure that black Missourians knew that, on issues of their concern, there was no daylight between him and his political benefactor, Boss Tom Pendergast. "Truman
was politically astute on the race question before he ever came to Washington," Roy Wilkins explained, "because the Pendergast machine was
politically astute."[48]

Like many who closely observed the remarkable paradox that was
Harry Truman, Wilkins was both accurate and inaccurate in his assess-
ment: Truman needed Pendergast to get elected to the Senate, but he
did not need the notorious Missouri boss to teach him the art of politics.
He knew he needed the support of African American voters, and he
understood that, because of his rural Southern heritage, they would eye
him with suspicion. Harry Truman was as shrewd a political actor as any
in the United States Senate.

By 1940, Truman appeared to have come as far in political life as
his ambition and abilities would take him. This is perhaps why Senator
Truman's colleagues, opponents, and pundits repeatedly underestimated
him. Most politicians at some point in their careers claim to have been
underestimated, and their retelling of the slight reveals their resentment.
Truman relished being underestimated. Humility came so naturally to
him that it became a sort of cloak, a disguise in plain sight. If he ever

read Roy Wilkins's observation about how he came to realize the value of black voters, he certainly would have smiled and understood how Wilkins had misread him. After all, there was nothing in Harry Truman's personal or professional life history that would suggest that he ever had or would give a second thought to the plight of black citizens struggling to survive in the American South.

Follow the Gleam

THE FUTURE PRESIDENT WAS BORN on May 8, 1884, in his parents' first home in Lamar, Missouri. There was no running water or plumbing in the small house. His father sold mules out of a barn across the street.[1] By the time Harry was six years old, he was wearing the eyeglasses that would become an ever-present trademark later in life. Young Harry Truman was an introverted child who preferred reading or playing his family's Kimball piano to playing ball outside with other children. When he did step outside to play, he would hide his sheets of music beneath his books on the ground.[2] He so rarely got into trouble that one childhood friend recalled that Harry "seemed to do whatever his mother told him."[3]

His father's successes and failures in business eventually brought the family to the town of Independence, Missouri. Harry attended the school for white children and was a good but not exceptional student. As one of his favorite teachers recalled, "Harry was always a very satisfactory pupil, always had his lessons." His eyeglasses often kept him from playing with the other boys. "While he was in school," his teacher continued, "he didn't get to play and have games with the other boys because he wore such heavy glasses, but he was interested in sports. You could see him watching the boys play."[4]

By the time he reached high school, Harry's insatiable reading habits were well-known among his teachers and friends. Biographies of military and political heroes were his favorites. "I think his steadfastness in always having his lessons and his proclivity for reading and particularly reading history in the library," his Latin teacher believed, "was indicative of something that was coming on in his life and character."[5] Truman later would write of how he was inspired by the books he checked out from the town library. He read nearly every book in the library and adopted Alexander the Great, Hannibal, Genghis Kahn, Stonewall Jackson, and Robert E. Lee as his personal heroes. Their true tales of triumph and tragedy revealed to him a world far beyond the town limits of Independence.

Harry was among several students in his high school who started an annual school publication. The *Gleam*, as they called it, was part yearbook, part newspaper, part literary magazine. The *Gleam* took its title from the poem "Merlin and the Gleam" by Tennyson, and, as Truman later proudly noted, "It is still published by the Independence High School after fifty years."[6] On the cover of the inaugural issue, framed by a student's artwork, were Tennyson's words:

Not of the sunlight,
Not of the moonlight,
Not of the starlight,
O, young mariner,
Down to the haven,
Call your companions,
Launch your vessel,
And crowd your canvas,
And, ere it vanishes,
Over the margin
After it, follow it,
Follow the Gleam.

In March 1952, when he was president of the United States, Truman baffled political observers and members of his own administration when he interrupted his vacation in Key West to fly 4,800 miles round trip to New York City to deliver an unwritten fifteen-minute address to three thousand schoolchildren. The students, members of Columbia's Scholastic

Press Association, eagerly awaited the president's arrival in the grand ballroom of the Waldorf-Astoria. *Time* magazine described President Truman as "beamish and bubbly" when he took the stage to deliver a "rambling and reminiscing" talk. "I came all the way up here," he told the student-journalists, "because the future of this great republic of ours depends on young people like you." He then described for them his time working on the *Gleam* and encouraged the young people to heed "that admonition in Tennyson's poem—After it, follow it, Follow the Gleam."[7]

Truman's high school Latin teacher followed his political career closely through the decades. She knew how lucky he had been but believed him to be "a self-made man in a great many ways" who deserved his good luck. The woman Truman forever called Mrs. Palmer concisely summarized the man she had known as a boy when she told an interviewer, "I think that motto, 'Follow the Gleam,' has really been Harry Truman's motto throughout his whole life."[8]

INDEPENDENCE, MISSOURI, was a harshly segregated town of six thousand. Black children enrolled in the one dilapidated school they could attend and were forbidden from using the town library. Stores and public accommodations were marked WHITES ONLY. African Americans knew that Independence was "Klan country."

Like most white families in Independence, the Trumans breezily used racial epithets when referring to African Americans. White supremacy was an unquestioned facet of their lives and their outlook. Journalists and editors for the county's local newspapers wrote approvingly of African Americans' being lynched, with one going so far as to predict that a black man soon would be tortured and murdered in Independence because "the conditions are favorable at this time. There are a lot of worthless young Negro men in town who do nothing."[9]

Harry Truman was not troubled by any of this. As a United States senator thirty-seven years later, he remarked to a Southern senator about the pending antilynching bill, "You know I am against this bill, but if it comes to a vote, I'll have to vote for it. All my sympathies are with you but the Negro vote in Kansas City and St. Louis is too important."[10] During their courtship Truman explained to his future wife that he believed all men were created equal, "so long as he's honest and decent and not a nigger or a Chinaman."[11]

Truman's family, particularly his mother, to whom he was very close, passed on to him their racist views. "I was raised amidst some violently prejudiced Southerners," he later recognized.[12] The Truman family's racism was not uncommon among whites in rural Missouri, many of whom, like the Trumans, spent a good deal of time listening to their older relatives fondly reminisce over the antebellum years. All four of Truman's grandparents were born in Kentucky, and about his forebears, Truman acknowledged, "They all had slaves. They brought them out here with them from Kentucky. Most of the slaves were wedding presents." One of his grandfathers owned two dozen slaves, who worked on his five-thousand-acre Missouri plantation. Harry's mother simply would say, "I thought it was a good thing that Lincoln was shot."[13] Decades later, when her son was president of the United States and she visited him at the White House, Martha Truman refused to sleep in the Lincoln Room. She was disappointed to see President Truman placing a wreath at the Lincoln Memorial.

FOR ALL HIS SOUTHERN PREJUDICE, Truman was glad the Union had won the war. "I am not sorry [Robert E. Lee] did surrender," he wrote to his daughter in 1941, "but I feel as your old country grandmother has expressed it—'What a pity a *white* man like Lee had to surrender to old Grant.'"[14]

His father's business failings rendered paying for college impossible so young Harry Truman decided to join the army. By the time he had turned thirteen, Truman had, in his words, "made up his mind that he would be a military man although he was afraid of a gun and would rather run than fight."[15]

The U.S. Military Academy at West Point rejected him on account of his bad eyesight, but he vowed not to let that keep him from becoming a soldier. Truman enlisted in a National Guard battery when he turned twenty-one. Despite his insular childhood, he took naturally to military life, beaming with delight even when a captain asked him to assist in removing his wet boots, because, as Truman explained, he "was very much pleased that so high an officer should notice him."[16] The young private soon received a warrant promoting him to corporal. "No commission in after life," Senator Harry Truman wrote about himself in 1940, "(and he got a dozen of them, one signed by President Wilson himself) ever gave him the thrill of that warrant."[17]

He drilled with Missouri's Light Artillery, Battery B, First Brigade unit, but, as a citizen-soldier, the young man spent nearly all his time working his family's farm. After receiving his promotion, Truman visited his grandmother's house, standing ramrod straight in his crisp blue National Guard uniform. She looked him up and down before admonishing him, "Harry, this is the first time since 1863 that a blue uniform has been in this house. Don't bring it here again."[18]

WHEN HARRY WAS still a boy, his mother enrolled him in Sunday school at the town's Presbyterian church, and here he met the girl whom he would love for the rest of his life. Elizabeth Wallace was, as he described her, "a very beautiful little lady with lovely blue eyes and the prettiest golden curls I've ever seen."[19] Elizabeth, whom everyone called Bessie, lived on the best street in Independence, just two and a half blocks from Harry. Unlike him, she was popular, athletic, and outgoing. Harry and Bessie attended Sunday school, grade school, and high school together. "If I succeeded in carrying her books to school and back home for her," he fondly recalled, "I had a big day."[20] Harry was smitten with Bess from the day they met, and, although it took many years to win her devotion, theirs was a lasting bond. As president he summarized it best when he wrote, "She was my sweetheart and ideal when I was a little boy—and she still is."[21]

WHEN AMERICA ENTERED the Great War in 1917, Harry Truman was thirty-three years old and desperate for a change in his life. His father had died and he was supporting his mother and sister by working the family farm in Jackson County. His beloved Bess still had not agreed to marry him. The war presented an opportunity for escape. Because he was both a farmer and his family's sole breadwinner, he was statutorily exempt from military service, but he was determined not to let this opportunity pass by. He left his sister with responsibility for their mother and the farm and reported to the National Guard office in Kansas City for a physical examination.

He was legally blind in his left eye and even with glasses, the vision in his right eye was less than optimal. At five feet eight inches tall and 151 pounds, Truman was slight but had a wiry strength gained by years working the farm. He knew his eyesight fell below military standards and may have been nervous about being rejected: During the physical his heart was thumping at a lively seventy-eight beats per minute.[22]

The fact that he possessed prior military experience likely contributed to his being accepted for service despite his poor eyesight. On September 14, 1917, Harry Truman officially accepted an army commission as a first lieutenant in the Second Missouri Field Artillery.[23] After extensive training, he set sail for France on Good Friday, 1918, with seven thousand other soldiers.[24]

UPON ARRIVING IN FRANCE, Truman partook of the food, wine, and accommodations enjoyed by many white officers in the American Expeditionary Forces before they reported to battlegrounds. For two weeks Lieutenant Truman resided at a posh hotel in Brest. He poured water from crystal decanters and reclined on plush upholstered furniture. By all accounts he resisted engaging the "ever-present" local women, whom one of his fellow lieutenants described as "so mysterious and seductive in the darkness."[25]

Instead, Truman religiously wrote letters to Bess. "Be sure and keep writing," he wrote to her, "because its [sic] sure lonesome over here when there's an hour to spare from work. I'll write as often as they'll let me even if I can only say I love you."[26] In his letters he described his training and the education he was receiving, happily reporting that he was excelling in college-level math classes. One exam was so difficult, it "would make the President of Yale University bald headed scratching his head trying to think of answers."[27] He acknowledged the fabled allure of French women but assured Bess, "Every fellow in this room is engaged to some fine girl back in the States and the French girls haven't a chance. None of us have ever seen any worth raving over yet. I guess all the pretty ones are in Paris anyway."[28]

ONE WEEK AFTER the Fourth of July, 1918, Truman was made commander of an all-white battery and placed in charge of 194 men. He was
visibly nervous as he stood before the notoriously unruly Battery D of
the second Battalion, 129th Field Artillery. The men initially derided
their bespectacled new leader, but Captain Truman's assertiveness and
experienced military bearing swiftly earned their respect. The demanding captain turned his battery of urban Irish Catholics into one of the
most squared-away units in the theater. One of the army's chief ord-
nance officers, after inspecting Battery D, told Truman that the unit
was one of the best he had seen in all of France. Harry wrote to Bess that
he was "plumb crazy" about "my Irishmen," who "sure step to when I ask
them to."[29]

Soon after Captain Truman drilled his soldiers into fighting shape,
they trudged through the mud into combat. They did not know "if we
would be heroes or corpses," but the young army captain quickly became a hero in the eyes of his men.[30] The first time Battery D fell under
enemy fire, nearly the entire company retreated after a sergeant mistakenly yelled that the Germans had them all but surrounded. Truman's
horse was hit and fell on top of him. He struggled for breath, could not
move, and therefore was unable to countermand the sergeant's order. A
fellow officer rescued him from beneath the horse and Truman regained
his breath. Then he uncharacteristically let loose a stream of profanity
and stood his ground amid the retreat. Only three or four soldiers stood
with him. The next morning back at camp, Truman wallowed in self-
loathing at the fact that his men had retreated. His superior officer assured him that such an ignominious reaction to heavy enemy fire was not
uncommon for green soldiers and that it bore no reflection on Truman's
leadership.[31]

Captain Truman later led Battery D in the great Meuse-Argonne offensive, the largest, most complex American army operation that had
ever been attempted. The sprawling battle plan, set forth by then colonel
George C. Marshall, was successful in large part because of the ability of
junior officers like Truman to lead and inspire their troops. Battery D
marched more than a hundred miles. They arrived at their destination,
a mud-soaked patch of woods, exhausted but prepared for battle. This
time the men performed valiantly amid enemy fire.

The Great War ended a few weeks later. The captain of Battery D was universally respected among his men. "We respected him and he earned it," one soldier later said of Captain Truman. "That's why we respected him, because he earned it . . . He's not a dramatic type or anything like it. He's no Patton, you know. He might have been a better soldier than Patton, but he was not a showoff."[32]

Truman arrived back in New York Harbor on Easter morning, April 20, 1919. He was ecstatic to be home in the States. "I made a resolution," he recalled, "that if old lady Liberty in New York harbor wanted to see me again she'd have to turn around."[33]

AFTER RETURNING TO MISSOURI, Harry Truman married Bess Wallace on the same day that the peace treaty at Versailles was signed. Their courtship had lasted eight and a half years—much longer than he had anticipated when he first fell in love with her. He was so anxious to marry that he initially suggested she travel to New York City to meet him. He had bought her a wedding ring in Paris and thought they could get married at a small Episcopal church near Broadway. Bess thought it best that their wedding take place in Missouri so their friends and family could celebrate with them. On their wedding day, Harry was thirty-five years old and Bess was thirty-four.

The *Indepedence Examiner* reported on the small and joyous ceremony:

A wedding of unusual beauty and interest was that of Miss Bess Wallace and Capt. Harry Truman, on Saturday afternoon at four o'clock, at Trinity Episcopal Church. Miss Wallace has lived in Independence all her life and has a large circle of friends. Independence also claims Capt. Truman although he has spent much time away. It was in this setting of love and devoted friendship that the marriage was solemnized. The church was beautifully decorated with garden flowers in pastel shades. The altar was a mass of daisies, pink hollyhocks and pale blue larkspur against a soft green background, lighted with tall cathedral candles.[34]

THERE WAS, IMMEDIATELY AFTER THEY celebrated their honeymoon in the Midwest and moved into her family's home in Independence, the

issue of how Truman would earn a living after being honorably discharged from military service. He had no intention of returning to
work the family farm. He had made arrangements with Eddie Jacobson,
a military buddy, to open a men's clothing store in Kansas City.

As impulsive as their plan might have seemed to his fiancée and future
mother-in-law, haberdashery had long been one of Truman's unspoken
interests. His father, even as he lost the family's modest fortune in pros-
pecting and trading, always prided himself on looking his best. Harry's
pince-nez glasses lent him a distinguished air that was accentuated by his
smartly cut hair and tailored shirts and slacks. One day he would be
world famous as a "common man," but Harry Truman's tastes and attention to detail in fashion were anything but common.

Truman & Jacobson opened on November 28, 1919, in an eighteen-
by-forty-eight-foot store on the first floor of a freshly renovated large
hotel. The spotless glass windows framed an array of handsomely ar-
ranged fedoras and shirts beneath a wooden transom advertising *SHIRTS
COLLARS HOSIERY GLOVES BELTS HATS*. Truman and Eddie Jacobson
were good friends and equally good business partners. They unofficially
divided duties to take advantage of each man's abilities. Jacobson tended
the store's books and usually could be found in the store during its daily
operating hours of eight in the morning until nine at night.

Truman was ill suited for such stationary duty. He had spent the prior
years plowing acres of farmland and then trudging through miles of battlefield mud. As proud as he was of the elegant store, the space seemed
confining to a man who, finally, in his mid-thirties, felt that he was coming into his own. So he became the store's rainmaker. He bounced around
downtown Kansas City meeting up with old friends and making new
ones. "Harry would get around a lot, you know," one of Truman's close
friends recalled, "and was mixing with people. He never stayed in the
store all day—he would get out and go to lunches and mix with people,
you know. He was very well known in that way and Eddie Jacobson
would stay around and take care of the business."[35]

Truman & Jacobson soon became something of a reunion hall for
former members of Battery D. Former corporal Harry Murphy recalled,
"I used to go there every time I was downtown. It was sort of a headquarters. You went in there to find out what was going on . . . [It] was a

news center."[36] Truman's old fellow soldiers enjoyed visiting the haberdashery, and, whenever they could, as one remembered, they "would
just come in to say hello."[37]

The sharp economic downturn of 1921 turned the profitable business
into one that attracted more friendly visits than clothing purchases. "A
lot of the fellows that could have bought something," Frederick J. Bowman, a Battery D sergeant, recalled, "would say, 'Well, I need a couple
of shirts, but I think I'll wear these a while longer,' because they just
didn't have the money to buy any."[38] In September 1922, Truman &
Jacobson held a going-out-of-business sale. Years later, the painful failure remained with Truman: "A flourishing business was carried on for
about a year and a half and then came the squeeze of 1921. Jacobson and
I went to bed one night with a $35,000 inventory and awoke the next
day with a $25,000 shrinkage . . . This brought bills payable and bank
notes due at such a rapid rate we went out of business."[39]

Now approaching forty years of age and still living in his mother-in-
law's house, Harry Truman again was in search of work. He was also
significantly in debt. When they closed their business, Truman and Jacobson decided not to file for bankruptcy protection, despite the fact that
doing so would have absolved them of paying a good deal of the store's
overdue obligations. Each man, they decided, would pay his share of the
store's debts. One debt proved particularly troublesome because its owner,
State Street Bank, pushed hard for large payments on the amount owed.
Jacobson was unable to make sufficient headway against his share of the
debt and in 1925 he filed for bankruptcy protection.

Historians often trumpet Truman's refusal to file for bankruptcy protection as an example of his moral rectitude and earnestness. This por-
trayal ignores Truman's own account of the matter. "Our creditors drove
Eddie into bankruptcy," he recalled, "but I became a public official and
they couldn't do that to me." Specifically, State Street Bank was legally
prohibited from garnishing Truman's wages after he was elected a county
judge. It was 1935 when he finally paid the last of the debt he owed on
the haberdashery store.

13

Some Minor County Office

THE DEMOCRATS IN JACKSON COUNTY, Missouri, had divided themselves into "Goats" and "Rabbits," and the Republicans had not mattered in longer than anyone cared to remember. The difference between Goats and Rabbits was more stylistic than substantive, but the rivalry was fierce. Each side was run by a machine boss. Buying and selling votes and stealing ballots were standard practice. Physical intimidation sometimes played a role in determining who won an election. Harry Abbot, one of Truman's fellow Masons and a political operative in Jackson County, summarized the era when he told an interviewer, "In them days, politics was awful corrupt."[1]

So when Mike Pendergast and his son Jim asked Truman to run for eastern judge of Jackson County, Truman, who was still working at the haberdashery, had a good idea of what their proposition entailed. Mike's brother Tom was known statewide as "Boss Tom"; he controlled much of Missouri's politics but rarely ventured beyond his home or office. "Besides his income from shakedowns from gambling joints and brothels," *Life* magazine wrote about Thomas J. Pendergast, "Tom owned a cement process called 'Ready-Mixed' and saw to it that Ready-Mixed was the only kind of cement that could meet the building specifications for the city and county."[2]

The county court to which Truman sought election was more of a county council than a judiciary body. Three judges sat on the court: the western judge from Kansas City; the eastern judge, who represented the farmland surrounding Independence; and a chief judge, who was elected at large.

Truman matched Pendergast's political needs in several ways. The failing small businessman was a Protestant where Pendergast was an Irish Catholic. Truman was an active Mason who was highly respected by his brethren. And Truman's family had settled in Missouri back in the 1840s and had fought in the Civil War. This mattered a great deal to rural voters. Moreover, Harry Truman had fought valiantly in the Great War. This was important not just because voters in 1922 were eager to vote for veterans but also because, as America's military units were organized locally, a Great War veteran had a cadre of fellow veterans nearby who were keen to work to get one of their own elected. In Missouri, Truman would be able to count on the 129th Field Artillery Regiment and all local Missourian members of the Thirty-fifth Division, to which the regiment had been attached.[3]

Truman immediately agreed to run on the Pendergasts' Goat ticket. As Truman & Jacobson spiraled further into arrears, he knew he had few other options. "Went into business all enthusiastic," he later wrote. "Lost all I had and all I could borrow. Mike Pendergast picked me up and put me into politics and I've been lucky."[4] He won election in 1922, but lost his reelection bid in 1924 to a political rival. His and Bess's first and only child, Margaret, was born a few months before he lost reelection and the suddenly unemployed Democrat again worried about money. This perhaps made his return to politics inevitable.

In 1926 Truman was elected to the first of two four-year terms as presiding judge. Because Tom Pendergast had settled his disagreements with the rival responsible for Truman's 1924 defeat, Truman's 1926 election was never in doubt. He served as presiding judge from 1927 to 1934, and it was in this office that he became a commanding figure in Missouri politics. He exercised primary control over the county's $7 million annual budget and its seven hundred employees. That he was a machine politician mattered little. Few voters expected the presiding judge to be otherwise. Despite the prevailing expectation of graft, Truman made a point to declare publicly on his first day as presiding judge that he would run the county in a way that benefited the taxpayers first and anyone else second.

For all his lofty ideals, Truman did not at all forget about the Pendergast machine that had by now elected him to two well-paying public offices. It was under Truman's watch that the county infamously contracted to use only Pendergast's Ready-Mixed Cement.[5] Truman saw nothing wrong with rewarding his patron with such spoils. "Tom Pendergast never asked me to do a dishonest deed," he insisted in 1939 after Pendergast was arrested on numerous federal charges. "He knew I wouldn't do it if he asked. He was always my friend. He was always honest with me and when he made a promise he kept it."[6]

To be sure, Judge Truman departed from typical machine politicians in that he did not award all the county's spoils to connected contractors. For several significant projects he solicited bids and, to the shock of local businessmen, issued contracts to the qualified companies that placed the lowest bids. This rankled some contractors, who visited Boss Pendergast's office to complain about this new presiding judge. Pendergast seemed amused by their outrage. "I told you he's the contrariest man in the country," he snapped. "Now get out of here."[7]

County citizens came to respect Truman most of all because, as his Latin teacher recalled, "He pulled Jackson County out of the mud." Mrs. W.L.C. Palmer was referring to actual mud. When Truman became presiding judge, Jackson County's roads were a muddy mess. Horses, buggies, and automobiles routinely became mired in the muck. Residents seeking to travel just a few miles often missed their appointments. Clothes were ruined trying to free tires from the sludge. Jackson County citizens considered theirs to be "about the muddiest county anywhere." Presiding Judge Truman made road construction a hallmark of his two terms in office. Palmer recalled that by 1934, "everybody was very proud of our roads. We have had good roads ever since."[8] With publicly approved bonds, he spent $10 million paving roads and streets and several million dollars more constructing public buildings, including a $4.5 million courthouse in Kansas City.[9]

TRUMAN DID NOT LIGHTLY CARRY the weight of his high-profile county office. The power to grant or reward men seeking to support their families in the depth of the Depression was not one that he cherished. He enjoyed the trappings of being presiding judge of Jackson

County. He also relished the responsibility attached to his title. The power that accompanied that responsibility, however, swiftly became a burden. It seemed as if every person he had ever known in Jackson County was calling him at work and at home asking for financial help from the county's coffers. He began to lose sleep and took pills to calm his nerves.[10]

The Pendergasts either did not know about or disregarded the apparent strain on Truman. They were more interested in his success in improving the county's infrastructure and the popularity it earned him. In May 1934, Boss Pendergast asked Truman to run for the United States Senate.[11]

The extent of Thomas J. Pendergast's political power in Missouri in 1933 is difficult to exaggerate. He controlled the state's congressional offices, the governor's mansion, and so much of the state house that many Missourians took to calling their capitol building "Uncle Tom's Cabin." With Boss Pendergast's blessing, almost anything was politically possible in the state.

Truman had been, at best, Pendergast's third choice for the Democratic Senate nomination. Because a decorated, popular Great War veteran was already running for the nomination, the first two men Pendergast asked declined to enter the race. Harry Truman was finishing his second term as presiding judge and was barred by long-standing custom from seeking a third term. Unlike either of Pendergast's preferred men, he had no professional office—no law practice, small business, or corporation— awaiting his return.

In part because of his professional insecurity, Truman constantly worried about money. His mother had taken out another mortgage on the family farm in Grandview. He agreed to run for the Senate. A few weeks later, on the night before he announced his candidacy, the presiding judge of Jackson County wrote a diary entry on hotel stationery: "I have come to the place where all men strive to be at my age and I thought two weeks ago that retirement on a virtual pension in some minor county office was all that was in store for me."[12]

He proved to be an inexhaustible campaigner. Crossing the state several times over, he made from two to ten appearances each day. "I went from town to town and from county to county and from daylight until midnight made speeches and shook hands with about a hundred thousand people."[13] That summer was the hottest on record in Missouri, but he preferred to campaign in his jacket, mopping the sweat from his brow with a white handkerchief. He drove himself around the state until he broke two ribs in a serious car accident. After that, friends drove him while he reviewed speeches and notes for the next campaign stop.

At rural campaign events Truman and his backers accentuated his farming background. "You folks won't get a chance very often," one supporter said as he introduced Judge Truman to a farming crowd at an annual picnic, "to vote for a farmer for United States senator. You'd better make the most of it and be for this man, Harry Truman. He's our kind of people." The *St. Louis Post-Dispatch* and the *Kansas City Star* both opposed him, but Missouri's rural population quickly rallied in support of Truman's campaign. The state's power long had been divided between the residents of Kansas City and those of St. Louis. Truman's hometown newspaper, the *Independence Examiner*, exemplified most rural voters' hopes in the coming election: "Missouri this year has an opportunity to get away from the two large cities and elect a country boy to the Senate. Judge Harry S. Truman of Independence is distinctively a product of the country. He was born and reared between the plow handles on a Jackson County farm."[14]

Not all of Missouri's farmers supported the candidate portraying himself as one of their own. The president of the Missouri Farmers' Association seethed, "For this bellhop of Pendergast's to aspire to make a jump from the obscure bench of a county judge to the United States Senate is without precedent. When one contemplates the giants of the past who have represented Missouri this spectacle is not only grotesque, it is sheer buffoonery."[15] Other opponents in the Democratic primary disparaged him as a puppet of the Pendergast political machine and blasted what they called his "record of subservience in Jackson County."[16] Truman refused to apologize for relying so heavily on Boss Pendergast's political machine, though it was financed by numerous criminal enterprises. He maintained years later, "Any man would have been foolish to turn down the support of the organization which at that time controlled 100,000 votes, and I acted as every other candidate would have done."[17]

His connection to the Pendergasts remained a persistent but surprisingly ineffective line of attack for Truman's political opponents for as long as he was one of Missouri's elected officials.

Judge Truman won the Democratic primary by 40,000 of the 660,000 votes cast. In the general election, he easily defeated the Republican candidate, Roscoe C. Patterson. He carried 88 percent of the largely urban black vote, despite African Americans' general wariness of a man from a town as rigidly segregated as Independence. "When Truman took office," Roy Wilkins later wrote, "there had been a raft of worries among Negroes—he was an untested haberdasher from Klan country. But I had known him when he was a judge back in Kansas City, and one of the things he had done back then was to save a home for Negro boys that the white folks thought as too good for colored children . . . Anyone who mistook Harry Truman for a pint-sized [famously segregationist Mississippi senator Theodore] Bilbo was making a big mistake."[18] On the day the Washington-bound senator-elect bade farewell to T. J. Pendergast in Kansas City, the Boss told him, "Work hard, keep your mouth shut and answer your mail."[19]

SENATOR HARRY S. TRUMAN quickly realized that because of his relationship with Pendergast, his fellow senators were loath to accept him. Some senators refused to speak to the man they called "the senator from Pendergast." Nevada's Pat McCarran spoke for many of his colleagues when he flatly declared, "I never considered him a Senator."[20]

"I was under a cloud," Truman recognized, but did himself no favors by handing out jobs to supporters of the Pendergast political machine and securing a job for his only sibling, brother Vivian, at the Federal Housing Agency in Kansas City. He also gave a job at the FHA to his high school Latin teacher. "I wrote him a letter," she told an interviewer, "after he became senator, for [a job] and that's what he got right away."[21] Moreover, despite the disdain that it brought him, Truman never disavowed his relationship with Boss Tom Pendergast. The freshman senator kept a picture of Pendergast placed prominently in his Senate office and posed for pictures standing in front of it even after Pendergast's corruption had begun to receive national attention.[22]

When the Department of Justice launched an extensive investigation into the Pendergast syndicate, Senator Truman's loyalty appeared to have become politically self-destructive. He took to the Senate floor to disparage the Justice Department and the U.S. attorney leading the investigation. He called the prosecutor crooked and the judicial system suspect. "I say, Mr. President," Truman bellowed, "that a Jackson County, Missouri, Democrat has as much chance of a fair trial in the Federal Court for the Western District of Missouri as a Jew would have in a Hitler court or a Trotsky follower before Stalin."[23] Senators, congressional aides, and political observers were stunned. Here was a man widely regarded as having been sent to Washington "by gangsters" standing on the floor not only defending his benefactors but denigrating the sworn law enforcement officials of his home state.

Pendergast pleaded guilty to income tax evasion in the spring of 1939. Shortly thereafter Senator Truman announced his intent to run for reelection. It seemed the act of a man who at best was disconnected from political reality and at worst was desperate to hold on to this job because he had no other prospects.

In August 1940 Senator Truman shocked political observers by winning the Democratic nomination over both the federal prosecutor he had maligned on the Senate floor and Governor Lloyd C. Stark. Truman's two opponents, according to one reporter, "join[ed] in attempts to brand Truman as 'the Pendergast senator' because he had been elected in 1934 as the personal choice of T. J. Pendergast, former Kansas City political leader."[24] Decided by just a few thousand votes out of more than half a million cast, it was Missouri's closest primary race since 1922. Truman's rural base all but deserted him. The Associated Press reported that "Stark carried [rural] Missouri by a fair margin, but a heavy Truman vote in St. Louis and Jackson County, the Senator's home, turned the tide in the unofficial tabulations of Tuesday's primary."[25]

That Truman carried St. Louis and Kansas City can be attributed in large part to black voters. African Americans overwhelmingly favored him over the openly segregationist Governor Stark. During his six years in office Senator Truman had supported federal antilynching legislation and a nondiscriminatory Selective Service Act. Walter White, the executive secretary of the NAACP, explained in 1948, "Few men in public life have ever had so consistent a record as has been that of President Truman. As a member of the Senate, long before he or anyone else ever dreamed that he would sit in the White House, he voted consistently for antilynching legislation and other measures . . . He did this in a quiet, diffident way without fanfare or publicity or boasting."[26]

As he sought reelection to the Senate, Truman understood that strong support from Missouri's 130,000 black voters could sway the statewide election. And so in 1940, in front of a nearly all-white audience in Sedalia, Missouri, Senator Truman made his political view plain:

> I believe in the brotherhood of man; not merely the brotherhood of white men, but the brotherhood of all men before the law . . . If any class or race can be permanently set apart from, or pushed down below the rest in political and civil rights, so may any other class or race when it shall incur the displeasure of its more powerful associates, and we may say farewell to the principles on which we count our safety . . .
>
> Negroes have been preyed upon by all types of exploiters, from the installment salesman of clothing, pianos and furniture to the vendors of vice. The majority of our Negro people find but cold comfort in shanties and tenements. Surely, as freemen, they are entitled to something better than this.[27]

As he explained to a nearly all-black gathering in Chicago, he did not favor integration. "I wish to make clear," he explained in his staccato, high-pitched public speaking voice, "that I am not appealing for social equality of the Negro. The Negro himself knows better than that, and the highest types of Negro leaders say quite frankly that they prefer the society of their own people."[28] The Constitution, however, demanded that black Americans enjoy the full rights of what Truman called "legal equality." At the 1940 Democratic national convention he declared, "We owe the Negro legal equality . . . because he is a human being and a natural born American."

———————

In November, Senator Truman won reelection along with President Roosevelt. The *Washington Post* noted that "Kansas City, voting without its fallen 'boss' T. J. Pendergast as a factor, returned its usual, top-heavy Democratic vote."[29] Having lost much of his base of rural voters but solidified his support among urban African Americans, Harry Truman was no longer the senator from Pendergast.

Thundering Resentment in the Voice of God

A FEW MONTHS AFTER the 1940 election that returned both Franklin Roosevelt and Harry Truman to Washington, African Americans had grown greatly dissatisfied with the president's apparent lack of interest in alleviating the discrimination they faced. Black voters had supported him again in 1940, but, aside from appointing a handful of prominent African Americans to War Department posts a week before the election, the president had done nothing to address their concerns. The president's reticence convinced many observers that his preelection appointments had been empty political gestures. In April 1941, A. Philip Randolph asserted: "President Roosevelt can issue an executive order tomorrow to abolish discrimination in the Army, Navy, Air Corps, Marines, and on all defense contracts awarded by the Federal Government, on account of race or color, and discriminations against colored people would promptly end." While he was perhaps overly optimistic about a president's ability to end discriminatory practices overnight, Randolph presciently described how segregation in the armed forces and the civilian defense industry eventually would end.[1]

In 1940 the nation's economy was emerging from the last of the Depression in part because, as war loomed on the horizon, the government was entering into large contracts with defense companies. Most of these, even in Northern states, refused to hire black applicants. The few that did restricted black workers to the lowest-level positions. "Negroes will be considered only as janitors," declared the general manager of one aviation contractor. The spokesman for another defense contractor said, "It is not the policy of this company to employ other than of the Caucasian race." In response to a query, Standard Steel's home office affirmed to the Urban League: "We have not had a Negro working in 25 years and do not plan to start now."[2]

By January 1941, Randolph had heard enough. He called for a march of ten thousand African Americans on the nation's capital. The protesters, who Randolph hoped would include men, women, and children from all walks of life, would march under the banner "We Loyal Colored Americans Demand the Right to Work and Fight for Our Country." By their numbers and their unity, the peaceful protesters "would wake up and shock official Washington as it has never been shocked before."[3] The march was scheduled for July 1, 1941. Notwithstanding his plan to rally ten thousand workers to march, Randolph publicly admitted, "even to get 2,000 Negroes to march on Washington would be a worthwhile accomplishment."[4]

To Randolph's surprise, African Americans of all classes embraced the idea of "a pilgrimage" to Washington. They were eager to protest segregation in the military and black workers' wholesale exclusion from a national economic recovery being paid for by the federal government. March to Washington committees were established in eighteen cities, and local committee members began to raise funds to transport marchers to the capital "by bus, train, private automobile and on foot."[5] One New York City reporter noted, "Negroes from all fields of endeavor are united behind the campaign and are solidly behind this 'March to Washington.'" After listing a slew of clubs, unions, fraternal orders, and civil rights organizations "comprising a cross-section of the Negro population" that had pledged to support the march, the reporter remarked, "This is, perhaps, one of the few times in the history of Harlem that all these organizations have been united in a single drive."[6]

Momentum for the march swelled rapidly. The public's response exceeded Randolph's most optimistic expectations. By May more than ten thousand marchers were expected from New York City alone and over one hundred thousand marchers were committed from cities and towns across the nation.[7]

Encouraged but unrelenting, Randolph exhorted black Americans "to keep in their minds night and day that all roads lead to Washington, D.C."[8] His Negro March on Washington Committee's official announcement vowed to "shake up white America, arouse official Washington and gain respect for our people." To black people in the North and South, the march committee proclaimed, "We summon you to mass action that is orderly and lawful, but aggressive and militant, for justice, equality and freedom."[9]

In speeches, interviews, and columns he wrote, Randolph began to use a kind of language new to African Americans' struggle for equal rights. He spoke as a Jeremiah, using a tone and imagery that at once harkened back to that of abolitionists, while foreshadowing the sermons of civil rights preachers to come. "Let the Negro masses speak!" he proclaimed. "When they speak, they will speak with the tongues of angels. When they thunder their resentment and revolt against the blighting bottlenecks of race prejudice and hatred, their voice will be the Voice of God." He challenged black Americans to "teach the gospel of justice, freedom and democracy" and swore to "tear the mask of hypocrisy from America's democracy!"[10] As the March on Washington movement gathered strength, it adopted as its official goal to persuade President Roosevelt to issue an executive order abolishing segregation and discrimination in the military, federal agencies, and national defense contractors.[11] "Let no black man be afraid," Randolph charged. "We are simply fighting for our rights as American citizens . . . This is our own native land. Let us fight to make it truly free, democratic and just."[12]

ADMINISTRATION OFFICIALS WERE ALARMED at the prospect of tens of thousands of black citizens staging such a spectacle. They worried that the march would make America appear to Tokyo and Berlin as a weak and divided nation. The president dispatched first lady Eleanor Roosevelt to meet with Randolph and ask him to cancel the march. In their meeting, she told the union leader that the march would be "a very grave mistake" that likely would result in "even more solid opposition" to federal desegregation from hardliners in Congress.[13] The first lady worried that the march "would tend to make Negroes lose the friends they now have."[14]

Randolph refused to cancel the march. He and other leaders believed that private meetings and conferences with federal officials, and even with the president himself, had accomplished very little. "Negroes cannot stop discrimination in National Defense," Randolph argued, "with conferences of leaders and the intelligentsia alone."[15] Roosevelt had appointed a handful of African Americans to federal positions, but these well-intentioned individuals were, according to Randolph, "helpless without the collective mass support of colored people. Aggressive, articulate, determined mass support will strengthen their hands."[16] The march would take place on July 1 as scheduled.

President Roosevelt now realized that if he stood any chance of convincing Randolph to cancel the march, he would have to get involved personally. Along with several advisers, he met at the White House with Randolph and Walter White on June 18, 1941. Randolph told the president that he would call off the march if the president issued an executive order outlawing segregation in the defense industry.

"Well, Phil," Roosevelt replied, "you know I can't do that. In any event I couldn't do anything unless you called off this march of yours."[17] The president offered to release a statement condemning discrimination in the defense industries.[18]

A statement, Randolph told the president, would not suffice. In previous weeks the White House had already released statements condemning racial discrimination to no discernible effect. An executive order was necessary and had considerable congressional support. In response to a questionnaire sent to them by the National Negro Congress, numerous congressmen and senators had stated their support for the issuance of an executive order desegregating the defense industry.[19] Randolph then told Roosevelt that more than one hundred thousand black Americans had committed to marching on the National Mall on July 1. This was far more protesters than the president had been led to believe were coming. He steered the discussion toward what specifics Randolph would like to see in an executive order.

One week later, on June 25, 1941, President Roosevelt signed Executive Order 8802: Prohibition of Discrimination in the Defense Industry. "I do hereby reaffirm," the order read, "the policy of the United States that there shall be no discrimination in the employment of workers in defense industries or government because of race, creed, color, or national origin . . ." Executive Order 8802 also established the Fair Employment Practices Commission and empowered it to investigate and grant redress for complaints of racial discrimination in defense industries and government. Importantly, the FEPC would answer only to the president, not to a congressional committee whose most senior members were likely to hail from segregationist Southern states.

Randolph was in Houston attending the annual convention of the NAACP when the White House announced the order. On behalf of the Negro March on Washington Committee, he "postponed" the march. "We hail this executive order," he said in a statement, "as a signal and profound step of a democratic process." Lest anyone mistakenly think that the committee was satisfied, he called upon all local chapters of the committee "in various sections of the country to remain intact to watch and check how industries are observing the executive order the President has issued."[20] NAACP executive secretary Walter White agreed that Executive Order 8802 was "not a complete victory" until industry practice changed to meet the order's mandates.[21]

African Americans were disappointed that the order appeared to leave untouched segregation and discrimination in the armed forces. The NAACP issued a resolution at its thirty-second annual convention in June 1941 lamenting the fact that the order, while "a step in the right direction," did nothing for the black American in uniform.[22]

DESPITE SUCH CAUTION, there was no denying the fact that the Negro March on Washington Committee had accomplished what much older, venerated institutions such as the NAACP and the National Urban League had been unable to do. This was partly because Randolph's committee was quite a different organization from those more established institutions. Committee members hailed from all classes and education levels. In the coming years the other organizations, particularly the NAACP, would experience dramatic increases in membership across class and education lines, but traditionally theirs was a middle- and upper-class membership. Second, unlike other civil rights organizations, the committee was all black, and ostentatiously so.

Most significant, the Negro March on Washington Committee

achieved its goal by threatening direct, nonviolent confrontation with the government. The prospect of one hundred thousand black men, women, and children marching down Pennsylvania Avenue so unnerved the president of the United States that he issued an order he did not want to issue. As James Ricks, a clerk in Harlem, told a reporter, "The President did not do it on his own goodness and generosity. He was forced to do it."[23] Randolph reflected on the success of the Negro March on Washington Committee: "We have aided in cleansing the soul of America of the poisons of hatred and thus have given added strength to the national defense effort at the time this strength is needed."[24]

The march committee's popularity made clear that black protest in America had developed a great deal since Woodrow Wilson was president. Indeed, much had changed in the months since President Roosevelt, while campaigning for a third term, managed to quell African Americans' uneasiness by appointing a few prominent black men to federal positions days before the election. African Americans' overwhelming embrace of A. Philip Randolph's committee, like the fiery language Randolph used to promote it, announced the birth of a new era in black Americans' struggle for equality. Amid the drumbeat of a second world war, the civil rights movement was coming to life.

THE USS *MILLER*

TODAY ONE CAN PURCHASE a United States postage stamp bearing the portrait of a Texas sharecropper's son who, until his death on Thanksgiving Day in 1943, served in the navy as a mess attendant. Cook Third Class Doris Miller, called Dorie by everyone who knew him, was born in Waco at the end of World War I. On December 7, 1941, Miller was twenty-two years old and the reigning heavyweight boxing champion of the USS *West Virginia*'s boxing league. The battleship was moored in Pearl Harbor. He arose at six that Sunday morning. One of his duties was to collect the sailors' laundry. Just before 0800, as he gathered khakis and blues, the *West Virginia*'s highest alarm sounded. A marine orderly yelled, "The Japanese are attacking us!"[1] Miller dashed up to the ship's deck.

Two thunderclaps burst from the hull on the port side. Torpedoes fired by Japanese warplanes had hit the ship. Within seconds, the *West Virginia* began listing to port. Flames reached fifteen to twenty feet high and explosions hurled sailors about the deck. Palm-sized metal debris rained from the sky, burning hot, slicing and scalding men struggling across the deck. Those sailors who were able to rise to their feet worked to push burning debris overboard and to extinguish the fires raging on the *West Virginia*'s gun turrets.

Once on deck, Miller joined Lieutenant F. H. White in hauling wounded sailors across the blood-, water-, and oil-slicked deck to a safer quarter of the ship. When officers learned that the captain had been seriously wounded, they ordered Miller to the ship's bridge to administer aid to him. Miller did all he could, but the captain was mortally wounded.

The Japanese planes continued to attack. On the *West Virginia* and nearby ships, ammunition-filled magazines exploded. Fires raged on oil slicks in the harbor.

Messman Miller seized control of a .50-caliber Browning antiaircraft machine gun. He aimed up at the swarming attack planes and fired. Miller had never been taught how to operate the weapon. "It wasn't hard," he said later. "I just pulled the trigger and she worked fine. I had watched the others with these guns." He fired until the machine gun ran out of ammunition. By then a fire belowdecks amidships was overwhelming the *West Virginia*. Officers ordered all hands to abandon the ship. "I guess I fired her for about fifteen minutes. I think I got one of those Jap planes. They were diving pretty close to us."

There were 1,541 men aboard the USS *West Virginia* when the Japanese struck. The attacking airplanes' torpedoes and armor-piercing bombs killed 130 men and wounded 52 others. Many more would have died had they not been ordered to abandon the *West Virginia*, which soon sank to the bottom of the harbor.

MILLER'S ACTIONS WERE TOO CONSEQUENTIAL to be omitted from Pearl Harbor's dispatches to the mainland. His fellow sailors had seen him shoot down enemy airplanes while under fire. Stories of Miller's heroic action and surprising accuracy quickly spread from the mainland military bases receiving Pearl Harbor's messages to black and white civilian communities, but, for months, navy officials would identify him only as "a Negro messman." The navy's peculiar reticence only heightened African Americans' desire to celebrate the anonymous hero. In a December 1941 letter that would not be made public until after Secretary of the Navy Frank Knox formally recognized Miller, NAACP leaders suggested to the navy that "the Distinguished Service Cross or other recognition be given to this hero of the battle of Pearl Harbor."[2] The letter was one of dozens the department received. Former Republican presidential candidate Wendell Willkie later recalled how "commentators began to speak of 'the unnamed Negro messman.'"[3]

It was spring by the time the Department of the Navy broke what one reporter called its "long silence" and revealed Doris Miller's name.[4] By then Miller was serving aboard the USS *Indianapolis*, again in the mess. His story resonated with Americans of all races. Miller was not a member of the bourgeoisie with a Howard or Tuskegee diploma hanging on a wall in his home in Washington, Baltimore, or New York City. Unlike the black officers and National Guardsmen who had fought in the Great War, he had not joined the military as part of a larger sociopolitical movement. Rather, Miller had joined the navy for the most traditional reason given by young men worldwide: He wanted to see the world.

Senator James Meade of New York joined Congressman John Dingell of Michigan in proposing that Miller be awarded the Congressional Medal of Honor.[5] Their fellow Democrat Alben Barkley joined in sponsoring the legislation in the Senate, but other senators defeated the bill in May.[6] In both houses of Congress, elected officials from Miller's native Texas were conspicuously silent.[7] Secretary Knox, a former Republican nominee for vice president, opposed granting Miller any formal award, contending that a letter he wrote to Miller commending the young man for his "extraordinary courage" was sufficient recognition.[8]

Leaders of black communities pressed the navy to present Miller with more than a letter. Former War Department official Emmett Scott wrote both to President Roosevelt and to Secretary Knox, urging them to use their "good offices in recognizing and rewarding Doris Miller."[9] Miller's parents were feted with "high honors" at the Fifth Annual All-Southern Negro Youth Conference on the campus of Tuskegee Institute.[10]

Due in part to his humble background and low rank, Miller's station in the mess became evidence for activists' arguments that segregation bred inefficiency in the military.

The navy's racist policy of restricting African Americans to food and custodial services had confined Miller to the mess. Neither black nor white reporters failed to mention that the former boxing champion served as a mess attendant, often referring to him as "the humble messman."[11] Miller's heroic turn raised the question of what he and others like him could accomplish in the navy if given the opportunity.

The NAACP wrote an open letter to Secretary Knox in which the organization exhorted Knox to abolish the navy's restrictions on black enlistees. This would be the most meaningful way in which the department could honor Doris Miller. "This action by the Navy," the NAACP contended, "not only would reward a hero, but would serve dramatic notice that this country is in fact a democracy engaged in an all-out war against anti-democratic forces."[12]

Prominent public figures also argued for the end of segregation in the navy. Speaking to two thousand guests attending the Freedom House inaugural dinner at the Hotel Commodore in New York City, Wendell Willkie called America's segregated navy "an injustice which makes a mockery of all our fine words." The Republican implored the dining guests, "Don't you think that as American citizens we should insist that our government and navy department eliminate the bar that prohibits any American citizen from serving his country?"[13]

Knox all but ignored these entreaties. Born in Boston and raised in Michigan, William Franklin Knox was a self-made man who had risen from working-class roots to become the Republican nominee for vice president in 1936. He was no Southerner, but neither was he a progressive. Secretary Knox considered the matter closed.

In early May, however, President Roosevelt overruled Knox and awarded Miller the department's highest honor, the Navy Cross. Admiral Chester Nimitz, commander in chief of the Pacific fleet, presented the sailor with the medal "for his distinguished devotion to duty, extraordinary courage and disregard for his own personal safety."[14] African Americans celebrated Miller's Navy Cross as a step toward equality in the armed forces. The *Chicago Defender* observed, "This is indeed encouraging and will sink deep into the hearts of our people. Let's hear three cheers for Franklin D. Roosevelt."[15]

Even after the award, however, the navy never permitted Miller to serve as anything other than a messman. African American journalists lamented the fact that the Navy Cross recipient was "waiting tables in the Pacific."[16] Doris Miller died in 1943 on Thanksgiving Day, when the *Liscome Bay* was torpedoed. Thirty years later, the navy commissioned a ship, the USS *Miller*, named in his honor.

BY THE TIME DORIS MILLER seized control of that mounted gun aboard a burning ship, African Americans were already making a concerted drive to integrate their country's armed forces. Their experience in the Great War had taught them that serving in a sharply segregated military—even fighting and dying in battle—would do little to advance their cause of achieving equality at home.

Indeed, it seemed to many that African Americans' communal plight had worsened considerably after the Great War. Homes and businesses burned down in race riots from the Northeast through the Midwest, and the South remained brutally segregated. All the while, federal officials remained uninterested in securing for black Americans the rights guaranteed to them by the Constitution. This was African Americans' reward for "closing ranks," for subjugating their own struggle to the war abroad.

Some time before Japanese warplanes attacked American sailors, African American leaders in communities across the country discerned that war again was coming to America. They decided that this time would be different for black soldiers abroad and their families at home. This time, in this new and larger world war, the military would not be just a means by which African Americans would seek to prove their loyalty and patriotism. This time, educated black men would not lobby Congress for a segregated officers' training camp, and working-class black men would not assent to serving overwhelmingly in labor battalions. Instead, the fight for equality would be brought to the armed forces.

As early as 1938, a group of black men who had served as officers in World War I formed the Committee for Participation of Negroes in the National Defense. The group wrote in a letter to President Roosevelt, "We are expecting a more dignified place in our armed forces during the next war than we occupied during the World War." The following year the National Bar Association, the largest organization of African American attorneys, established a committee to end black applicants' exclusion from most states' National Guard units, and the National Negro Insurance Association announced its official opposition to restrictions on black Americans' service in the army and the navy.[17] In 1940 the *Crisis* magazine, demanding that the War Department eradicate its race-based limitations on military service, declared, "This is no fight merely to wear a uniform. This is a struggle for status, a struggle to take democracy off parchment and give it life."[18]

Black newspaper editors and civil rights leaders echoed the call for the military's racist structure to be changed. In 1939 editors of the *Pittsburgh Courier* demanded that "the color bar be abolished in the armed forces," reminding its considerable readership that "there will be a hard-fought Presidential election campaign within twelve months, and our vote will be solicited."[19]

There were four primary reasons why African Americans in 1939 and 1940 were focused so keenly on eliminating segregation and racial discrimination in the armed forces. First, because nearly four hundred thousand of them had served in the military during the Great War twenty years earlier, there was an enormous pool of veterans who remembered the bitter experience of serving in uniform beneath the yoke of Jim Crow. Newspapers published popular serialized remembrances written by black officers. These stories recounted not just the drama of battle, but also the continual fight the men waged against racist policies and practices in their own military. Serialized articles such as the *Baltimore Afro-American*'s "Road to War, from the Diary of Clifton S. Hardy" vividly connected the soldiers' bravery in battle to their courage in battling discrimination.[20] Charles Hamilton Houston, the widely influential attorney, civil rights leader, and Great War veteran, told Secretary of War Harry Woodring in 1940 that "there are thousands and thousands of Negroes who will make very poor material as labor battalions and mess attendants. We mean to be fighters, no less."[21]

Second, military service members, unlike civilians, could be ordered to implement social changes. As one army historian later wrote, "The armed forces could command where others could only persuade."[22] For all the angst exhibited by War Department officials and senior military officers over how and whether to permit black Americans to serve, the fact was that the president could desegregate the armed forces without leaving his desk. Congress likewise could pass a bill desegregating the military. In either case, unlike in civilian arenas, officers could command compliance with the orders they received from Washington.

Third, again recalling their experiences in the Great War, African Americans knew that after Congress enacted the draft, the military soon would employ more African Americans than any other single institution. For all its problems, the military offered steady employment for African

Americans at a time when civilian opportunities were few. In 1939, well before the war, 80 percent of black soldiers reenlisted in the army. This contrasted with a 48-percent reenlistment rate for white soldiers. The War Department's acting chief of public relations, Major Ward Maris, released a statement asserting that the numbers "indicate that the colored soldiers are very well satisfied with conditions in the army." Black veterans disputed Maris's explanation but could not dispute the high reenlistment rate among black servicemen.[23]

Last, the nature of the coming conflict, with Germany's overtly white supremacist casus belli, necessarily internationalized African Americans' struggle for human rights in a way that the Great War never did. Germany's Nazi government already had ordered all Polish Jews over the age of twelve to wear a white armband with a blue Star of David, had destroyed synagogues, had restricted Gypsies to their homes, and had established ghettos. As black Americans learned more of the injustices Nazi Germany inflicted on Jewish Europeans, they came to view the Jews' plight as similar to their own. One black journalist reported that in Poland the Germans had designated "jim crow streetcars for Jews . . . How much like our dear old Southland this sounds. First Germany robs the Jews of property, jobs and schooling and then insists that they are inferior as a race and diseased."[24] A black Chicagoan declared, "To hate the Negro or to hate the Jew is to hate humanity."[25]

Citizens and expatriates of African nations also linked their national defense to African Americans' struggle for equality. A French priest claimed that black people worldwide "hate the Nazi Germans" because of "Hitler's race policy."[26] In the Great War many African Americans joined the military to prove their collective loyalty to the nation, but if America were drawn into this war, they would fight against a racist regime seeking to conquer most of the world.

"If not now, then when?" became the rallying cry for greater equality in the military. The *Baltimore Afro-American*'s editorial board summarized the gathering mood with an April editorial: "We've been fighting our country's wars since 1775, always getting a slap on the back when the fighting begins and a kick in the pants when it's over. One hundred and sixty-five years is a long time, long enough to win a square deal."[27]

THE DAY AFTER THE JAPANESE ATTACK on Pearl Harbor, President
Roosevelt addressed a joint session of Congress to request a declaration
of war on Japan. He opened his short speech by declaring, "Yesterday,
December 7, 1941—a date which will live in infamy—the United States
of America was suddenly and deliberately attacked by naval and air forces
of the Empire of Japan." The draft of the speech presented to the president had read, "a date which will live in world history." In black ink
Roosevelt crossed out "world history" and wrote "infamy."[28] Congress
approved the war declaration with near unanimity. The only nay vote
was cast by Montana Republican Jeannette Rankin, the first woman ever
elected to Congress.

16

THE DOUBLE V

THE SUCCESS RANDOLPH ACHIEVED by challenging the administration from without contrasted sharply with the frustration William Hastie was experiencing within the government as he labored as the civilian aide to the secretary of war. By the time Randolph had cornered the president into issuing Executive Order 8802, Hastie was coming to realize how little influence he had in Roosevelt's War Department. He repeatedly threatened to resign, but, after cajoling him into staying on the job, War Department officials always returned to ignoring his recommendations. Because he was ignored despite his exceptional education and professional experience, William Hastie's frustrating tour in the War Department had come to resemble the experiences of many African Americans throughout the armed forces.

Some leaders of the black press were disappointed by Hastie's inability to garner results. John Sengstacke, the powerful editor of the *Chicago Defender*, allowed that Hastie was "a very capable gentleman," but the former federal judge had "no appreciable authority and scarcely any influence with the big wigs of the War Department." As much as Hastie had sought to avoid becoming as ineffectual within the department as Emmett J. Scott had been, it appeared to some close observers that he had. The fact was that Hastie could "make no commitments [regarding black troops]," Sengstacke continued, "and he cannot explain away segregation and discriminatory practices to which the high officials of his own department are clinging." Sengstacke's remarks stung Hastie, who was working tirelessly, if sometimes in vain, on behalf of African American servicemen.[1]

No struggle better exemplified the War Department's bureaucratic obduracy than its 1941 decision to use only blood collected from white donors. In October 1941, the surgeons general of the army and navy delivered a confidential memo to the American Red Cross. In it the military's senior doctors advised Red Cross officials that the War Department would accept only blood donated by white people. This was because most of the men in the armed forces were white and the majority of them preferred to receive blood from white donors. If black soldiers or sailors needed blood, the memo decreed, "they will be given normal transfusions from Negro donors if they do not desire the use of blood or plasma from white donors."[2] Major General James Magee, the army's surgeon general, explained that army officials were "afraid the indiscriminate use of white and Negro donors would militate against the success of our blood plasma program."[3]

The Red Cross promptly began refusing any donated blood from African Americans for military use. Red Cross officials assured the public that this new policy would not affect "the total amount of blood plasma available to the armed forces."[4] The American Medical Association was among the first organizations to protest: "There is no factual basis for the discrimination against the use of Negro blood or plasma for injection into white people."[5] A Red Cross spokesman in a *New York Times* article claimed that the organization staunchly opposed the prohibition but nonetheless was bound by the War Department's policy. In response to outraged protest from the NAACP, the director of the Red Cross War Drive agreed that there was no scientific basis for rejecting the blood of African Americans, but later averred that "the feelings and perhaps even the prejudices of those to whom transfusions are given should be respected as a symbol of democracy."[6] The director of Washington's Red Cross office, a physician and professor at Johns Hopkins, told reporters, "We have thousands of Southern whites in our forces, and they are absolutely against having the blood of colored donors let into their system."[7]

Black Americans were incredulous. In Baltimore, mere days before the Japanese attacked Pearl Harbor, the Red Cross was seeking fifteen thousand blood donors, but its staff began turning away African Americans who arrived at its collection center.[8]

"FOR PURE, UNADULTERATED, INSULTING GALL," Roy Wilkins seethed, "the American Red Cross takes all honors." Noting that the Red Cross was in the midst of a drive to raise $50 million, Wilkins remarked, "It would not refuse any Negro money to make up the fifty million dollars but it will not take any Negro blood."[9] A. Philip Randolph compared the Red Cross's policy to "the cult and curse of Hitler and Hitlerism."[10]

African Americans were not alone in their anger. Two influential white columnists wrote, "Because [the Red Cross] holds a unique place among humanitarian agencies, enjoys semi-public status and is possessed of enormous power," its decision to turn away black blood donors would be "bad enough in peacetime but utterly inexcusable in a time of war."[11] Some would-be white blood donors told reporters that the military's need for plasma must not be serious if one tenth of America's population could be excluded from the donor program.[12]

THE GREATEST IRONY OF THE MILITARY blood drive policy was that the man selected by the Red Cross to lead its blood plasma collection in New York was a black man. Dr. Charles Drew was universally recognized as one of the world's leading authorities on drawing and saving human blood. He had taken a leave of absence from the Howard University School of Medicine to manage more than two thousand physicians and nurses in the Red Cross's blood donation program.

Although Drew unequivocally stated that there existed "no scientific basis for the separation of blood from different races," his view on the Red Cross's policy initially was more nuanced than his friend William Hastie would have liked. The famous doctor told a reporter for the *Baltimore Afro-American* that "there is a definite social problem that cannot be overlooked. I think that it is almost as wrong to say that a man must take blood of a certain type as it is to deny an individual the opportunity to give his blood. Where persons express a preference for a blood of a certain type, I think their wishes should be respected if it is at all possible."[13]

After Hastie privately met with him to discuss the issue, however, Charles Drew resigned his position with the Red Cross.[14]

Hastie continued to pressure Undersecretary of War Robert P. Patterson until he at last relented. After conferring with Red Cross officials, the War Department issued a statement declaring that the charity "is prepared hereafter to accept blood donations from colored as well as white persons. In deference to the wishes of those from whom the plasma is being provided, the blood will be processed separately so that those receiving transfusions may be given plasma from blood of their own race."[15]

Hastie immediately warned Patterson that this new policy of accepting, but segregating, black Americans' blood was just as bad as the previous policy. Prominent voices from diverse communities soon echoed Hastie's criticism. Congressman Vito Marcantonio met personally with Norman Davis, the chairman of the board of the American Red Cross, and told him that segregating human blood according to race was "a violation of the Constitution and the principles of this war" and "that the Red Cross should lend its great weight to such a policy is unthinkable." The Spanish-language New York newspaper *Anco Antillano* published editorials lambasting the policy. Union leaders and the Catholic Church excoriated the Red Cross for undermining the very principles for which the nation's troops were fighting.[16]

Despite the widespread condemnation, neither Secretary of War Stimson nor Red Cross chairman Davis changed the policy. Davis insisted that it was "not the job of the Red Cross to settle racial controversies or to take sides in racial controversies."[17] It was not until eight years later, on December 1, 1950, that the War Department and the American Red Cross would stop separating the blood of black and white American donors.

THE SEGREGATION OF BLOOD according to the race of its donor shocked African Americans into realizing that, for all the political and economic progress they had made since the Great War's end, the military and its civilian leadership still held them in low regard. Military officials remained as intransigent as ever on the issue of segregation, continuing to claim that the armed forces could not exceed the nation's well-established racial customs without endangering support from white civilians and would-be recruits. "The Army is not a sociological laboratory," an army colonel and War Department spokesman told a group of black reporters. "To be effective it must be organized and trained according to principles which will ensure success. Experiments to meet the wishes and demands of the champions of every race and creed for the solution of their problems are a danger to efficiency, discipline and morale and would result in ultimate defeat."[18] Now that the nation was at war, senior officers contended, Congress and the president should take special care not to disrupt the regulations and traditions under which the nation's military had succeeded in the past.

The prospects for making any progress toward civil rights in the armed forces appeared bleaker than at any time since the Civil War. African American communities had felt greater hope in the opening days of World War I, when they "closed ranks" with a segregationist federal government and asked only that they be permitted to train in their own segregated officers' training camp. Their national demand for "colored officers to lead colored troops," once granted, did not disrupt the entire army.

Conversely, their current demand to eliminate segregation and discrimination, if granted, would affect the entire army, navy, and marine corps. After America entered World War II, this seemed unlikely. "I was never optimistic," William Hastie admitted later, "that it would be possible to persuade the military to eliminate existing racial segregation while World War II was in progress."[19]

With War Department officials repeatedly stating that the military should not move ahead of the population it defended, African Americans decided that, as their sons and brothers enlisted to fight in a segregated military, they would continue to agitate for equal rights at home. The *Atlanta Daily World* editorialized, "Slogan of the first World War was: 'Drop all grievances and pull together to make the world safe for democracy.' . . . Wiser and more determined now than he was in the first World War, the Negro is saying that giving up his grievances should be accompanied by [white Americans'] giving up discriminations against him."[20] African Americans were determined during this war, as Roy Wilkins wrote, "to fight on for the full freedom of 100 percent democracy at home while we are fighting a war for democracy abroad."[21]

In February 1942, the *Pittsburgh Courier* christened this drive the Double V campaign. Black Americans and their allies of all races would fight for victory overseas and victory at home. A cafeteria worker at a defense contractor eloquently summarized the Double V campaign's call: "The first V for victory over our enemies from without, the second V for victory over our enemies from within. For surely those who perpetuate these ugly prejudices here are seeking to destroy our democratic form of government just as surely as the Axis forces."[22]

Such declarations distressed many whites. One white newspaper editor wrote that the Double V campaign was "a war against our enemies abroad and against the whites at home," while another criticized black Americans for not closing ranks as they had during World War I, declaring, "The Negro must not regard [World War II] as a shining opportunity to right his wrongs."[23] One white editor who boasted of being "one of the Negro's best Southern friends" counseled that the campaign, by demanding "the impossible," was "endangering the war effort."[24] The director of the Office of War Information, Archibald MacLeish, blasted the Double V campaign and drew condemnation from both black and white columnists when he told reporters that "the great majority of colored Americans are lukewarm toward the war."[25]

Some African Americans refused to join the call for an end to segregation in the military. More conservative leaders were content to endure continued segregation if the army and navy lifted all other restrictions on black servicemen. Navy officials, they figured, would be more willing to permit black sailors to serve as more than just messmen if these sailors were willing to serve in all-black units. Black conservatives deemed it unrealistic to expect the marine corps to change from an entity that excluded blacks entirely to one that not only admitted black men but allowed them to train and fight alongside whites.

Judge Hastie recognized the potential appeal of this gradualist thinking and sought to stifle it. Gradualism only buttressed military leaders' own arguments for continued segregation. Hastie reasoned that "as long as people who are opposed to mixed units are able to point to Negroes as also agreeing with this position, our problem is extremely difficult." African American newspaper editors and other leaders railed more forcefully against what they called the "defeatism" of "ask[ing] for a Negro division, Negro this and Negro that," because "segregation has always led to discrimination."[26]

Like the Negro March on Washington movement before it, the Double V campaign quickly became popular in black communities across the nation. One poll concluded that the campaign enjoyed a 91-percent approval rating among African Americans.[27] The idea of fighting for victory abroad and at home swiftly wove itself into the fabric of black American life. In Atlanta, the Business and Professional Women's Club hosted a "Double V Dance," the highlight of which was one young lady's winning "the honor of being crowned Miss Victory."[28] North Carolina A&T was one of several colleges to declare "Double V" as the theme for its spring festival. The college declared its May Queen to be the "Queen of the Double V," and she rode atop a float adorned with a twenty-feet-tall V and several American flags.[29]

Many progressive white American leaders and organizations supported the Double V campaign. At its annual convention in Chicago, the United Auto Workers endorsed the campaign and called upon the federal government to integrate all branches of the military "as a strong and vital blow against racial segregation and discrimination."[30] Former presidential candidate Wendell Willkie delivered a widely covered speech in New York City in which he called for an end to segregation in the military. "Don't you think," he asked his audience, "that as American citizens we should insist that our Government and Navy Department eliminate the bar that prohibits any American from serving his country?"[31]

The popularity of the Double V campaign demonstrated to administration and War Department officials that African Americans would continue to fight to integrate the armed forces even as the nation waged war. The campaign's supporters believed the war presented the military with a prime opportunity to end segregation. Some of these supporters, particularly those on active duty, suggested that it would behoove America to address black soldiers' concerns before the war's end. None wanted a reprise of the bloodshed that engulfed American cities after World War I. One African American corporal warned, "A new Negro will return from the war—a bitter Negro if he is disappointed again. He will have been taught to kill, to suffer, to die for something he believes in, and he will live by these rules to gain his personal rights."[32]

HARVEST OF DISORDER: THE ARMY

JUST AS SCHOLARS OFTEN ANALYZE America's involvement in World War II by considering the European and Pacific campaigns separately, it is useful to examine African Americans' struggle to end military segregation during the war by considering the army and the navy separately. The two branches segregated their service members differently and, ostensibly, for different reasons. Their future paths to integration would differ widely as well.

BETWEEN SEPTEMBER 1939, when war erupted in Europe, and Japan's attack on Pearl Harbor in December 1941, the army expanded its ranks significantly. The number of black soldiers grew from 3,640 to 97,725. This twenty-seven-fold increase presented logistical problems to an institution committed to maintaining racial segregation. The army lacked both the facilities and the organizational structure to absorb so many African Americans. By the time the United States officially entered the war, it was becoming clear to many army senior officers that segregation posed a threat to military efficiency.

Segregation in the army was considered a firmly entrenched policy. Just as segregation was a fixed part of most Americans' civilian lives, it was fixed in the United States Army.[1] William Hastie lamented after joining the War Department, "The traditional mores of the South have been widely accepted and adopted by the Army as the basis of policy and practice affecting the Negro soldier."[2] The African American newspaper reporter Ollie Stewart, on assignment at Fort Monroe, Virginia, exclaimed, "The War Department is still too over-run with narrow-minded Southerners!"[3]

Most of the army's training camps were in Southern states whose elected officials remained adamantly opposed to African American soldiers training in their states. In 1942 the Southern governors' conference unanimously passed a resolution formally declaring their opposition to the army's stationing black troops in their states. Mississippi's congressional delegation protested the posting of black soldiers there, and Arkansas's governor said sending black recruits to Arkansas would be a "grave mistake."[4]

The army's most senior officers believed that this opposition would disappear as soldiers took to war. Inducting so many African Americans in such a short time was unprecedented. Logistical difficulties were to be expected. Army brass considered themselves ready and willing to adapt. They already had changed regulations to open more diverse service opportunities to black soldiers. The army would change as necessary to fulfill its mission. All options except desegregation would be considered.

SECRETARY OF WAR HENRY STIMSON and army chief of staff General George C. Marshall were bulwarks against efforts to desegregate the army. When Roosevelt sought his advice on the matter, Stimson professed to President Roosevelt to be "sensitive to the individual tragedy which went with it to the colored man himself" but advised the president to avoid placing "too much responsibility on a race which was not showing initiative in battle." As Stimson saw it, "foolish leaders of the colored race" were seeking to desegregate the armed forces in an effort to achieve "social equality," which was impossible "because of the impossibility of race mixture by marriage."[5] Southern hardliners consistently invoked the specter of interracial sex to defend segregation. Although Secretary Stimson was no such hardliner, even he believed that maintaining segregation in the military was inextricably linked with preventing interracial sex.

General Marshall supported maintaining segregation for reasons bound in both American tradition and military efficiency. "The settlement of

vexing racial problems," he believed, "cannot be permitted to compli-
cate the tremendous task of the War Department."[6] Less than one week
before the Japanese attack on Pearl Harbor, Marshall explained his support of the army's racial segregation policy. First, separation of the races
was a well-established custom in much of the country. Second, the education level of most African American recruits and draftees was below
that of most white recruits, and efficiency demanded that the army employ personnel according to their abilities. Last, "experiments within the
Army in the solution of social problems are fraught with danger to efficiency, discipline and morale."[7]

Marshall's concern regarding black soldiers' low education level was
well founded. Officers administered the Army General Classification
Test to all new soldiers. Results of the AGCT divided soldiers into five
grades. Soldiers who tested into grades I, II, and III were classified as
potential leaders, specialists, and technicians. Men who tested into
grades IV and V were classified as semiskilled soldiers and laborers.

More than 80 percent of black soldiers scored in the two lowest
grades. Nearly 50 percent of black men drafted between March 1941 and
December 1942 scored in AGCT grade V, the lowest category—this
compared with the 8.5 percent of white soldiers who tested into the
lowest AGCT grade. There were far more white soldiers than black soldiers, and, importantly, black and white soldiers with comparable education levels achieved similar scores. The soldiers with the lowest scores,
black or white, hailed from Southern states.

Army officials regarded the AGCT as an accurate indicator of natural
cognitive ability. Despite the fact that similarly educated white and black
soldiers achieved similar scores, the high number of African American
soldiers who scored poorly confirmed many senior officers' assumptions
about black soldiers' ability to absorb technical training.[8] They believed
that most black soldiers scored poorly not because of their limited educa-
tions but because they were innately less intelligent. This was a primary
reason why, they argued, segregation must be maintained.

Segregation therefore required placing the large number of uneducated black soldiers into the comparatively few black army units. Although more white soldiers than black soldiers tested into grades IV and
V, the uneducated white men were dispersed among the great many

white army units. This ameliorated the degree to which white men in grades IV and V could hamper their units' training. In comparison, segregation concentrated lesser-educated black soldiers in African American army units, limiting both the effectiveness of those units and the types of assignments for which they were deemed eligible.

Shortly after the attack on Pearl Harbor, NAACP executive secretary Walter White presented General Marshall with an idea endorsed by several black newspaper editors. White asked General Marshall to create within the army an experimental integrated division. Black and white soldiers could volunteer to serve in the division. White insisted, "This was not idle speculation on my part." His proposal had support from Undersecretary of War Robert P. Patterson and William Hastie. The everresourceful NAACP official also had names of white men from Northern and Southern states who were "gravely bestirred by the conflict inherent in their country's declaration that it was fighting a war against dangerous Nazi racial theories, while a similar racial philosophy dominated our Army and Navy."[9]

The NAACP rallied popular support for the establishment of the integrated division. Association executives contended that many white Americans believed that "racial segregation in the Army is undemocratic and dangerous to our national morale."[10] Indeed, several prominent white Southerners vocally supported White's proposal. Howard Kester, general secretary of the Fellowship of Southern Churchmen, told reporters that an integrated army division "would greatly strengthen the position of the democratic forces among the colored peoples of the entire world." The president of the University of North Carolina, Frank P. Graham, likewise endorsed the establishment of a voluntarily integrated division.[11]

The War Department rejected the proposal, stating that it "would not indulge in social experimentation in time of war." Walter White was proposing a new way of organizing a division and General Marshall believed that "the urgency of the present military situation necessitates our using tested and proved methods of procedure, and using them with all haste."[12] When White asked the army's commanding generals to hold a conference on the idea, the adjutant general of the army, Major General E. S. Adams, replied, "The War Department does not contemplate the organization of such a division such as suggested, and consequently a conference on the subject is not deemed necessary." White ruefully declared that "the tradition-bound and prejudice-indoctrinated majority" had won again.[13]

THE ARMY'S INTRANSIGENCE BRED growing frustration among African Americans, a majority of whom had come to believe that equality and segregation were incompatible. The NAACP's membership grew dramatically during this time. In 1940 the organization had nearly 51,000 members. By 1946 there were 450,000 members in 1,073 NAACP branches, and, importantly, this vast membership spanned traditional class boundaries in black communities.

Roy Wilkins exemplified popular black thinking when he associated Nazi fascism with America's institutionalized racism. Black Americans were perfectly willing, even eager, to fight, he wrote, for a "new world which not only shall not contain a Hitler, but no Hitlerism. And to thirteen million American Negroes that means a fight for a world in which lynching, brutality, terror, humiliation and degradation through segregation and discrimination, shall have no place—either here or there."[14]

Edgar G. Brown, the director of the National Negro Council and president of the United Government Employees, telegraphed the president: "Twelve million American Negroes renewed today their pledge of 100 percent loyalty to their country and our Commander in Chief against Japan and all other invaders. Negro youth await your call for an unrestricted and full opportunity to serve their country at this critical hour in all capacities of the United States Army, Navy, Marines, Coast Guard, Air Corps and national defense."[15] The Brotherhood of Sleeping Car Porters mailed to President Roosevelt a resolution pledging its "unshakable determination to support the government . . . for complete victory over Japan and Hitler and his Axis allies. When in uniform in the Army, Navy, Air corps and Marines, members of the Brotherhood will give unstintingly of their toil, sweat, blood, brain and brawn . . ."[16] The *Baltimore Afro-American* published a passionate editorial:

We have said before and we say now that we colored people are Americans, and as Americans who have as much at stake in this our land as any other citizens, we will do our share to defend it . . . But we cannot defend America with a dust brush, a mop and an apron.

We cannot march against enemy planes and tanks and challenge warships armed only with a whiskbroom and a wide grin . . .

Twelve million colored people, without bitterness for what has happened in the past, offer themselves to the Chief Executive in this crisis and say, "Mr. President, you can count on us."[17]

As much as they feigned otherwise, War Department leaders recognized that they could not ignore African Americans' persistent protests. For one thing, there were a great many African Americans now serving in the army. One year after the Japanese attacks on Pearl Harbor, an Army spokesman informed reporters, "The requirements of military security prevent disclosing the exact number of Negro units or the exact number of Negroes in the army. Negroes, however, are serving in every arm and service of the army and the number of Negro soldiers practically equals the ratio of the Negro race to the total population of the United States."[18]

Led by Colonel Edwin W. Chamberlain, several top army officers concluded that segregating soldiers by race "aggravated if not caused in its entirety" racial friction in the army. More important, they argued, segregation hindered mission readiness because it wasted manpower, money, and equipment. Colonel Chamberlain recommended that the army cease creating new all-black units. Instead, black soldiers who scored into the two lowest AGCT grades should be assigned to white units at a ratio of no more than one black soldier for every nine whites. The grades IV and V black servicemen would work as cooks, drivers, and orderlies. The more educated black soldiers who scored in grades I, II, and III would continue to be assigned to existing black units. This would mitigate the concentration of low-scoring soldiers in those units.

Predictably, Chamberlain's recommendation met with opposition from segregationists. To such criticism Chamberlain replied that his plan presented no more integration than that found in "the employment of Negroes as servants in a white household."[19] His superior officers on the army staff, although intrigued with his plan, could not bring themselves to accept its recommendations. They rejected his ideas. After the defeat of Colonel Chamberlain's plan, no military leader made a serious attempt to revise the army's racial policies until after the end of World War II.[20]

On January 11, 1943, the United States Army commissioned an officer whose life up to that point had been remarkable only for its misfortune. Vernon J. Baker was born on December 17, 1919, to one of just a dozen African American families in Cheyenne, Wyoming. Both his parents died in a car accident four years later and young Vernon was raised by his grandparents. He spent a couple of his teenage years at Father Flanagan's Boys Home in Omaha, Nebraska, before graduating from high school in Iowa and finding work as a railroad porter.

Baker hated working as a porter. When his grandfather died in 1939, the grandson fell adrift. He quit the railroad and accepted manual labor where he could find it. Back in Cheyenne in April 1941, before America entered the war, Baker tried to enlist in the army. "We don't have any quotas for you people," the recruiter said, sending him away. Baker returned a few weeks later and a different recruiter accepted his application. After he completed Officer Candidate School, the army commissioned him as a second lieutenant, assigning him to the 370th Regiment of the Ninety-second Infantry Division.[21]

Baker and his fellow soldiers fought in Italy in the summer and fall of 1944. On patrol one night Baker discovered a German sentry. A fierce firefight ensued. Baker, who stood five feet five inches tall and weighed 145 pounds, killed the enemy but suffered a severe arm wound that required him to be hospitalized for months.

By April 5, 1945, he had rejoined his fighting unit as the only African American officer in Company C. His orders were to help lead an attack on a German mountain stronghold. The battle was intense. The Americans sustained heavy casualties. As he and Captain John Runyon huddled to discuss strategy, a German soldier appeared just beneath them. Baker recalled that the soldier "threw a hand grenade at the two of us. The grenade missed us and failed to explode. The enemy soldier tried to duck back into the concealed entrance of a dug-out but before he made it, I shot him in the back, twice. He fell just outside the entrance."[22]

Lieutenant Baker borrowed a staff sergeant's submachine gun and crept down the path to the entrance where the German soldier lay dying. He peered inside and killed four enemy soldiers in the hideout before they could react. Baker scampered back up the path to rejoin the captain and other soldiers, who by then had fallen under heavy enemy fire.

For hours the men fought the enemy with grenades and artillery, but the German mortar fire came so consistently that the Americans first mistook the mortar shells for birds. Company C called for reinforcements. Hellfire rained on them for hours as they fought back as best they could. Finally they realized that no reinforcements were coming. The army's official history acknowledges that the officers who received the request for reinforcements refused to believe that the all-black company had successfully advanced as far as it had. The official report concludes, "The regimental executive officer informed Captain Runyon not to expect reinforcements for a long time, perhaps for days."[23]

Runyon ordered his men to retreat. "I told him I would remain," Baker later said, "and help to get the wounded out and follow him and the executive officer later. Eight men stayed with me and the wounded while I covered their evacuation." Two of Baker's eight men, including the medic, soon lay dead. With machine guns and white phosphorus grenades, Baker and his six remaining men destroyed six enemy gun nests, two observer posts, and four dugouts, and killed twenty-six enemy soldiers. Baker awoke the next day and led a battalion assault that captured the top of the mountain.

Baker's commanding officers did not so much as acknowledge that he and his men had completed their mission. "Our thanks was an ass chewing and an assignment to scout for white soldiers," he recounted in his memoir, *Lasting Valor*. "It was a way of life for my men. It made me furious."[24] They were fighting in an army that seemed to despise them. "I was an angry young man. We were all angry. But we had a job to do, and we did it."[25]

More than fifty years later, on January 13, 1997, Vernon Baker became the only living African American World War II veteran to receive the Medal of Honor. President Bill Clinton awarded the medal to Baker and six deceased African American veterans. A *Washington Post* reporter who spoke with Baker at the White House reception noted that the celebrated veteran "appeared melancholy." Baker explained, "I just wish the other guys were here."[26]

AS THE ARMY HAD a torrent of African American volunteers and draftees to deploy, the War Department reverted to the creation of all-black divisions. It reactivated the Ninety-third Infantry Division on May 15, 1942, and reactivated the Ninety-second a few months later. In February 1943 it reestablished the all-black Second Cavalry Division.

Lest they appear to be regressions to the Great War era, these reactivations were greeted with considerable fanfare. When the War Department reactivated the Ninety-second Division on October 15, 1942, at Fort McClellan in Alabama, Governor-Elect Chauncey Sparks was among the speakers. Elected officials, a military band, and thousands of spectators looked on as the Ninety-second's white commanding officer, Major General Edward Almond, proudly received the colors of the unit that reporters were calling "the Black Buffalo Division."[27] In keeping with the War Department's practice of appointing Southern white officers to command black troops, General Almond was a Virginia native who had attended the Virginia Military Institute. His career path was reported widely in African American newspapers, with journalists taking care to note that Almond had been awarded a Purple Heart and the Silver Star for gallantry in action.[28] Guarded as it was, their optimism was unmistakable. After all, as one reporter wrote, "The 92d Division had a glorious record in World War I."[29]

War Department civilians worked with army senior officers to ensure that black soldiers' training, facilities, and recreation were better than they had been during World War I. By the end of 1943, the area for African American soldiers at Arizona's Fort Huachuca boasted five movie theaters showing first-run films, a well-equipped soldiers' lounge, and a fully stocked officers' club with original artwork decorating the rooms.[30] A football stadium able to hold twenty thousand fans, two baseball stadiums, and an eleven-thousand-seat arena helped make Fort Huachuca one of the nation's finest army camps.[31]

Sergeant Joseph Barrow, a cavalryman better known as the world heavyweight champion Joe Louis, delivered motivational speeches across

U.S. Army Eighth Illinois Volunteer Regiment, ca. 1899. (LIBRARY OF CONGRESS)

Integrated crew of the Civil War–era vessel USS *Miami*. (U.S. NAVY)

The lead troops of the famous Ninth Cavalry pass in review at Camp Funston in May 1941. (U.S. ARMY)

Admiral Chester Nimitz pins the Navy Cross on Steward's Mate First Class Doris Miller, Pearl Harbor, May 27, 1942. (U.S. NAVY)

An African American recruit unit at Naval Training School,
Great Lakes, Illinois, August 1943. (U.S. NAVY)

Private First Class Victor Tampone, a military police officer,
in Columbus, Georgia, in 1942. (U.S. ARMY)

The first African American
Navy WAVES officers,
Lieutenant (Junior Grade)
Harriet Ida Pikens and
Ensign Frances Wills.
(U.S. NAVY)

Legendary African American
drill instructor Sergeant
Gilbert "Hashmark" Johnson,
USMC, at Montford Point.
(USMC)

Corporal Cornelius R. James, Sr., the author's grandfather,
a military police officer during World War II. (JAMES FAMILY)

Fighter pilots of an Army Air Force squadron credited with shooting down eight
German aircraft discuss the day's exploits on base, February 1944. (U.S. ARMY)

Officers of the Ninety-second Infantry Division—Company F,
370th Combat Team, reviewing maps and orders in Italy. (U.S. ARMY)

Brigadier General Benjamin O. Davis, Sr., the first African American flag officer, supervising Signal Corps soldiers in France, August 1944. (U.S. ARMY)

President Harry S. Truman. (LIBRARY OF CONGRESS)

The Golden Thirteen, the first African American naval officers, March 1944. From bottom row, left to right: Ensign James E. Hair, Ensign Samuel E. Barnes, Ensign George C. Cooper, Ensign William Sylvester White, Ensign Dennis D. Nelson; middle row, left to right: Ensign Graham E. Martin, Warrant Officer Charles B. Lear, Ensign Phillip G. Barnes, Ensign Reginald E. Goodwin; top row, left to right: Ensign John W. Reagan, Ensign Jesse W. Arbor, Ensign Dalton L. Baugh, Ensign Frank E. Sublett. (U.S. NAVY)

the country and trained with black troops. White commanding officers enthusiastically received the Brown Bomber, with one white colonel publicly telling him, "You are . . . admired by everyone with whom you have come in contact; by all who have seen you in the ring and out of it and by everyone who has read about you in the press."[32] The world-famous singer and actress Lena Horne entertained soldiers and praised their discipline and bravery.

Rather than being rushed into service units, as they had been in World War I, black soldiers in World War II received combat training. At Fort Huachuca, drill instructors trained twenty thousand black soldiers in hand-to-hand combat.[33]

Even with the improved facilities and training, black Americans continued to protest the segregated army. The Manhattan Central Medical Society, an African American doctors' group, condemned what it called "the jim-crow hospital at Fort Huachuca, Arizona." The physicians dispatched a telegram to the surgeon general of the army. "We insist on recognition as physicians," they declared, "not segregation as 'Negro physicians.' We are more than anxious to serve the country but demand a democracy for which to work and fight."[34] Their protests were all but ignored by the War Department.

Near the end of 1942, the army conducted an extensive survey of 13,000 soldiers in ninety-two units. Of those questioned, 88 percent of white soldiers and 38 percent of black soldiers preferred serving in segregated units. Half the black soldiers and 85 percent of white servicemen favored separate service clubs.[35] Most white officers assigned to black units desperately tried to get reassigned, even if doing so meant being demoted. "Please relieve me from this assignment," one brigadier general wrote, "reduce me to my permanent grade and send me to a combat unit on the European front."[36] In the wake of this survey, it became clear to African American activists that neither the army nor the Roosevelt administration would do any more than the little they already had done.

ONE OF THE FEW REASONS for African Americans to feel optimistic about progress in the army during World War II was that the army decided to continue commissioning African American officers. Surveys of

African American soldiers illustrated that by large margins they preferred being commanded by black officers rather than white officers.[37]

Reserve Officers' Training Corps units were established at Howard, Wilberforce, West Virginia State, North Carolina A&T, and Tuskegee universities.[38] Louisiana's Southern University in 1942 boasted twenty alumni in officers' training camps and four officers serving in the Ninety-third Division, including Ora Pierce, a nurse who, although born into a poor family as one of seventeen children, served with such distinction that she rose from the enlisted ranks to become a major.[39] The victory achieved by the World War I–era Committee of Negro College Men was lasting.

Perhaps more significant than the army's decision to continue commissioning African American officers, during World War II the War Department's leaders decided that, except for those in the army air corps, all army officer candidates would train in integrated programs. The department's experience during World War I showed that training black officer candidates in a separate school was expensive and inefficient. During this new war, black and white officer candidates would be selected and trained according to the same standards. They would train in the same schools. The army adjutant general ignored race when he announced in 1941, "The basic and predominating consideration governing selections to OCS [will be] outstanding qualities of leadership as demonstrated by actual services in the Army." General Benjamin Davis, when asked for his opinion on the race-blind new policy, replied, "You can't have Negro, white or Jewish officers, you've got to have American officers."[40]

Predictably, segregationists objected to integrated training facilities. Everyone from Florida's congressmen to the president of the White Supremacy League lodged protests, with the latter claiming that white officer candidates having "to eat and sleep with Negro candidates [was] the most damnable outrage that was ever perpetrated on the youth of the South." Army officials answered these protests by stressing that segregated officers' training camps were "decidedly uneconomical."[41]

African Americans greeted news of integrated officers' training schools as a welcome instance of the Roosevelt administration backing its rhetoric with action. "Continuing reports of Negro soldiers qualifying and graduating from officer candidate schools," a *Chicago Defender* journalist reported, "demonstrate that members of the race are being taken into the army in accordance with President Roosevelt's proclamation: 'It is the policy of the United States to encourage full participation in the national defense program by all citizens regardless of race, creed, color or national origin.' "[42] Secretary of War Stimson told reporters that many black officers would command troops in the newly reconstituted Ninety-second Division.[43]

During World War II and thereafter, men training to become army officers slept, ate, and trained together in integrated camps. William Hastie remembered this as long-overdue progress: "We were able to get significant numbers of black soldiers admitted to officers' candidate schools, and earning their commissions, who theretofore would have found their application for one reason or another, pigeonholed or rejected."[44] After Hastie forcefully argued in 1942 that the army was accepting far too few black officer candidates—just twelve in the preceding three months—President Roosevelt ordered Secretary of War Stimson to commission more black officers.[45] At the NAACP's annual convention, its leaders extolled "the training together of Negro and white officers, even at Army schools in the South, which shows that it can be done."[46] Integrated officer candidate schools, the army's first experiment with integration, succeeded even in the face of political opposition.

ONCE THEY RECEIVED THEIR COMMISSIONS, however, black officers were hurled into a segregated army whose regulations and customs seemed to mock the very notion of an African American officer. In many ways they were officers in name only. Army policy dictated that no black officer could outrank a white officer in the same unit. This meant that only black officers who worked exclusively with other black officers— an extraordinarily small group of men—could rise above the rank of first lieutenant. As Walter White lamented, "James Crow is more firmly entrenched than ever in our armed forces."[47] Despite the fact that black and white officers had trained together, the army refused to permit black officers to command white enlisted men. One white officer noted that "Negro officers were often judged by whether they had the 'right attitude' toward race problems, so that obsequious and bootlicking individuals were favored far more than in white units."[48]

_____

AT AGE SIXTY-FOUR IN 1941, the nation's only black flag officer, Brigadier General Benjamin O. Davis, was deemed too old to command combat troops. He served in the army's inspector general's office but was frequently dispatched to review black soldiers' facilities, providing black recruits and draftees with what one reporter called "the thrill of being inspected by the highest-ranking member of their race in the army."[49] The thrill was unlikely to be mutual, as General Davis understood perhaps better than the soldiers he inspected how deeply entrenched was the army's disregard for its black troops. In 1943 Davis wrote in a memorandum, "The colored man in uniform is expected by the War Department to develop a high morale in a community that offers him nothing but humiliation and mistreatment."[50]

America's fighting army of World War II was just as segregated as the one it sent to fight in World War I. The War Department refused to permit African American soldiers to enter its WHITES ONLY cafeteria. At his desk in the department, rather than be refused service at the government-run cafeteria or forced to sit in the COLORED section of one of the diners near his office, General Davis fasted every day during the lunch hour.[51]

ON ACCOUNT OF THE BETTER EDUCATION they received in Northern states, most African American officers were from the North. They resisted the confines of the army's Southern-style segregation. A few officers resigned their commissions rather than continue to subject themselves to gross discrimination. One such officer wrote, "I am unable to adjust myself to the handicap of being a Negro officer in the United States Army . . . Sins of omission, sins of commission, humiliations, insults—injustices, all, are mounted one upon another until one's zest is chilled and spirit broken."[52]

In February 1943, the white commanding general of the Ninety-third Division mustered all his black officers for a rare Saturday night meeting. Delivering news that was even worse than most of the officers' suspicions, General Fred Miller informed his men of the War Department's policy regarding the promotion of African American officers. He announced that no black officer would be promoted above the rank of first lieutenant.[53]

In response to the many incredulous queries and letters it received from African Americans across the country, the War Department clarified that the order applied only to African American soldiers at Fort Huachuca. These soldiers remained technically eligible for promotion beyond the rank of first lieutenant, but if they received such a promotion, they would be transferred out of the Ninety-third Division and away from Fort Huachuca. As one journalist explained, "This means that if a commander recommends a good officer for promotion, he is lost to the 93d."[54] Because no other military unit was subject to this order, civil rights activists and military observers alike wondered whether the Ninety-third Division was merely a token military outfit set up to appease colored people who were complaining that they were not being given adequate opportunity in the army. Several of the division's officers anonymously admitted to a reporter that they believed this to be the case.[55]

The order devastated morale among the Ninety-third's black officers. Aside from the medical corps, whose all-black staff was commanded by one of Chicago's most prominent physicians, Colonel Midiam O. Bousfield, all but two officers in the division above the rank of first lieutenant were white. An unusually high number of these white officers were recent college graduates. Their being placed in command of more experienced black officers at Fort Huachuca, according to one report, "has thrown consternation in the ranks of Negro soldiers here."[56]

There were more than twenty thousand men stationed at Fort Huachuca, which some black Americans had taken to calling "the world's largest Negro combat training camp."[57] Reaction to the no-promotion policy reverberated nationwide. "It is tough enough for Negroes to be jim-crowed and kept back," Walter White remarked upon learning of the policy. "But expecting us to be so unintelligent as not to know what is being done to us adds gross insult to grievous injury."[58]

18

THE ARMY AIR CORPS

IN APRIL 1941, the body of a black man was found hanging from a sapling on a U.S. military base in Georgia. He was a soldier, still wearing his uniform, and there was a bullet hole through his temple. His family had not heard from him in two months. A medical examiner concluded that he had been dead for at least four weeks.[1] Private Felix Hall had served Company E of the Twenty-fourth Infantry. After his father traveled to Fort Benning to identify his body, the remains of the nineteen-year-old were returned to his hometown of Montgomery, Alabama.

During World War II, racial violence surged in the United States. Sadistic lynchings horrified even some segregationists. Thousands of black and white Detroit residents fought brutal battles in 1942 and 1943. Thirty-four people were killed in the latter conflict, seventeen of them black residents killed by police officers.[2] A few weeks later, on a sweltering Sunday night, Harlem erupted into flames. New York's mayor, Fiorello La Guardia, requested white military police officers to quell the melee. Deadly racial clashes broke out in Los Angeles and Mobile, Alabama, as well.

Segregated military camps were not immune to the violence. "Weather conditions and the availability of land meant that a disproportionately large number of the training centers were in the deep South," Hastie recalled, "and this created, of course, a great number of very serious racial problems; and I think we were able to ameliorate conditions, though they remained really very bad throughout the war."[3] In Little Rock, Arkansas, a white police officer shot a black soldier. At Fort Dix, New Jersey, three men were killed when white military police exchanged gunfire with black soldiers. Violence between white and black army units disrupted training at other large camps.[4] Race riots erupted on military camps in Georgia, Texas, Mississippi, and California. A black soldier stationed at Fort Sill, Oklahoma, wrote, "The cross-section of the Negro soldiers' opinions here is that we had just as soon fight and die here for our rights as to do it on some foreign battlefield."[5]

After military police officers shot and killed a black soldier named Ned Turman at Fort Bragg, North Carolina, army leaders at last realized that they were facing a crisis. On account of its racist policies, the army was reaping what one black officer called the "harvest of disorder."[6] MPs, or military police, were particularly feared and despised by black soldiers because, as one journalist reported, they did "not hesitate to beat up and kill Negroes in the streets and in the jails." The *Pittsburgh Courier* sharply charged that the impunity with which the MPs acted proved that the army "has bowed . . . to the doctrine of white supremacy and racial separatism with a zeal that Dr. Joseph Goebbels would regard as commendable."[7] In a move that was both symbolic and substantive, the army established black military police units.*

LESS THAN TWENTY-FOUR HOURS after the Japanese attacked Pearl Harbor, the army deployed troops to the Panama Canal. War Department officials deemed the Canal Zone a probable "next target" for either Germany from the Atlantic side of the isthmus or Japan from the Pacific.[8] Among the men deployed to the canal were four hundred black soldiers of the 275th Signal Construction Company. They labored in Panama's steaming jungles under the command of Lieutenant General Daniel Van Voorhis.

The men of the 275th were also among the first to experience racism's scourge while on tour. Panamanian law prohibited non–Spanish-speaking black people from immigrating or from staying too long on a visit.

---

* My grandfather, Corporal Cornelius R. James, Sr., served in one of these newly created military police units at Tuskegee Air Base in Alabama.

Despite the fact that the soldiers' mission was to protect Panama from invasion, Panamanian government officials worried about the effect that the relatively well-paid black Americans would have on local workers. They asked America to take its black soldiers home. This request was too much even for Secretary of War Stimson, who ordered army officers to tell Panamanian bureaucrats that the black soldiers "must complete their work. It is ridiculous to raise such objections when the Panama Canal itself was built with black labor."[9] After the governments of Chile and Venezuela protested the presence of African American soldiers in their countries, however, Stimson capitulated, noting that the United States had asked to station troops in those countries; Panamanian officials had asked for American forces to defend their nation against Axis invasion.

Brigadier General Dwight D. Eisenhower drafted a memorandum for his boss, General Marshall, titled "The Colored Troop Problem." In it the future president presented a list of nations and territories that objected to African American troops being stationed on their soil. Australia, Hawaii, Bermuda, Iceland, and Trinidad were among those on Eisenhower's list.[10] The War Department then developed a new policy: African American soldiers would be stationed in any nation so long as that nation was not in the far north latitudes and its government had asked the United States to place troops on its soil. Although Stimson's was an ostensibly evenhanded policy, the practical result was that few African American soldiers were stationed overseas during the early years of World War II.[11]

In 1942, when the American military desperately needed more combat troops, 75 percent of the army's African American soldiers were assigned to labor battalions. The War Department's Advisory Committee on Negro Troop Policies recommended to Secretary Stimson that "Negro combat troops be dispatched to an active theatre of operations at an early date," but Stimson's staff urged him to "quit catering to the Negroes' desire for a proportionate share of combat units."[12] The secretary decided, because white commanders more readily accepted black soldiers as laborers than as combat troops, to increase the number of black soldiers assigned to labor duty. To satisfy the army's need for more combat troops, he would transfer white soldiers from labor units to combat battalions, and, to replace the white laborers, Stimson would order the storied all-black Second Cavalry Division to become a service corps.

William Hastie urged his boss not to repeat "the tragedy of World War I."[13] The former judge, having grown tired of political half measures, told Stimson:

> It is respectfully submitted that it is time and past time that the matter of utilization of Negro combat units pass out of the hands of those who deal with this matter as a distasteful search for compromise born of political necessity, and into the hands of those who have the will and the understanding to exploit the great combat potential of the Negro soldier as a valuable asset in the winning of the war.[14]

Stimson replied that the average African American's inferior education greatly limited his ability to serve in a combat unit. Placing so many uneducated soldiers into combat units would put lives at risk. Conversely, Hastie viewed the African American soldiers as untapped assets. By now it was clear to both men that they possessed opposing views on how to solve what Hastie viewed as a fundamental flaw in America's armed forces.

African American soldiers who were stationed overseas were likely to be service and supply troops. Other African American servicemen found themselves stuck on American soil years after completing their combat training. Combat units that had trained for warfare were converted into stevedore units. The Twenty-fourth Infantry transported cargo, and the Ninety-ninth Antiaircraft Artillery Regiment returned home after a brief tour in Trinidad.[15] Closer to the battlefront, in Italy, nearly every African American soldier in the country was unloading ships, constructing airfields, or driving trucks.[16] General George Marshall simply refused to send black units into combat.[17]

Men in the all-black Second Cavalry Division were ecstatic when they received orders to report to an Allied base in North Africa. They had trained for close combat duty. Upon arriving in theater, however, the cavalrymen were assigned to labor duty, loading and unloading ships. Adding to their resentment was the fact that near the labor port was a camp housing between forty thousand and fifty thousand white soldiers who had, for various reasons, been relieved of combat duty. Army generals preferred that these white soldiers remain idle rather than perform work typically reserved for black soldiers. Morale became so low in the Second Cavalry Division that Major General George Barr, chief of staff of the Mediterranean theater, brought in Walter White to assuage the men's wounded pride. White told the men "that I shared their anger. I promised to do whatever I could to enable them to serve in [combat]."[18] Despite White's personal appeals to the War Department, the Second Cavalry Division remained in port.

New York congressman Hamilton Fish, who had led black troops into battle in World War I, took the fight to the floor of the House of Representatives. "It is astonishing," he told his fellow representatives, "that after 26 months of World War number two virtually no Negro units have been engaged in combat except the Ninety-Ninth Pursuit Squadron and a few anti-aircraft units." Eleanor Roosevelt urged the War Department to grant "the colored people . . . a chance to prove their mettle."[19]

Secretary Stimson sent a widely read letter in reply to Congressman Fish. He conceded that black combat units had been converted, after months of training, into service units, but denied that this was due to the soldiers' race. Instead, Stimson, whom many progressives and African Americans already held in low regard on account of his thinly veiled racist views, insisted that black troops were not smart enough to use contemporary weapons: "Many of the Negro units . . . have been unable to master efficiently the techniques of modern weapons."[20]

The outcry to Stimson's letter was immediate and widespread. He attempted to ameliorate the damage by announcing, "There are now more than 75,000 colored American troops in various theaters of operation. They include not only service troops but combat troops such as coast artillery and infantry." In contrast with its experience during World War I, when the Ninety-third was split into numerous separate units for training, Stimson told reporters, the "division is now undergoing maneuvers as a division. This is an advanced stage of training for this unit."[21] Stimson believed that this was proof of the War Department's policy "to utilize the Negro soldier in combat as well as in active theaters of war."[22]

It was clear despite Stimson's announcement that the army was reluctant to employ black troops in combat. That these units would remain segregated was accepted under protest by many activists and soldiers, but the fact that the army would either leave them idle on bases at home or convert them into labor battalions abroad was an insult too great to bear. There was what one army historian called "a glut of black soldiers stationed in the United States."[23] The 75,000 black soldiers stationed overseas constituted but a fraction of the 504,000 African American troops in uniform. The fact that African American combat troops and most service units remained idle at camps in the American South was a flagrant waste of manpower.

The War Department appointed Assistant Secretary John McCloy to chair its Advisory Committee on Negro Troop Policy. McCloy was a Harvard Law graduate whose considerable self-made fortune survived the 1929 stock market crash because the cautious lawyer had not invested any of his money in the markets. Personnel directors for the army air forces, army ground forces, and army service forces served along with General Benjamin Davis on what became known as the McCloy committee. Judge Hastie was pointedly excluded.[24]

Testimony by witnesses appearing before the committee convinced McCloy that the army needed to make better use of its black soldiers. On March 2, 1944, McCloy informed Secretary Stimson: "It is the feeling of the Committee that colored units should be introduced in combat at the earliest practicable moment."[25] Secretary of War Stimson and General Marshall finally accepted the recommendation, agreeing that black soldiers who had been trained for combat should be assigned to combat duty. Combat teams were chosen from the Ninety-second and Ninety-third Divisions. Soldiers from the Ninety-third landed in the South Pacific by the end of March 1944, and Ninety-second Division troops arrived in Italy in July. As their combat assignments were publicized in the black press, the units quickly became a source of pride for African Americans.

The army deployed more black soldiers overseas, but remained reluctant to commit them to battle. When the NAACP pressed the army about black combat troops being converted to labor units, General Douglas MacArthur personally assured Walter White, "The 93d Division is and will remain a combat unit and will be used as such as circumstances warrant. Race or color has nothing whatever to do with failure to use this division to date. Lack of ships, among other circumstances, has prevented us from moving the 93d and several other divisions to forward areas. We hope to remedy that soon."[26] The McCloy committee disbanded shortly after the war ended. By then committee member General Benjamin Davis, normally a voice of moderation, had joined many African Americans in concluding that the members had no intention of desegregating the military.[27]

THE UNITED STATES ARMY AIR CORPS, created in 1926, was reorganized as the U.S. Army Air Forces in the summer of 1941. Before America entered the war, civil rights activists lobbied the War Department to include black servicemen in what was regarded as one of the more glamorous arms of the military. Judge William Hastie believed that if the black soldier found equal footing anywhere, it would be in the army air forces.* Hastie surmised that "the Air Force was the place where we should have made the most progress, because the Army Air Force was essentially new. It did not have the traditions that the older arms of the Service did, and it would have been entirely feasible, as it developed and new institutions and new organizations in the Air Force developed, to have planned and organized them differently from the old Army way."[28]

Hastie soon learned that his rare flash of confidence in the War Department was misplaced. The army air corps was commanded by General Henry Arnold, a decorated officer who believed that "having Negro officers serving over white enlisted men . . . would create an impossible social problem." General Arnold enjoined the air corps from training black Americans as pilots because pilots were officers and forbade them from enlisting as mechanics because they would serve alongside white air corps mechanics.[29] As a result, nine separate black aviation squadrons were formed in 1941 and all were assigned to maintain existing airfields for the nation's white pilots.

This harsh adherence to separate and manifestly unequal service opportunities for black and white Americans dismayed many civilian ob-

---

*The United States Air Force became a separate branch of the military in 1947.

servers. The NAACP and other leading liberal groups besieged Congress and the War Department with protests. In response, on January 16, 1941, the army air corps announced the formation of an all-black pursuit squadron. These pilots would be trained in Tuskegee, Alabama, just forty miles away from a state-of-the-art training facility for white pilots at Maxwell Field.

The Tuskegee Army Flying School would train some of the air forces' best pilots. Frank Lambert, a white flight instructor at Tuskegee, frequently extolled his students' skills in interviews with reporters. "An airplane does not react," he noted, "to the color or appearance of its pilot, either favorably or unfavorably."[30] In recent decades, the Tuskegee airmen have received overdue recognition for their grace under pressure in the segregated South as well as in the skies of war.

When the flying school was established, however, it made clear to all Americans that despite decades of struggle and protest, the nation's military remained as segregated as it ever had been. Walter White called the establishment of the segregated flying school a "sorry experience."[31]

When the army air forces made clear that they would remain as segregated as the army, it was the last straw for William Hastie. He finally resigned his position in the War Department on January 15, 1943. The air forces continued to funnel black recruits into labor battalions and, to Hastie, it became "inescapable that the air command does not propose to inform, much less counsel with, this office about its plans for Negroes."[32] He at last had accepted that his influence in the War Department was fatally marginalized by Secretary Stimson's commitment to maintaining a segregated military. He told Stimson that, after two years and two months, his presence in the War Department was not effective, that he would be of greater help to black soldiers as a private citizen, and that the department had waged a campaign to minimize his effectiveness.[33] Hastie returned to his office as dean of Howard Law School.

Judge Hastie's resignation sharpened criticism of the army air forces' policies. As one observer wrote, "Judge Hastie's resignation . . . certainly is the type of protest that must say to the world that we are not unmindful of what is happening to us and we want a better day not some time in the future but now!"[34]

DURING WORLD WAR II, the number of African American soldiers in the army grew from fewer than five thousand to over seven hundred thousand. When the war began, one could count the number of African American officers on one hand, but, as the war drew to a close, nearly six thousand black men had become officers. The army air forces employed 678,000 black airmen and over one thousand officers. Four thousand black women served in the U.S. Women's Army Corps (WACs) and the U.S. Women Accepted for Volunteer Emergency Service (WAVES). More than a half million African American men and women in uniform had served in Europe, Africa, and the Pacific.[35] Despite the fact that most black military men and women still worked in labor or service units, the tireless efforts of black community leaders, journalists, government officials, and, of course, African Americans in uniform combined to make the military a better place for black people than it had been before the war.

In the end, though, the army remained a segregated institution. For all the medals awarded to African American soldiers, they served in battalions and units whose very existence contradicted the cause for which they were fighting. Because War Department officials were so intent on sending very few black units into combat, more black soldiers in service and labor units than in combat units actually experienced combat.[36] America's military remained as segregated as ever. In June 1944 a letter to the Democratic and Republican national parties signed by leaders of twenty-five African American organizations warned America's political leaders, "No injustice embitters Negroes more than continued segregation and discrimination in the armed forces."[37]

"Entitled to a Showdown": The Navy Under Secretary Knox and the Truman Committee

James Hairston, a native of Madisonville, Virginia, enlisted in the navy when he was seventeen and served from 1938 to 1960. The proud black Southerner was in his eighties when he quipped, "If anyone my age [who is African American] tells you they were in the Navy and say they were anything more than a steward they are telling you a lie." It was inconceivable that the United States Navy's senior officers or civilian leaders would permit a black sailor to serve as something other than a steward or messman. "If you asked the Navy to do anything else," Hairston remembered, "they'd want to analyze you. They'd think you were crazy."[1]

There were 5,026 African Americans in the navy when America entered World War II, accounting for 2.4 percent of the navy's total manpower. These seamen were restricted to serving in the Steward's Branch, an all-enlisted unit organized outside the navy's general service. Steward's mates and messmen wore different uniforms than sailors and were forbidden to give orders to sailors whom they outranked. Except for an Asian contingent consisting mostly of Filipinos, every last man in the Steward's Branch was black. African American journalists called them "seagoing bellhops."[2] In March 1943 the *Baltimore Afro-American* published a striking photograph depicting nearly a hundred African American men ranging in age from their twenties to middle age standing in their chef's whites on the steps at the United States Naval Academy in Annapolis, Maryland. Centered in front of the cooks were three white men—two officers and a civilian. Above the photograph read the headline: "We Can Cook in the Most Prejudiced Branch of the U.S. Navy." The brief note beneath the photograph reminded readers that the naval academy refused to accept black applicants. In its caption, the *Afro-American* declared, "Here are 93 cooks in the U.S. Naval Academy, all of whom are buying war bonds."[3]

The U.S. Coast Guard, which provided maritime law and safety enforcement, was part of the Department of Transportation until it was brought into the navy as part of the military's war preparation.* Like the navy, the coast guard boasted a long tradition of employing both black and white sailors. Unlike the navy, however, the coast guard always had restricted African American sailors to low-ranking duty and the Steward's Branch. There were rare exceptions, such as Captain Michael Healy, who retired in 1903 as the third-ranking officer in the service, but earlier all African Americans in the coast guard, like their navy brethren, served in the mess.

IN JULY 1940 PRESIDENT ROOSEVELT, a former assistant secretary of the navy, appointed Frank Knox as secretary of the navy, which at that time was a cabinet-level position. Knox, a partial owner of the *Chicago Daily News*, had been the Republican Party's nominee for vice president in 1936. Roosevelt appointed the Boston native in part to drum up bipartisan support for his defense and foreign policy initiatives in the wake of France's fall to Nazi Germany.[4]

Although he was a skilled administrator, Knox knew very little about the navy. He therefore deferred even more than typical appointees to military commanders' recommendations. The navy's senior admirals ardently opposed allowing African Americans into the general service. During Knox's first weeks in office, they explained to him the reasons for keeping the general-service navy all-white. Black men could serve only in the mess because the navy had no way to segregate them aboard

---

*After the attacks of September 11, 2001, the coast guard became a component of the Department of Homeland Security.

ships if they worked as general-service sailors. Segregation aboard ships was impracticable, they reasoned, and therefore exclusion was necessary. Integration was not an option.

This made sense to Secretary Knox, who added that "it is no kindness to Negroes to thrust them upon men of the white race." African Americans who wanted to serve as anything other than mess attendants could join the army.[5]

The navy's racial policy drew widespread criticism. Immediately after America entered World War II, the NAACP sent a telegram to Secretary Knox demanding: "Because our country is in peril we ask revision of the navy's policy with respect to the use of Negroes and the limitation upon their use. Thirteen million American Negroes want to know if only white Americans are to be permitted to fight and perhaps die for our country in the navy."[6] The navy replied with a letter that read, "There has been no change in the navy's policy of enlisting men of the colored race, and for the time being no change is contemplated."[7]

Radio stations beamed commercials and public service announcements asking young men to join the navy, but, as one editorial board noted, "Negroes who answer the appeals made through the radio and the press are either turned down or assigned to the messmen branch. These men want to fight, not cook."[8] Peering down at a line of white applicants stretching down the block, a navy recruiting officer in Baltimore told a reporter, "We are in great need of all the men we can get, but we can use colored boys only as messmen." A marine corps recruiter stated that he was accepting absolutely no enlistments from black men.[9]

As the years passed and the war raged on, the navy's policy—and African Americans' response to it—had a debilitating effect on the morale of African American men already serving. One chief petty officer with decades of service complained that when he tried to encourage young men to join the navy and see the world, "they ask me how they can see the world scrubbing floors and washing dishes. They make fun of me."[10] William M. Renard, a messman who had served aboard a ship that had nearly been sunk in the Pacific, told reporters that his regular duties consisted of "shining shoes, making beds, and serving officers at the table."

Renard nonetheless acknowledged, "I like the service very much. I've been in now for more than two years and after the war I am going to enlist again for another hitch." The messman wanted a career in the navy. He hoped one day to attain the rank of first class steward. With 20 percent overseas pay he earned just $64 per month. Anyone who hoped to earn any more would have to "play politics if you want to get a break."

"What do you mean by playing politics?" journalist Richard Dier asked.

"As a colored man," Renard explained, "you've got to know your place at all times. Obey and respect the officers and treat them like they expect to be treated . . . a colored man has to be particularly careful how he handles himself." Despite the limitations on his advancement and the nature of his duties, Renard asserted that he had "been in action many times" and was "concerned with licking the enemy."[11]

AFTER RECEIVING THE TERSE REPLY that the navy contemplated no change in black sailors' status, the NAACP asked President Roosevelt to issue an executive order ending the navy's racially exclusive policy.[12] The president declined to issue such an order, but he did write to Secretary Knox: "I think that with all the Navy activities the Bureau of Navigation [which controlled personnel assignments] might invent something that colored enlistees could do in addition to the rating of messmen." Likely anticipating Knox's reiteration of the admirals' rationale for excluding black men from the general service, Roosevelt added, "Officers of the U.S. Navy are not officers only but are American citizens. They should, therefore, be expected to recognize social and economic problems which are related to national welfare . . . It is incumbent on all officers to recognize the fact that about 1/10th of the population of the United States is composed of members of the Negro race who are American citizens."[13]

Three months later, in April 1942, Secretary Knox announced that the navy, marine corps, and coast guard would begin accepting black recruits who would be trained for the general service. Navy officials hoped to enlist 14,000 African Americans during the first year. Recruits would train in segregated facilities and could rise in rank no higher than petty officer. If enough black recruits ranked highly enough, the navy would consider permitting them to work as crew on destroyers or other small ships. Knox had good reason to believe that this proposal would satisfy Roosevelt because, although the president believed the navy's current policy was unjust and politically unsustainable, he also believed that "to go the whole way at one fell swoop would seriously impair the general average efficiency of the Navy."[14]

Newspaper editorial boards strained to accentuate the positive aspects of the new policy. The *New York Times* board could have been writing on behalf of African Americans when it declared that the navy's announcement was "good as far as it goes." The "unhappy" fact was that the navy still employed a policy of discrimination "for which no warrant can be found in the Constitution, the statutes or the democratic traditions of the United States."[15] The *Philadelphia Inquirer* called the new policy "a beginning from which further liberalization of policy can develop," and the *New York Herald Tribune* agreed that "it is a step in the right direction and it has important symbolic value, not only for colored Americans, but for every citizen of a democracy pledged to a life-and-death struggle with a monstrous evil which has made racial discrimination one of its chief tools of destruction." The *Chicago Sun*'s editors contended that "something more substantial is needed" to stem the "serious loss of faith among nonwhites in the white race."[16] A. Philip Randolph more pointedly concluded that the navy's new policy "accepts and extends and consolidates the policy of Jim-Crowism in the Navy as well as proclaims it as an accepted, recognized government ideology that the Negro is inferior to the white man."[17]

GENERAL SERVICE IN THE UNITED STATES Navy opened to African Americans on June 1, 1942. Black recruits trained at Camp Robert Smalls, a post named for an African American Civil War hero and located on the outskirts of the Great Lakes Training Center. Fully separated from the surrounding all-white facility, Camp Robert Smalls was a base within a base. Lieutenant Commander Daniel Armstrong, a naval academy alumnus whose father founded Hampton Institute, a leading college for African Americans, commanded the recruit program at Camp Smalls. A number of the officers serving under his command held progressive racial views.[18] Even though they were segregated from the larger navy base, African American recruits and draftees training at Camp Smalls endured a more bearable experience than did those at boot camp in Norfolk, Virginia, which black sailors had taken to calling "the asshole of creation."[19]

Navy chief specialist John F. Potts told reporters that black recruits were joining the navy for three reasons: First, black enlistees on leave from training or duty were delivering positive reports to their friends and families. Second, trainees enjoyed the benefits of the navy's physical training program. Third and most important, young black men were eager to learn trades that would earn them good wages in the civilian workforce after the war ended.[20] Potts worked toward his stated goal of recruiting and successfully training enough African American sailors to comprise 10 percent of the navy's general service.[21]

Unfortunately, the navy was nowhere near attaining that goal. African Americans remained wary of the service that for so long had restricted them to food service duty. Most African Americans did not view Secretary Knox with the same mix of suspicion and derision with which they viewed Secretary of War Stimson, but Knox had capitulated repeatedly to the conservative whims of his military advisers. Knox's apparent willingness to yield led civil rights observers to view him as unable to effect the sort of dramatic change in the navy that African Americans sought. The army remained segregated, but young black men registering for the draft and reporting to recruiting stations believed that they were more likely to find meaningful service in a segregated army unit than in the navy.

The president was losing patience with the navy's recruiting shortfalls among black men. On February 22, 1943, he wrote to Knox:

> The point of the thing is this. There is going to be a great deal of feeling if the Government in winning this war does not employ approximately 10% of negroes—their actual percentage to the total population. The Army is nearly up to this percentage but the Navy is so far below that it will be deeply criticized by anybody who wants to check the details.
>
> Perhaps a check by you showing exactly where all white enlisted men are serving and where all colored enlisted men are serv-

ing will show you the great number of places where colored men could serve, where they are not serving now—shore duty of all kinds, together with the handling of many kinds of yard craft.[22]

President Roosevelt's memorandum agreed with the solution Knox believed best for putting more black sailors to work outside the mess halls. Knox replied to the president that the navy would continue to segregate black sailors and would restrict them to serving in certain billets: Overseas they would serve in twenty-seven new all-black Seabee construction battalions and as stevedores, cooks, and port hands. Black sailors would serve aboard ships only in harbor crafts and local defense forces. In other words, black sailors would remain restricted to shore duty in segregated units, working jobs with little chance for promotion. President Roosevelt assented to this plan.[23]

THOUSANDS OF AFRICAN AMERICAN recruits graduated from the Great Lakes Naval Training School during the first year of the navy's new policy. Many of them went on to attend an advanced naval training program at Hampton Institute in Virginia, where they became electricians' mates, machinists' mates, and first, second, and third class firemen. When they were stationed at domestic American bases, these specially trained new sailors, like nearly all black sailors regardless of their rank or education level, were assigned to labor or custodial work. In East Boston, for example, educated black sailors waxed floors and cleaned toilets.

Although the navy's official policy was that all positions were "open to colored men in every branch of the service," the fact was that black sailors were employed almost exclusively to lift and carry cargo and to clean up after white sailors. Half of all black sailors were assigned to shore billets within the continental United States. They worked as laborers on sharply segregated naval bases. Because the draft produced many more white sailors than had existed before the war, the navy needed many more stewards and messmen to serve those sailors.

Reporters for the *Baltimore Afro-American* asked the navy why it assigned even specially trained black sailors to menial tasks. A navy spokesman responded, "Although it is the policy of the Navy Department to use men in the trades for which they were trained, colored sailors can expect to be used in accordance with the needs of the service." If a base commander elected to put all his black sailors to work in labor units, the spokesman claimed that there was nothing the Navy Department could do. A base's commanding officer "is in complete charge and is at liberty to use men as he sees fit."[24]

This issue of menial duties only intimated the larger problem faced by African American sailors: In 1943, a full year after the navy opened the general service to black sailors, there were no general-service black sailors serving aboard any of America's seagoing vessels. A navy spokesman confirmed that nearly all black sailors "are still assigned to shore duty and some to defense and harbor craft, but, no colored sailors are on duty on large combat vessels except in the steward branch." The spokesman added, "I do not know why it is that colored sailors aren't being used. They surely are needed."[25]

Black sailors on leave from duty at Pearl Harbor brought to the mainland stories of how their superior officers in Hawaii were completely ignoring official navy policy and assigning college-educated African Americans to stevedore and labor duty. Newspapers reported that every one of the fifteen hundred black sailors at Pearl Harbor, regardless of rank or training, worked in a labor unit. One sailor visiting family in Illinois hoped to find a way to avoid being sent back to Pearl Harbor. "If I can," he said, "I'm going to try to stay right here."[26]

NAVY OFFICIALS SOUGHT TO PROVIDE more opportunities to African American sailors without integrating American ships. President Roosevelt had made clear that restricting black sailors to menial tasks was no longer militarily or politically acceptable. But Roosevelt had also told the navy's senior leadership, "I do not think it the least bit necessary to put mixed crews on the ships."[27] Navy officers' insistence on maintaining segregation posed something of a riddle to planners tasked with diversifying the force's use of African American sailors.

Civilian and uniformed leaders believed they found the answer in the USS *Mason*—the nation's first naval warship manned almost entirely by black sailors. Initially, white officers would be assigned to lead the ship's crew, but navy officials planned to replace them with African American officers as the force implemented its plan to train and commission black men as officers. Among the African American officers who would serve aboard the USS *Mason* was Ensign Samuel Gravely, who would become America's first black admiral.

First Lady Eleanor Roosevelt had introduced the idea of manning a seagoing vessel with an all-black crew; for this reason, detractors called the ship under construction at the Boston Navy Yard "Eleanor's Folly." When she was completed, however, no one could deny that the USS *Mason* was an impressive vessel: An elite Evarts-class destroyer escort, she was 289 feet long and weighed 1,140 tons. She could reach speeds of twenty-one knots while carrying a crew of 150 men and six officers. The numerous weapons and gun turrets trimming her decks left no doubt that this ship was bound for warfare.

The forty-four white officers and petty officers selected to command the USS *Mason* were granted the opportunity to decline the assignment, not because of the danger involved, but because they would be commanding black sailors. Navy officials required the officers to sign documents stating, "I consent to and accept this assignment . . . after having been advised of the fact that a colored crew will be assigned to the vessel."[28]

Lieutenant Commander William "Big Bill" M. Blackford agreed to be commanding officer of the USS *Mason*. A naval reservist who already had skippered a minesweeping ship off the Alaskan coast, the tall, hefty Seattle resident was two semesters shy of earning his Ph.D. in chemistry when the navy summoned him to active duty. About being asked to command the USS *Mason*, Blackford wrote to his parents, "Can't figure out why I was picked but will do the best I can—really quite an opportunity to do something."[29] Blackford's optimism may have been hereditary: His great-grandmother had been a prominent abolitionist in Virginia.

It snowed in Boston on the first day of spring in 1944. A bitter wind blew drifts across the Navy Yard and snow piled high on the docks. None of the more than five hundred men and women gathered for the commissioning ceremony minded the snow, however, and a respectful silence fell as Captain Ronan C. Grady, commander of the Boston Navy Yard, rose to read the commissioning orders for the USS *Mason*. After the ship was officially commissioned, the governor of Massachusetts addressed the crowd. He was followed by the mayor of Boston and the president of Boston's NAACP chapter. Several men became visibly emotional when the mother of Newton Henry Mason, an ensign killed in battle and the ship's namesake, gave Lieutenant Commander Blackford a picture of her son.[30]

After the guests and dignitaries departed and the journalists had taken enough pictures, Blackford finally was alone with his crew. The USS *Mason*'s commander told his men that, by taking this assignment, he was not "trying to solve the race problem." He would treat them fairly as sailors. They would be traveling through treacherous ocean waters littered with enemy submarines. Their race was not his concern.

On June 14, the USS *Mason* assembled in formation with other destroyer escorts to guard a convoy of merchant vessels loaded with matériel bound for Allied troops in Europe. The *Mason* and her crew returned safely to America's East Coast three months later. A war correspondent embedded with the crew reported that their successful completion of this first mission fulfilled "the Navy's promise to send colored bluejackets to sea as fighting men on a fighting ship."[31]

The USS *Mason*'s crew respected their fair-minded commander. After he led them safely across the treacherous Atlantic and back, they vowed they would "follow him to hell and back" and noted that "he treated us man to man."[32] Blackford was equally impressed with his men. Their bravery and work ethic were impeccable. In a letter to his parents he wrote, "There has been a lot of bunk about the Negro crews . . . They are anxious to make a name for themselves and actually work harder."[33]

The sailors aboard the USS *Mason* got the chance to work very hard when their shop joined Convoy NY119. It was a convoy of seagoing tugboats, harbor tugboats, yard tankers, and barges owned by the U.S. Army. Convoy NY119 would become legendary in the annals of naval warfare. It left New York Harbor for the northern European war zone in September 1944, protected by the *Mason* and other navy vessels.

On account of its tugboats and barges, the convoy's progress was treacherously slow. German submarines aggressively patrolled the open North Atlantic, and sluggish Allied merchant and resupply vessels were their favorite targets. The fight that would launch Convoy NY119 into history, however, was not against Axis warships; it was against the harshest ocean storm recorded during the war. Waves reaching fifty feet in height battered the steel ships. Hurricane-strength winds assailed the American ships relentlessly for thirty days and nights. The waves and winds exceeded some vessels' capabilities: Three tugboats, eight car floats, and five cargo barges sank in the maelstrom.

AT LAST, on October 18, 1944, sailors on watch aboard the USS *Mason* spied Bishop Rock, England.[34] But with safe harbor in sight, the bad weather turned even worse. Winds became so strong that *Mason* sailors finally issued radio calls for assistance. Storm winds posed a greater threat to their ship now that it was close to shore. Visibility dropped to zero. No ship, military or civilian, answered the *Mason*'s calls for help. Waves thrashed against her hull and the wind snapped off her radio antenna.

Moments later, the ship's deck split. Two beams belowdecks collapsed. Water flooded her engine room. The *Mason* was in danger of breaking apart and sinking. The sailors worked furiously to save their ship. They pumped water from the engine room and repaired the broken beams. Specialists replaced the antenna and restored communication.

With the storm still tossing her about, the *Mason* turned back to sea to aid twelve more convoy ships. Two British ships were ordered to accompany the American destroyer escort, but once they saw the violent seas beyond the harbor, their captains ordered them back to port. Blackford and his men remained at sea for three more days, guiding convoy ships into port. The USS *Mason* then set course for the coast of France. The men had powered through an enormous storm. They would live to say, as sailor James Graham later did, "I was there. I was aboard the *Mason*."[35]

News of the incredible storm reached far and wide. In his official report, Commodore Alfred Lind, commander of Convoy NY119, wrote that he "considers the performance of the USS MASON, her Commanding Officer, Officers and men outstanding and recommends that this ship be given a letter of commendation to be filed in the record of each officer and man on board the vessel." Blackford officially recommended his men for individual commendation. Navy officials in Washington ignored both recommendations.[36]

The USS *Mason*'s sailors at last stepped on English soil in Plymouth.

They made their way to a nearby canteen where the Red Cross was serving hot dogs and Coca-Cola. When the sailors arrived at the canteen in their United States Navy uniforms, the Red Cross workers refused to admit them. The canteen for colored men, Red Cross personnel explained, was located several blocks away.[37]

NEITHER THE WHITE HOUSE nor the Department of the Navy could ignore the calls for the navy to commission black men as officers. By the end of 1943 there were nearly one hundred thousand enlisted African American sailors, and navy officials expected many more to enlist the following year.[38] The overwhelming majority of black men in the navy were Southerners. In 1943 only about one quarter of black sailors hailed from the North, because black Northerners continued to prefer serving in the army, which commissioned qualified black recruits as officers.

The fact that thousands of African American men from Northern states, a sizable percentage of whom were college-educated, would soon be forced into the navy weighed heavily on the minds of millions of African American families. One commenter lamented, "A half million colored boys who will be called into the navy next year (because the army has met its quota of new colored units and will need no more colored draftees except as replacements), therefore face the discouraging prospect of joining a branch of our armed forces in which educated colored men are not wanted."[39]

Navy officers and civilian leaders recognized that an influx of Northern black men could affect the navy's ability to maintain segregation. In response to a journalist's questioning the depth of training the navy provided to black inductees, Secretary Knox bristled. "Well, you know exactly what we are trying to do," he answered. "We are trying to avoid mixing crews on ships. That puts a limitation on where we can employ Negro seamen. Using them for crews of small shore and harbor craft, and things of that sort, and for shore duty. But we are not mixing crews."[40] Aside from cooks and stewards, U.S. Navy ships at sea would continue to employ only white sailors.

As the 1944 election year drew near, members of Congress pressed the Navy Department to alter its discriminatory policies. As the draft delivered more African American sons and husbands to the navy, African American voters made clear that changing the navy's race-based policies was high on their political agenda. Editors of the *Baltimore Afro-American* wrote in a widely read editorial:

> Colored people stand to suffer grievously from the Navy's indifference to national welfare and its defiance of President Roosevelt's oft-expressed pronouncements that there must be the fullest use of all our human and national resources to win the war . . .
>
> [Black] navy recruits enter the service with the full knowledge that they are barred from fighting ships except as flunkies and that there is no promotion in the coastal command.
>
> This brings us down to the question: Who is commander in chief of the United States Armed Forces? If the President is boss, we expect him to direct the Navy to end its race discrimination . . . We are entitled to a showdown now.[41]

Although it was true that black sailors were largely confined to the lowest ranks, a significant number had risen to become petty officers. Navy officials realized that black senior enlisted sailors' leadership improved the morale and performance of lower-ranking black sailors. In 1943 the navy actively began recruiting African American men who were well established in their communities to serve as petty officers.

There were in 1943 only three ways to become a United States Navy officer: graduate from the naval academy, complete the V-12 training program while enrolled in college, or be commissioned directly from the civilian world or from the enlisted ranks. The first two of these were closed to African Americans. The navy commissioned a handful of black officers for the naval reserves, but during the autumn of 1943 the navy was inducting twelve thousand African American sailors each month. The absence of officers was beginning to present a morale issue as well as an image problem. During the preceding summer months, black sailors outside the messmen's branch were beginning to let officers know how much they resented serving in segregated units. When sailors at the naval ammunition depot at St. Julien's Creek, Virginia, learned that they would be segregated while attending a radio broadcast, violence erupted.[42] Racial unrest on naval bases had increased enough for Knox and his staff to worry.

Adlai E. Stevenson, an Illinois lawyer and future Democratic nominee for president, served as a special assistant to Secretary Knox. He strongly favored increasing opportunities available to black sailors. Because of the navy's policies and reputation, he repeatedly told his boss, the navy was losing America's most highly educated and best-qualified black recruits to the army. The time had come, Stevenson contended, for the navy to commission black men as officers. Failure to do so exposed the president to unnecessary political risk: The editorial board of one black-owned newspaper already had openly declared, "If Wendell Willkie or Thomas E. Dewey were President, we would not have lily-white fighting ships."[43]

Navy officials' first concern, like army officials before them, was how to avoid the possibility that black officers might command white sailors. The Bureau of Naval Personnel (formerly known as the Bureau of Navigation) studied the issue and, in a December 1943 memorandum, concluded that there were enough all-black units that black officers could be employed without undue risk of supervising white sailors. The bureau recommended that the navy commission twenty-two officers from its finest enlisted black sailors. In part because of Adlai Stevenson's lobbying, Secretary Knox approved this plan, but cautioned personnel officers, "After you have commissioned the twenty-two officers you suggest, I think this matter should again be reviewed before any additional colored officers are commissioned."[44]

THE NAVY DEPARTMENT ANNOUNCED that it would begin accepting black officer candidates in its V-12 college program. Young African American men were encouraged to obtain a copy of the pamphlet "The Qualifying Test for Civilians" from their colleges and high schools.[45] On New Year's Day, 1944, sixteen African American men commenced training as officer candidates at the Great Lakes base. Navy commanders selected the candidates from among the highest-rated senior enlisted men. All had demonstrated exceptional leadership qualities and most had been stellar athletes. Extensive background checks on the men revealed no propensity for civil rights advocacy. Several lacked college degrees, but others held graduate degrees. They were drawn from geographically diverse locations. The sixteen sailors would not receive the customary sixteen weeks of officers' training school; instead they would train for only eight weeks.

Very soon the men came to believe, on account of the restrictions on their training, that the navy was setting them up for failure. They covered their windows with blankets after lights out each evening so that they could continue studying late into the night. "We knew to a man that if we failed in this endeavor," George C. Cooper, one of the candidates, recalled in 1987, "the evil of segregation in the Navy, as related to black officers, would be set back for God only knows how long."[46]

The candidates took their examinations after weeks of rigorous training and relentless studying. Cooper told an interviewer, "When our grades were sent to Washington, we came out two-tenths of a point ahead of any indoctrination class they'd ever had."[47] Convinced that there had been a mistake, Navy Department officials ordered the men to take the exam again. This time the candidates scored even higher. Navy officials then decided, without warning or explanation, to commission only twelve of the sixteen candidates. A thirteenth was permitted to become a warrant officer.

On March 17, 1944, the candidates became officers. *Life* magazine published a group photograph of the men immediately known as the Golden Thirteen: Ensigns Jesse W. Arbor, Phillip G. Barnes, Samuel E. Barnes, Dalton L. Baugh, George C. Cooper, Reginald E. Goodwin, James E. Hair, Graham E. Martin, Dennis D. Nelson, John W. Reagan, Frank E. Sublett, William Sylvester White, and Warrant Officer Charles B. Lear.[48]

The navy immediately marginalized the new officers by designating them "Deck Officers Limited—only," a label typically reserved for officers with physical or mental impairments preventing them from performing the full duties of a line officer. Commanding officers assigned two of the ensigns to teach at the navy's school in Hampton, Virginia. Four were ordered to harbor craft duty. The remaining seven were assigned to training sailors at Great Lakes.[49]

Frank Knox died suddenly of a heart attack on April 28, 1944. So long as Knox was secretary of the navy, Walter White wrote, "no change of the status of Negroes in that service was considered."[50] The fact is that change in the navy's race-based policies was considered during Knox's tenure, but the secretary's widely known opposition to increasing opportunities for black sailors stymied what little progress did occur. Black sailors at last were ordered to fight at sea, but only aboard a destroyer escort specifically designated for an all-black crew. President Roosevelt on numerous occasions prodded Knox to alleviate the black sailor's plight, but the secretary, out of excessive deference to military commanders and his own stilted views of African Americans' abilities, would commit only to half measures.

Compared with the navy's prewar policies, however, these half measures were welcome steps forward. Progress toward equality in the navy was slow but steady. Despite their unexplained decision to limit its first black officers to onshore duty, Navy Department officials a few months later enrolled ten more African Americans in its officers' training program. Unlike the Golden Thirteen, however, these candidates were not forced to train and study in a segregated facility. Instead they trained alongside white officer candidates, and, once commissioned, they became staff officers in the civil engineer, chaplain, dental, medical, and supply corps. By January 1945, there were thirty-four African American naval officers, and the navy was continuing to train more alongside white officer candidates.[51]

Although its spokesmen would never say so publicly, the Navy Department's decision to integrate its officers' training program was an experiment with desegregation. On bases on both American coasts, black and white sailors worked together on projects. Perhaps more significant, black and white sailors on some bases began using the same recreational facilities, eating in the same mess halls, and bunking in the same barracks. No less an activist than Roy Wilkins felt compelled to admit, "There is more than a little indication that the Navy is making a sincere effort to give the Negro in uniform a better break. This does not mean, of course, that everything is rosy in the Navy . . . but it does mean that the Navy is aware of some matters and is devising and following a policy of correction."[52]

EVEN AS THE NAVY FACED dramatic shortfalls in onshore jobs, it remained steadfast in its refusal to admit African American women. Even members of Congress who did not normally involve themselves in issues of racial equality believed that this was an inexplicable waste of resources. Black women comprised a considerable part of the federal civilian workforce. To many lawmakers it made no sense that these same women were forbidden from serving in the Department of the Navy.

One such woman appeared to have received the chance in 1943. Amuncia J. Tucker's father had died when his U.S. Navy ship was torpedoed in World War II, and, as one journalist reported, she "wanted to get a crack at the Nazis." A civilian employee in the War Department, she received an invitation to apply to become an officer in the new navy division called Women Accepted for Voluntary Emergency Service, or WAVES. "Realizing your interest in the WAVES," read her letter from the naval office of officer procurement, "we know that you are anxious to contribute as much as you possibly can to ending this war with victory, and soon." Tucker scheduled an afternoon off from work to take the exam, but before reporting to the recruiting center she called the office of the *Baltimore Afro-American* to ask if the navy's policy had changed.

When an *Afro-American* reporter contacted the office of officer procurement, he learned that Tucker had received an invitation to join the WAVES because navy officials believed she was white. "I guess it was a mistake," an ensign at the office explained. "Colored people are not being accepted. Miss Tucker does have an appointment for this afternoon, however, and I'm afraid I shall have to clear that up."

Tucker arrived at the recruiting center a few hours later, and navy officials assured her that she had every right to take the examination. When she asked when she should expect to hear from them, they told her that "no promise could be made." She respectfully declined the examination.[53]

Navy officials announced in the summer of 1943 that black women would be permitted to join the WAVES. Because there were no black officers in the navy, black WAVES would not be eligible to become officers. Like white WAVES, they would work shore duty posts so that more sailors could be sent out to sea. Also like white WAVES, applicants were required to be between the ages of twenty and thirty, college-educated, "childless, and if not married must agree not to marry for the duration."[54] In keeping with navy policy, African American WAVES would train and serve in segregated units apart from all other WAVES.

Alpha Kappa Alpha, the oldest and largest African American sorority, immediately protested the new, segregated WAVES corps. The women were tired of "steps in the right direction"—of the military granting limited opportunities to black Americans in segregated units. "We would rather not have Negro women in the WAVES," a sorority spokeswoman informed reporters, "than have them taken in on such conditions as this plan proposes."[55] Alpha Kappa Alpha's protest was significant not just because of the sorority's vast membership but because of its role as a standard bearer for middle-class African American women. Numerous civil rights groups soon joined Alpha Kappa Alpha in urging President Roosevelt to overrule Secretary Knox's decision to segregate the new auxiliary corps.[56]

Despite the first lady's support for their cause, the White House ignored the groups' protests. Rather than establish the previously announced segregated units, Secretary Knox and his commanders reversed their earlier decision and instead decided to exclude African Americans from the WAVES entirely. Knox wrote that although he "tentatively approved" the idea of black women serving in the WAVES, the matter required further study.

The navy did not allow black women to enter the WAVES until after Knox's death in April 1944.[57] African American WAVES then served alongside white WAVES in integrated units: the first two African American WAVES officers, Harriet Ida Pikens and Frances Wills, were sworn in on December 22, 1944.

As CONGRESS APPROPRIATED BILLIONS of dollars for contracts with defense industry companies to build the ships, planes, and weapons necessary for defending the nation, Senator Harry Truman received word that many of these contracts and contractors were rife with inefficiency and sometimes outright corruption. He embarked on a ten-thousand-mile-long tour of military bases and defense industry sites, on which he learned that the situation was worse than he suspected: The government was guaranteeing defense contractors fixed profits on their contracts. The contractors in turn had little incentive to operate efficiently. Truman returned to Washington determined to challenge what he viewed as the systematic waste of taxpayers' money. He asked his fellow senators to create a committee to investigate the nation's military and defense industry.

On March 1, 1941, the Senate voted by unanimous consent to create the Special Committee to Investigate the Defense Program. Truman would serve as chairman of the committee, which swiftly became known as the Truman committee. His work on the committee, more so than his impressive 1940 reelection, changed Truman's reputation from that of a political machine's flack to an official intent on protecting the taxpayers' dollars by eliminating waste and corruption from government contracts.[58]

All but one of the committee's members were relatively junior senators seeking to establish themselves. Truman bragged that they conducted their work with "no pre-conceived notions, no partisan views to promote, no beliefs to prove."[59] Over the course of three years, the Truman committee spent approximately $400,000 in operating expenses and, by Truman's estimate, saved taxpayers $15 billion.[60]

The national media extolled the efforts of both the Truman committee and its plainspoken chairman. Truman appeared on the cover of *Time* magazine in 1943. Like any politician, he enjoyed the great deal of positive coverage he was receiving. "I am working night and day—still standing the boys on their heads," he wrote to a friend, "and getting more favorable publicity in the papers than all the rest of the Senators put together."[61] In 1944 *Look* magazine took a poll of Washington correspondents asking them which civilian leader, after President Roosevelt, had been most helpful to the war effort. The majority answered Senator Truman of Missouri.[62]

It is unlikely that many African American journalists were in the majority of the *Look* magazine poll. Truman's work on the special committee actually hurt his standing among African Americans. The committee twice scheduled hearings to investigate racial discrimination in the military and the defense industry and twice "indefinitely postponed" those hearings.[63] The NAACP contended that the Truman committee never intended to conduct a serious inquiry into the military and defense industry's race-based policies. When reporters asked the committee's chief counsel about its plans to investigate racial discrimination, the lawyer replied, "The Committee hearing on race discrimination has been postponed and no definite date has been determined for hearing."[64] Edgar G. Brown of the National Negro Council, an organization influential in the fight to diversify the civil service, told reporters, "The race has been double crossed."[65]

The Truman committee held hundreds of hearings during its three-year existence, but not one of these hearings explored racial discrimination in the military or civilian defense industry. In its final report, the committee detailed the armed forces' failure to utilize the skills of drafted men. It ignored the military's largely inefficient use of black troops. Defense contractors' discriminatory practices, which violated President Roosevelt's Executive Order 8802, likewise were ignored. Although given ample opportunity to do so, Senator Truman's special committee refused to question the race-based policies and inefficiencies that had become for millions of African American voters a significant blight on the nation's war effort.

In the short term, the committee's decision was politically expedient. The report of the Democratic-led Truman committee was so broadly accepted in the Senate that Republicans issued no opposing report. National approval of the committee's findings paved the path for Truman's nomination for vice president. Had the committee investigated racial discrimination, it would have lost the support of Southern Democrats. The convenient decision to ignore institutionalized racism would haunt Harry Truman's candidacy for vice president.

The Navy and Marine Corps
Under Secretary Forrestal

O N May 19, 1944, a wealthy former banking executive who had
served as undersecretary of the navy during Knox's tenure became
the secretary of the navy. James V. Forrestal was a trim, dark-haired
fifty-year-old whose father had emigrated from Ireland shortly before
America's Civil War. Forrestal had attended Princeton University but
left without a degree, in part due to financial difficulties. He went to
work for an investment banking firm, where he worked his way up from
bond salesman to president. His career in public service began in 1938,
when he became the first undersecretary of the navy, and ended eleven
years later in 1949.[1]

During his years working on Wall Street, Forrestal had joined the
National Urban League. He believed that the navy's race-based policies
were as indefensible as the Jim Crow laws of Southern states. His four
years as undersecretary had convinced him that the navy's policies were
not only immoral but inefficient as well. This the former businessman
could not countenance. Special assistant Adlai Stevenson now had an
ally in the secretary's office.

Secretary Forrestal quickly saw that assigning black sailors to labor
units on shore duty was no different from restricting them to serving in
the messmen's branch. He wrote that, under this policy, African American sailors had merely "swapped the waiter's apron for the stevedore's

grappling hook." It was time for the navy to "expand the use of Negro personnel by assigning them to general sea duty."[2]

After accepting a request from senior admirals that he not attempt to integrate combat vessels during the war, Forrestal devised a plan that would integrate some fleet auxiliary ships. To President Roosevelt he explained, "From a morale standpoint, the Negroes resent the fact that they are not assigned to general service billets at sea, and white personnel resent the fact that Negroes have been given less hazardous assignments." Forrestal proposed assigning black sailors to large auxiliary vessels where they would not comprise more than 10 percent of the ship's crew. If these crews were able to integrate without affecting mission readiness, black sailors would be assigned to smaller vessels "as necessity indicates"—that is, without regard to race. The president scribbled his reply: "OK, FDR."[3]

With Roosevelt's approval secured, Secretary Forrestal turned to the task that he imagined would be more difficult: obtaining the support of the navy's highest-ranking officer. Admiral Ernest J. King served as both the chief of naval operations and commander in chief of the U.S. fleet. The Lorain, Ohio, native and U.S. Naval Academy alumnus had served in the submarine service and in the naval aviation corps. By the time Forrestal became secretary, King was widely recognized as one of the most powerful and gifted naval officers in American history. A portrait of King's narrow, stern face graced the cover of *Time* magazine two years before Forrestal's did.[4] In December 1944 Congress took the rare step of appointing him fleet admiral, a five-star flag officer.

Forrestal scheduled a meeting with King. He approached the venerated admiral respectfully but firmly. "I don't think," he began, "that our Navy Negro personnel are getting a square break. I want to do something about it, but I can't do anything about it unless the officers are behind me. I want your help. What do you say?"

Admiral King sat silently in his chair for a moment, staring out the window. Forrestal did not attempt to fill the ensuing silence. King finally turned his gaze back to the former banker. "You know, we say that we are a democracy," King replied, "and a democracy ought to have a democratic Navy." The admiral pledged to support Forrestal's program "all the way."[5]

The Bureau of Naval Personnel chose ammunition ships, cargo vessels, and oilers—twenty-five ships in all—to participate in the pilot program. The twenty-five selected ships did not even amount to one third of 1 percent of the navy's seventy-five thousand maritime crafts, but the black sailors and their new white commanding officers understood that they were a part of a significant test.[6] Because there was not enough room on board to establish separate quarters for black and white sailors, segregation was all but impossible aboard ships. This was the navy's—and the United States military's—first official attempt at integration.

This attempt took place amid increasing racial strife in the navy. Despite Forrestal's efforts to liberalize the service, black sailors' resentment at the daily insults and restrictions they faced was reaching a boiling point. In Norfolk commanders forced them to obey signs in city parks reading NIGGERS AND DOGS KEEP OFF THE GRASS. On the island of Guam in the western Pacific, violence erupted between black sailors and white marines. Black sailors in California engaged in a hunger strike to protest the conditions imposed on them by their Mississippi-born commanding officer. The most serious event involving black sailors, however, was the one that accounted for 15 percent of all African American naval casualties during World War II. It was the deadliest domestic event of the war.[7]

WHAT WOULD BECOME KNOWN as the Port Chicago mutiny began on July 17, 1944, near San Francisco at Port Chicago, California. Black sailors were loading ammunition onto navy cargo ships shortly after ten P.M. when over ten thousand tons of ammunition exploded. The massive blast collapsed a 1,200-foot pier, sank two ships, and could be felt as far away as Nevada. The explosion killed 320 ammunition loaders, 202 of them African American.

A sailor named William Farrio, who, before joining the navy, had lived on 135th Street in Harlem, told a reporter how strongly the blast reverberated across the base. "I was in the barracks just getting ready to go to work when the explosion took place about a mile away." From Farrio's description, it was as if an earthquake had hit the base: "I was knocked from my bed to the floor, in a daze. I got myself together and ran outside. I was cut on the forehead, face, arms and back and on the sole of my foot." Whitfield Pollard, a sailor from Pittsburgh, recounted, "I was hurled clean across the barracks, and am now being treated for a compound fracture of the left leg."[8]

One journalist succinctly captured the devastation: "The United States Navy did not have to sound taps or perform last rites this week for the 250 Negro seamen who died in the line of duty here in the explosion last Monday night, for not a single body of the sailors . . . has been recovered either on land or sea."[9] Freddie Meeks, an African American sailor who had been on leave in Oakland on the day of the explosion, was ordered to return to Port Chicago to help recover body parts. "You see, there weren't any bodies," he told an interviewer decades later; "there were just pieces of flesh they shoveled up, put them in those baskets and brought them into the warehouse."[10]

Commanding officers granted thirty days of leave to white sailors who survived the explosion. Black survivors, along with Port Chicago's other black sailors, were ordered back to work loading ammunition under conditions similar to those on the docks that fateful Monday night.

Over 250 of these sailors refused to load the ammunition. Officers ordered fifty of them arrested and charged them with mutiny. Among them was Freddie Meeks, who likely would have been killed in the explosion if he had not been on leave in Oakland. Their trials and appeals enthralled millions of African Americans. The NAACP's legal team, led by Thurgood Marshall, represented the defendants. All fifty sailors were found guilty and sentenced to fifteen years in prison. In January 1946, the Navy released all of the sailors from prison but refused to discharge them, ordering them to serve "probationary periods" overseas. The men soon received "discharges under honorable conditions." But their convictions remained.

In 1994 the Department of the Navy reviewed the sailors' cases and concluded that race played no part in their convictions. "Sailors are required to obey the orders of their superiors," Secretary of Defense William J. Perry explained, "even if those orders subject them to life-threatening danger."[11] President Bill Clinton pardoned the three surviving mutineers, including Freddie Meeks, in December 1999. Meeks, who died a few years later at the age of eighty-three, wept when the president signed the pardon. "I knew God was keeping me around for something to see," he said, "but I am sorry so many of the others are not around to see it."[12]

FORRESTAL'S PILOT PROGRAM to integrate twenty-five vessels was a resounding success. Commanders unanimously reported to Admiral King that integration had worked aboard their ships. There were no incidents to report, morale among all sailors remained high, and, as the commander of the USS *Antaeus* wrote, the entire experiment was "remarkably successful."[13] In March 1945 Rear Admiral Randall Jacobs, chief of the Bureau of Naval Personnel, proposed to Admiral King that the navy "assign Negroes gradually to all auxiliary ships of the Fleet" with the limitation that "the number so assigned to any one ship should not exceed 10% of the allowed general service complement." Admiral King agreed.[14] A few months later, the navy announced that all recruiting centers would begin accepting inductees without regard to race.[15] Secretary Forrestal was transforming the navy.

Upon assuming office, Secretary Forrestal also took immediate steps to permit African American women to enlist in the WAVES. Not only should they be allowed to train to join the WAVES, he decided, but they should do so in integrated units. On July 28, 1944, he recommended to President Roosevelt that African American women be permitted to serve in the WAVES. They should be assigned "wherever needed within the continental limits of the United States, preferably to stations where there are already Negro men." As both reason and caveat, he reminded the president that protests against the current WAVES policy had gained considerable momentum over the past year. "I consider it advisable," Forrestal wrote, "to start obtaining Negro WAVES before we are forced to take them." Roosevelt was not persuaded. When Republicans charged the president with discriminating against black women who wanted to serve their country, he quickly relented and instructed navy commanders to admit African Americans into the WAVES.[16]

BY V-J DAY, there were 165,000 black men serving in the navy. Forty percent of them worked as messmen or stewards and nearly all the rest served in construction, maintenance, or labor units. Only fifty-three were officers. But there was no denying that the navy was changing from being the most harshly segregated branch of the military to the most integrated. Unlike the War Department, the Navy Department instituted an official desegregation policy during World War II. Secretary Forrestal established in the navy a culture that was beginning to strive openly for racial equality. Slow as progress had been coming to the navy, Secretary Forrestal would face even more resistance from senior officers of the all-white United States Marine Corps.

THE U.S. MARINE CORPS was, and to this day remains, a component of the Department of the Navy. As even many contemporary civilians know, however, the marine corps is culturally its own organization. During World War II the corps proudly was an all-white, all-male fraternity of fierce warriors who resented the suggestion that they begin training black men.

Major General Thomas Holcomb, the corps's commandant from 1936 to 1943, was born in 1879 to a Delaware family that could trace its roots to the Revolutionary War. He joined the marines three years after graduating from high school and one year shy of earning his bachelor's degree. Nearly forty-four years after being commissioned as a second lieutenant, Holcomb retired as the marine corps's first four-star general. Secretary of the Navy Frank Knox had enthusiastically written to his friend, "You will be the first officer of the Corps to hold the rank of general—the highest rank in our armed forces. I know of no other officer to whom that distinction more fittingly belongs."[17]

By the time America entered World War II, Holcomb already had solidified his place as a transformative military figure in the nation's history. There were only 18,000 marines when he became commandant of the depleted Depression-era corps. At its wartime zenith, the corps was 385,000 strong. Holcomb managed the corps's metamorphosis from a navy subbranch smaller than some army units into a truly global fighting force.

That this fortified marine corps might include African Americans was a possibility that Holcomb fought with all his considerable clout. In April 1941 he told the navy's General Board that African Americans had no "right" to join the corps. "If it were a question of having a Marine Corps of 5,000 whites or 250,000 Negroes, I would rather have the whites." There could be no black marines, he explained, because the corps was simply too small to form segregated units.[18] As Holcomb saw it, "there would be a definite loss of efficiency in the Marine Corps if we have to take Negroes."[19] He understood that many young black men wanted to fight for their country. "The Negro race has every opportunity now to satisfy its aspirations for combat," Holcomb insisted, "in the Army. And their desire to enter the [marine corps] is largely, I think to break into a club that doesn't want them."[20]

The commandant did not relent until Secretary Knox announced, on orders from President Roosevelt, that the corps would begin accepting African American inductees in April 1942. The next month, Navy Department officials ordered marine corps officers to commence inducting nine hundred African American men each month. The corps was the last American military service to accept black volunteers. In understated military fashion, the marine corps's official historian wrote that this order "was unpopular at Headquarters Marine Corps."[21] General Ray A. Robinson, one of the corps's battle-hardened senior officers, confessed his fear of what now appeared inevitable: "Eleanor [Roosevelt] says we gotta take in Negroes, and we are just scared to death; we've never had any; we don't know how to handle them; are afraid of them."[22]

General Holcomb realized that, once the decision had been made to induct African Americans, the corps needed to prepare for what promised to be a challenging transition. He wanted to avoid the violence and discipline problems related to integration that plagued the army in both world wars. He instructed marine commanders: "All Marines are entitled to the same rights and privileges under Navy Regulations." African American marines would neither be coddled nor harassed but instead were expected "to conduct themselves with propriety and become a credit to the Marine Corps."[23]

Holcomb decided, as the corps prepared to absorb its first black inductees, that he would not employ the new marines in existing units. Instead, he would seek to impose segregation in a manner similar to that found in the army. Black recruits would train at a single, all-black facility in North Carolina. As one military historian succinctly wrote, "black marines would train and serve in isolation."[24]

The inductees would train at the Montford Point marine training camp, a mosquito- and snake-infested woodland near Camp LeJeune. Seventy-five percent of the marines' African American inductees were college-educated, but the corps's senior leaders resolved that no African Americans would be commissioned as officers. Instead, nearly all 17,000 African American marines would serve as messmen, stewards, or laborers. As they completed their training and were placed into the Pacific theater, the black laborers would replace white labor units, which would allow more white marines to turn to combat.

Two defense battalions, the Fifty-first and the Fifty-second, were the only African American units intended for combat. The men trained for eight weeks under drill instructors like Sergeant Germany, who greeted his recruits with a greeting at once so racist and colorblind that it was as curious as his last name: "I did not come here to make friends. I came here to undertake the impossible assignment of making Marines out of you goddamn people. When the first load of y'all got here it made me want to puke, then go get drunk! The material gets worse with each platoon. The Marine Corps is not for cooks and janitors, which is about all you son of a bitchin' people are qualified to do as far as I can see. Just remember that I am going to try and get as much out of you people as I would from a platoon of white recruits. If I have to kill you to do it then you are dead."[25]

Despite the unwelcome news that most African American marines would serve in mess and labor units, African Americans celebrated the fact that the last branch of military service was finally open to them. Most news articles in the black press reported that the men were training at Camp LeJeune, rather than in an area that the marine corps considered an entirely separate training camp. Instead of focusing on the segregated boot camp or mess and labor assignments, many African Americans accentuated the fact that, as reporter Alfred A. Duckett wrote, there would be "Negro leathernecks" in "the most difficult possible kind of service under the flag of the United States."[26] He and other African American journalists excitedly wrote of inductees' grueling schedule of "hard and tough physical exercise, bayonet work, maneuvers and night problems, chemical warfare, demolition, jiu jitsu and Commando tactics."[27] Black-owned newspapers printed photographs of men in boot camp training with high-caliber weapons, often commenting that the recruits were "set for action."[28] One correspondent succinctly captured the marines' boot camp experience when he wrote, "In a few words, they are given a start in the terribly vital matter of how to kill quickly and efficiently and exercise all means of personal security at the same time."[29]

When the first African American marines completed their training, African Americans nationwide extolled the men's tenacity and promise. Four marines, two of them college graduates, made national news when they were promoted to the rank of sergeant.[30] The *Chicago Defender* published a photograph of Private First Class Edward Swann in his dress marine corps uniform, smiling proudly as he rang his parents' doorbell at 192 Decatur Street in Brooklyn.[31]

The marine corps's senior officers shrewdly took advantage of opportunities to publicize the efforts and successes of their new African American servicemen. Colonel Samuel A. Woods, a twenty-six-year corps veteran and a commander of black marines, told reporters, "I have found that any soldier anywhere will respond to his duties if he is treated like a human being. The same is true of the colored marines as of all other persons in the service." In his May 1943 interview, Colonel Woods also announced that the first black marines had already been sent overseas—"less than a year," one newspaper could not resist noting, "after the 167 year-old ban against their enlistment was lifted."[32] A photograph of marines boarding a military ship was published in one black-owned newspaper with the caption "Here's a group of Negro Marines, hardened for combat against the Japs, boarding a U.S. Coast Guard manned transport."[33]

DESPITE BEING STATIONED in the Pacific, none of the black marines in combat units ever saw combat. The experiences of the Third Marine Ammunition Company and the Eighteenth and Twentieth Depot Companies exemplified the ironic fact that African American marines assigned to labor units experienced the danger of combat. They were assigned to the hazardous duty of unloading ammunition and hauling supplies, sometimes under fire, on captured shores. The first African American marine killed in World War II was Private Kenneth J. Tibbs, who served as Captain William C. Adams's orderly. Tibbs was killed by enemy fire, Adams recalled, as his company landed on the island of Saipan in the Japanese-held Mariana Islands on June 15, 1944.[34]

On Saipan, African American marines, all of whom served in labor, steward, or mess units, proved their combat mettle. Japanese soldiers fought ferociously against the invading Americans, firing on them on the beach and in the trees. The marines, black and white, fought back with the discipline and resolve that characterized the USMC. "They were under intense mortar and artillery fire," one of their officers told *Time* magazine about the black marines, "as well as machine gun fire. They all kept on advancing until the counterattack was stopped."[35] On the island of Guam, African American marines in noncombat units performed heroically as U.S. forces recaptured an island that remains strategically important today.[36]

DESPITE THE MARINE CORPS'S ADHERENCE to segregation, the Department of the Navy significantly altered its race-based policies during World War II. When the navy allowed black sailors into its general service, integrated its auxiliary fleet, and inducted black men into the marine corps for the first time, African Americans collectively could believe that they were making progress in their struggle for the rights of full citizenship. To them, ending discrimination and segregation in the armed forces was an issue of "democracy." There remained a great deal of work to be done, but in the eyes of many African Americans there was no denying that, as one reporter wrote, "Democracy is on the march in the armed forces."[37]

This sentiment promised to be politically valuable to President Roosevelt as he sought an unprecedented fourth term in office. In seventeen states with 281 electoral college votes, African American voters were poised to play a pivotal role.[38] "Roosevelt remains individually popular with the Negro," one commentator noted, and they appeared ready to support him again in the 1944 election.[39] This was before the president announced that he was replacing liberal vice president Henry Wallace with Senator Harry Truman from Missouri.

21

FROM SENATOR TO VICE PRESIDENT TO PRESIDENT IN ONE HUNDRED DAYS

For all the times that Truman used Midwestern modesty as a cleverly convenient cloak, he was almost certainly telling the truth when he wrote in his *Autobiography,* "When the 1944 election was approaching mention began to be made about Truman for vice president. Every effort was made by me to shut it off. I liked my job as a senator and wanted to stay with it." By way of explanation, Truman continued, "It takes a long time for a man to establish himself in the Senate. I was a member of three very important standing committees—Appropriations, Interstate Commerce, and Military Affairs—and was well up on the list on all of them for seniority, which was very important. My Special Committee was doing good work and I wanted to stay with it."[1]

What Truman, by then out of office, chose not to mention is that when the powerbrokers of the Democratic Party set about choosing a vice presidential nominee in 1944, they understood that they likely were choosing the next president of the United States. Roosevelt remained popular, but his health had become a matter of growing concern as he visibly weakened. Vice President Henry Wallace's widely known liberal views on racial matters rendered the prospect of his remaining on the ticket unacceptable to Southern Democrats. Southern delegates traveled to Chicago for the 1944 Democratic national convention intent on removing Wallace from the ticket. "Hell's fire," one such delegate proclaimed, "the man nominated as Vice President at this convention may be President one day. The South knows that. President Roosevelt may not serve out this term. And we won't have Henry Wallace."[2]

Democratic activists at the convention spoke openly of Roosevelt's ill health even as they prepared to nominate him for an unprecedented fourth term in office. Walter White, who was no stranger to realpolitik, was taken aback by such open talk of the president's expected death. "I have never seen such cold-blooded speculation," he later wrote, "as there was among Democrats, particularly those from the deep South, as to how many years of a fourth term President Roosevelt could last."[3]

At the convention, Vice President Wallace delivered an impassioned address in which he declared that "there must be no inferior races" in American life. Moreover, Wallace contended in a speech decades ahead of its time, the government should guarantee "equal wages for equal work regardless of sex or races."[4] The fact remained, however, that Wallace was woefully unpopular among elected politicians and voting delegates alike. Black Americans appreciated his progressive views but understood that, on account of his reputation as an introverted bureaucrat who dabbled in mysticism, Wallace had little influence on legislation or the administration's agenda. On the convention floor African American Democratic activists wondered, as one journalist reported, whether "the rejection of Wallace was a rejection of his liberal theories as well."[5]

Truman professed to have no interest in the vice presidential nomination. He pledged his support to South Carolina's James F. Byrnes. Truman remembered "the week at Chicago" as "the most miserable I ever spent, trying to prevent my own nomination to be Vice President." Truman knew that President Roosevelt faced serious health issues and "was afraid of what would happen" if he became vice president. It soon became clear, however, that Senator Truman was, as Roosevelt told a friend, "the one fellow that Southerners like, and the one fellow that labor could accept." If Democrats' political coalition were to hold, Truman would have to be the party's nominee for vice president. He accepted the nomination, becoming what the *New York Times* called "the second Missouri Compromise."[6] A *Washington Post* political columnist observed that the senator's career "has been the product of political miracles," and that being nominated for vice president "found Truman emotionally disturbed, reluctant, totally unprepared."[7]

African American Democrats were nervous about Truman's nomination. Adding to their concern was Southern delegates' unabashed glee at having succeeded in electing the man they called their "compromise candidate." Alabama's powerful delegation leader said at the convention, "I hope Truman doesn't forget Alabama was the first to start the ball rolling for the landslide." Alabama governor Chauncey Sparks asserted, "The South has won a substantial victory. I find [Truman] safe on states' rights and the right of the states to control qualifications of its electors. In the matter of race relations, Senator Truman told me that he is the son of an unreconstructed rebel mother."[8] Mississippi's delegation chairman added, "Though we Southerners have been tossed about with many conflicts and many doubts, yet we have been victorious in the selection of a Vice-President."[9]

THE NEWLY NAMED DEMOCRATIC NOMINEE for vice president immediately sought to assure African American voters that they had nothing to fear from his replacing Henry Wallace on the ticket. "Of course," Senator Truman breezily guaranteed the renowned African American reporter Harry McAlpin, "Negroes will lose nothing by my nomination as vice-president." Notwithstanding his consistent record of supporting civil rights legislation, Truman found himself counting on allies to make his case to black voters. His voting record in the Senate did not protect him from attacks on his alleged "indifference" to the difficulties most of them faced. "Truman will work in close harmony with Roosevelt, will do everything in his power to aid and assist him in carrying out those liberal ideas and principles which made him President of the United States for three terms and assures his reelection for the fourth," Representative William Dawson, an Illinois Democrat and the only black member of Congress, told journalists. However, Dawson had supported Vice President Henry Wallace at the convention until it was clear that Wallace had lost his place on the ticket to Truman.[10]

The very activity responsible for his rapid ascent to prominence in the Senate, his work in leading the special committee, was what gave pause to millions of black voters. Far from being an abstruse issue of interest only to political pundits, the Truman committee's decision to ignore racial discrimination in the military and defense industry became a prominent national news item once Truman was his party's vice presidential nominee. "The big hurdle facing Democrats, however," wrote the *Baltimore Afro-American*'s Washington correspondent, "is the failure of the Truman committee, which has been investigating the national defense program for three years, to inquire into discrimination against colored people in the armed service and war industries."[11] The article was published beneath the headline "GOP to Use Truman's Nomination as Weapon."[12]

Republicans indeed highlighted the committee's silence on racial matters. Senator Truman would vote for an antilynching bill doomed to fail, they argued, but he would not use his committee to help African Americans in uniform or in the civilian defense industry. This reticence was particularly loathsome, Republican spokesmen contended, because African American leaders had directly asked Truman to investigate whether the military's policy of segregation had a deleterious effect on its mission readiness.

Political though these attacks might have been, they were based on facts Truman was unable to dispute. "While the Truman Committee investigated war contracts," charged Perry W. Howard, the chairman of Mississippi's Republican Party, "it completely ignored discrimination against colored people in the armed forces, in the vocational training program and in industries having national defense contracts." Truman's decision to decline requests made by distinguished African Americans such as the noted intellectual and activist Dr. Rayford W. Logan, according to Republican spokesmen, directly affected the plight of African Americans in uniform. "If [the Truman committee] had made a forthright inquiry into these matters when petitioned to do so, certainly some of the bars against colored men's serving in various branches of the armed forces would have been dropped sooner and colored men would have been better trained to serve their country in this war."[13] Chairman Howard concluded, "I can find nothing in the entire record of Senator Truman in the nine years he has served in the Senate which would commend him to colored voters."[14]

As always, Truman campaigned with boundless energy. He met with African American reporters on numerous occasions, telling a gaggle in Detroit, "I feel that the improved conditions of Negroes are going to improve even more as we swing into the peacetime era." He sought to shift the focus from his special committee's inaction on race discrimination to Roosevelt's record after twelve years in office. "Negroes have never had a better friend in the White House and I know that they are going to continue him there."[15]

Rumors abounded about whether the Missouri senator personally held racist views. His low regard for African Americans was so ingrained in his thinking that it invaded his most casual descriptions. In a letter to his daughter, Margaret, telling of a dinner at the White House, he described the wait staff as "an army of coons" who were "evidently the top of the black social set in Washington."[16] In another letter lamenting how messy his desk was, he wrote: "Just killed a cockroach. He walked right out on the armrest . . . as impudently as a sassy nigger."[17]

Word that he bragged about being the "son of an unreconstructed rebel mother" endeared him to many Southern whites but served only to reinforce black voters' apprehensions. With the election just a few weeks away, Truman was accused of being a member of the Ku Klux Klan. The NAACP sent him a telegram asking if the charges were true and asking about his claims of belonging to an "unreconstructed rebel" family.

In his reply telegram, Truman flatly denied being a Klan member or sympathizer and claimed that the widely circulated quote regarding his mother was inaccurate. He asked to be judged not just by his own words but by his "lifelong public record." His words struck an exasperated tone as he sought to convince black voters to assess his career as a senator beyond his chairing the Truman committee.

> You can turn to the Congressional Record and see exactly how I voted and what I supported. You will find that I have fought for fair treatment of every minority, every labor group, every interest that has been underprivileged. Especially I believe that on issues affecting fair treatment of Negroes, there is no legislation that has not had my support.
>
> I supported [the Fair Employment Practices Committee], I voted for cloture on the anti-lynching bill. I voted for . . . every bill to give a fair deal to minorities racial and economic, on all subjects, whether economic or political. I cannot control the opinions

of other people as to whether they think my voting record favors
states' rights or national rights or should be given some other theo-
retical classification. All I ask is that I be judged by my record.[18]

A few weeks later, Franklin Roosevelt and Harry Truman defeated
Republican challengers Thomas Dewey and John Bricker, 432 electoral
college votes to 99. They captured 53 percent of the popular vote with
25.6 million ballots cast in their favor. African American voters strongly
supported the Democratic ticket. They now closely watched the new
vice president. The editorial board of the *Atlanta Daily World* accurately
assessed the mood when it wrote: "Now that Negroes have ignored the
charged bandied about the country against him and supported the Roosevelt ticket, Mr. Truman has his finest opportunity to demonstrate to
them, as did Justice Hugo Black, that he stands four square for equality
and justice for all."[19]

PRESIDENT FRANKLIN ROOSEVELT'S HEALTH had been deteriorat-
ing steadily since his summit with British prime minister Winston
Churchill and Soviet premier Joseph Stalin near the end of 1943. Among
other ailments, he suffered from dangerously high blood pressure, heart
disease, and left ventricular cardiac failure. His sinuses pained him.
Having been infected with polio, the president could not stand or walk
without metal leg braces. He moved more easily in a wheelchair, in
which, except for two known exceptions, he never was photographed.
His breath grew short at the slightest exertion. Gaunt and weakened,
President Roosevelt did not appear healthy, but, with a press corps that
agreed not to discuss his ailments or photographically document his inability to stand or walk, he won reelection in November 1944. Most
Americans had no idea he was so physically incapacitated.

When he addressed Congress on March 1, 1945, the president did so
while seated behind a desk. It was the only time he publicly acknowledged the metal braces gripping his legs. "I hope that you will pardon
me for this unusual posture of sitting down during the presentation of
what I want to say," Roosevelt began, "but I know that you will realize
that it makes it a lot easier for me not to have to carry about ten pounds

of steel around on the bottom of my legs; and also because of the fact that I have just completed a fourteen-thousand-mile trip."[20]

By the end of the month he had returned to the "Little White House" on his property in Warm Springs, Georgia. On April 12 he was in good spirits and enjoying the sunlight through the windows of his living room when he suddenly leaned forward in his wheelchair. His hands fumbled about as if seeking something.

"Have you dropped your cigarette?" a companion asked.

"I have a terrific pain in the back of my head." He grimaced as his head rolled from side to side. The president was suffering a cerebral hemorrhage.[21]

At 5:48 p.m. the White House announced that the president had died. Hours later newspapers reported that Chief Justice Harlan F. Stone had administered the presidential oath of office to former vice president Harry S. Truman. Franklin Roosevelt's funeral would take place at 4:00 p.m. in the East Room of the Executive Mansion and his body would be interred in Hyde Park, New York. His body would not lie in state.

The first official statement from the Truman administration was a vow to win the world war: White House press secretary Jonathan Daniels declared, "The world may be sure that we will prosecute the war on both fronts, East and West, with all the vigor we possess to a successful conclusion."[22] A writer for the *New York Times* wrote of the four-term president, in a front-page article, that no president in American history had died "in circumstances so triumphant and yet so grave."[23]

Harry Truman became president of the United States on Thursday, April 12, 1945, at 7:09 p.m. Sworn in by Chief Justice Stone a little more than two hours after Franklin Roosevelt died in Warm Springs, Georgia, Truman had been vice president for just eighty-two days.[24] He had met with Roosevelt only twice during that time. Serving as vice president had come naturally to Truman, who relished the fact that, as presiding officer of the United States Senate, he could retain his old office. He was enjoying his new position. The prospect that he might one day become president, which caused him considerable anxiety on the campaign trail, had all but vanished from his daily consideration.[25] As

Washington Post columnist Drew Pearson remarked two days after Roosevelt's death, "Harry Truman will be known as the man who didn't want to be President."[26] Truman himself privately told a supporter, "If there ever was a man who was forced to be President, I'm that man."[27]

Upon returning to his apartment on Connecticut Avenue that night after being sworn in, the new president was understandably in a bit of a daze. "I was very much shocked," he wrote in his diary. "I am not easily shocked but was certainly shocked when I was told of the President's death and the weight of the Government had fallen on my shoulders." Roosevelt had been an extraordinary president, "a man whom they all practically worshipped. I was worried about the reaction of the Armed Forces." There were countless issues suddenly weighing on his mind, so many that President Truman, eating turkey in the apartment he and his family soon would vacate, decided to wrestle with them tomorrow. He "went to bed, went to sleep, and did not worry any more."[28]

THAT AN ORDINARY, plebeian man was now president of the United States was almost as shocking to most Americans as news of Roosevelt's death at age sixty-three. Unlike the Harvard-educated patrician elected to the presidency four times, Harry Truman had never attended college and was far from wealthy. The *Atlanta Daily World* celebrated Roosevelt's ability to appeal to the common man, calling him "the People's President," but could not resist marveling at the fact that "Harry S. Truman, former senator, Missouri county judge and one-time Kansas City haberdasher, by Mr. Roosevelt's death, moves up to the highest office in the land."[29]

White Southerners were satisfied with Truman's becoming president. The coup they had orchestrated at the Democratic convention was complete. South Carolina's Democratic senator Burnet Maybank told a supporter, "Everything's going to be all right—the new President knows how to handle the niggers." The speaker of the Mississippi House of Representatives wrote, "I am glad I was given the opportunity to play a small part in the events which contributed to his elevation to the presidency."[30] Segregationist congressman John Rankin serenely told reporters, "Everyone who knows President Truman as I do knows the nation is in safe hands."[31] The managing editor of the *Kansas City Star* reminded readers, "The country thinks of Truman as a Kansas Cityian. He isn't. He's a rural Jackson County-ite—down where they really fought the Civil War . . . In the Senate Truman's closest friendships were with the Old South."[32]

African Americans greeted the new president with what can best be described as optimistic trepidation. As a senator, Truman had proven to be relatively liberal on civil rights issues, but his reelection to the Senate had depended on support from Missouri's sizable population of black voters. Now that he was president, African Americans such as Chicago physician Julian Lewis could only "sincerely hope that [Roosevelt's] successor, Harry Truman, will conduct the office of the President with equal vigor and consideration for oppressed peoples."[33] The Harlem political columnist Carolyn Dixon advised her readers, "Remember this prediction: President Truman is going to surprise the world with respect to his views on the so-called Negro question, some of his ideas will sound more radical than FDR's and HST will not seek the nomination in '48. He's a 1-term man."[34] Dixon presciently predicted that President Truman would work to secure civil rights for all Americans even as other observers more closely affiliated with official Washington viewed the new president with silent skepticism. Judge William Hastie, when asked by a reporter, refused to comment on Harry S. Truman's becoming president.[35]

President Truman himself knew that African Americans perhaps loved Franklin Roosevelt more uniformly than any other group. Roosevelt consistently refused to risk his governing Democratic coalition by challenging the segregationist demands of his party's Southern contingent, but the late president, with his New Deal programs, had done more to improve the lives of average black Americans than any chief executive since Abraham Lincoln. The day after Roosevelt's death, Truman marveled at how the "old and young were crying in the streets." Particularly, he was struck by the sight of an "old Negro woman sitting down on curb with apron up [and] was crying like she had lost her son."[36]

Everyone agreed, however, that the most important issue facing the new president was winning World War II. A few hours before Truman was sworn in as president, senior military officers had informed him and several senators during a briefing that victory was at hand in the war against Germany.[37] Roosevelt, despite possessing the most intimate knowledge of his own failing health, had done little to prepare Truman for the presidency. Truman had no foreign policy experience. Roosevelt had not kept him informed of the most basic negotiations or developments in America's relationship with its allies Great Britain and the Soviet Union, nor of the massive effort under way to develop an atomic bomb. "I knew the President had a great many meetings with Churchill and Stalin," Truman recalled. "I was not familiar with any of these things."[38] The new president was undeniably ill-equipped for the international issues he suddenly faced. The *Washington Post* plainly stated in an editorial, "It is needless to say that President Truman comes into this gigantic assignment under a handicap . . . We should be less than candid at this grave moment . . . if we did not recognize the great disparity between Mr. Truman's experience and the responsibilities that have been thrust upon him."[39]

PRESIDENT TRUMAN ADDRESSED a joint session of Congress on Monday, April 16, or, as he put it, "I went to the Congress with a message."[40] For fifteen minutes the new president told the packed chamber and millions listening on the radio that there would be no change in the United States' war policy. He spoke as he did when campaigning: fervently, in a staccato chop of words that rose in tone as he reached the ends of key sentences. "So much blood has already been shed for the ideals which we cherish and for which Franklin D. Roosevelt lived and died," he pronounced, "that we dare not permit even a momentary pause in the hard fight for victory." The reporter Bernard John Poll wrote that the president was "speaking with all the emotion at his command" when he declared, "Both Germany and Japan can be certain—beyond any shadow of doubt—America will continue the fight for freedom until no vestige of resistance remains."[41] Lest there be any mistake, Truman avowed that America's goal had not changed: "Our demand has been, and it *remains*—Unconditional Surrender!"[42]

V-Day Deferred

At nine in the morning on May 8, 1945, President Truman addressed the nation from the Radio Room in the White House. "This is a solemn but glorious hour," he declared. "I only wish that Franklin D. Roosevelt had lived to witness this day. General Eisenhower informs me that the forces of Germany have surrendered to the United Nations."[1]

War had raged in Europe for more than half a decade and much of the continent lay in ruins. Unlike his revered predecessor and nearly every other president in history, Harry Truman had fought in an army combat unit. As he spoke, the president did not know exactly how many American soldiers, young men as he had been, would be buried where they fought. He exhorted the millions of Americans listening to their radios to "repay the debt we owe to our God, to our dead and to our children . . ."

He then reminded them, "We must work to finish the war. Our victory is but half-won. The West is free, but the East is still in bondage to the treacherous tyranny of the Japanese."[2] It was winning this war in the Pacific to which the president, the nation, and its military now turned their full concentration.

The weaker the Japanese military became, the bloodier and deadlier the battle was for America's soldiers, sailors, and marines. This paradox sobered administration officials and military leaders, all of whom realized that an invasion of the island nation, even if successful, would result in an extraordinary number of American casualties. Truman believed that invading Japan would cost the lives of 250,000 American servicemen. It was a dreadful proposition. "We had only too abundant evidence in those days," recalled one military intelligence officer, "that surrender was excluded from the Japanese ethos."[3]

Although he had ordered one million American troops to be prepared to invade Japan, President Truman did not intend to order an invasion. By the end of July, he had resolved to use what he called "the most terrible bomb in the history of the world. It may be the fire destruction prophesied in the Euphrates Valley Era, after Noah and his fabulous Ark." After billions of dollars and years of research, American scientists in New Mexico had successfully tested an atomic bomb. "This weapon," Truman wrote in his diary on July 25, "is to be used against Japan between now and August 10th. I have told the Sec. of War, Mr. Stimson, to use it so that military objectives and soldiers and sailors are the target and not women and children." The president expressly forbid dropping "this terrible bomb" on Kyoto or Tokyo, "even if the Japs are savages, ruthless, merciless and fanatic."[4]

The first atomic bomb exploded over Hiroshima on August 6. When Japan did not immediately surrender, the American military, without receiving an express order to do so from the president, exploded a second atomic bomb over the city of Nagasaki. Tens of thousands of civilians died in each blast. Truman ordered that no more atomic bombs be deployed except on a direct order from him.

On Tuesday, August 14, five days after the atomic bomb devastated Nagasaki, Japan surrendered. At 7:00 P.M. Eastern War Time, President Truman addressed reporters at the White House. Referring to the message the government had received from Emperor Hirohito, Truman said, "I deem this reply a full acceptance of the Potsdam Declaration which specifies the unconditional surrender of Japan." Army general Douglas MacArthur would receive the official surrender.[5]

More than ten thousand people, many of them servicemen and -women in their uniforms, gathered in Lafayette Square across the street from the White House. Young soldiers and sailors climbed atop stalled cars on Pennsylvania Avenue to cheer for victory and for their president. Black and white revelers celebrated together in the middle of segregated Washington.[6] "We want Truman! We want Truman!" they shouted. The president, resting in the residence with Mrs. Truman, obliged them by stepping onto the porch and addressing them through a microphone. "This is a great day, the day we've been waiting for. This is the day for free governments in the world. This is the day that fascism and police government ceases in the world." The thousands gathered roared their approval; President Truman later said he was "deeply moved by the excitement."[7]

U Street was Main Street for black Washingtonians, a vibrant corridor akin to Harlem's 125th Street. Shortly after President Truman's seven o'clock announcement, the movie theaters, jazz clubs, and restaurants lining U Street emptied. Residents and revelers poured onto the four-lane boulevard until cars, like those on Pennsylvania Avenue three miles to the south, could no longer move. For seven blocks between Seventh and Fourteenth Streets, U Street, as one reporter described it, "was one tremendous explosion." Servicemen in uniform received kisses from women left and right. The only businesses into which celebrators were flowing in and not out were bars, which struggled to keep pace with the stream of patrons waving money. One newspaper reported that U Street's saloons "were literally spilling with persons falling in to drink a cocktail or two to victory."[8] Although America's official V-J Day celebration would not take place until September, the nation rejoiced that cool summer night.

THERE WERE, ON V-J DAY, 695,264 African Americans serving in the United States Army. Most of them had been transferred to the Pacific theater. Had President Truman decided differently, these men would have invaded Japan and many of them would have been killed.[9] Instead, they were returning home.

To War Department officials' surprise, a large number of African American soldiers soon would decide to remain in the army. Two primary factors contributed to the high retention rate of black soldiers. First, for all its entrenched discriminatory practices, the army was, by American standards in 1945, a progressive employer. It placed African Americans in leadership positions and professed to promote them according to performance and ability. The army's African American noncommissioned officers were invaluable assets and its commissioned officers were commanding troops. Compared with private employers and even other government agencies, the army provided qualified African Americans with a decent opportunity for a rewarding job.

The second reason for the surprising retention rate was that employment prospects for African Americans declined swiftly after V-J Day. With the war over and the defense industry contracting, there were far fewer private sector jobs to be had. Boeing Aircraft was laying off 21,000 workers at the same time Ford was letting go of 50,000 employees. Senior military officials canceled $15 billion worth of defense contracts in less than one month.[10] Many employers refused to hire African Americans for most of the few jobs that remained. Businesses listed job vacancy notices for "White Only" or "White Gentile Only" applicants. Sears Roebuck agreed to hire 250 workers through the Veterans Administration but would accept only white veterans.[11]

Just one week after V-J Day, the NAACP reported that black Americans had been laid off by the thousands across the country. Lines of the newly unemployed stretched for blocks outside relief offices in Detroit. The director of the Fair Employment Practices Commission's New York regional office concluded that, during the months after V-J Day, black workers were laid off at twice the rate of white workers. At twenty-five major New York plants, nearly half of all black empoyees were laid off, while 21 percent of white workers lost their jobs.[12] In such a bleak job market, army leaders realized that black soldiers were here to stay.

Robert Patterson, the new secretary of war, was a former president of the *Harvard Law Review*, a decorated army officer in World War I, and a federal appellate judge. He believed that the army had to understand and accept the black soldier's future role. Secretary Patterson appointed three general officers to a committee charged with investigating the effects of the army's current racial policies and, importantly, recommending a new policy. The panel became known as the Gillem board, named for its chairman, Lieutenant General Alvan C. Gillem, Jr.

The Gillem board held its first meeting on October 1, 1945. Over the next six weeks, Lieutenant General Gillem, a Tennesseean, Major General Lewis Pick from Virginia, and Brigadier General Winslow Morse from Michigan pored through thousands of documents, interviewed witnesses, and debated proposals in the most thorough examination ever of the army's racial policy.[13] They worked very quickly, questioning more than sixty witnesses in six weeks.

In March 1946, the Gillem report, titled "Utilization of Negro Manpower in the Postwar Army Policy," was made public. The board stated that black Americans had a constitutional right to fight in the army and that the army bore an obligation to use each soldier as effectively as possible.[14] It declared that its "Ultimate Objective" was that "manpower . . . be utilized, in the event of another major war, in the Army without regard to antecedents or race."[15] This declaration was significant because the army at last stated as its goal the elimination of racial lines and boundaries. Unfortunately, the Gillem report offered no plan to reach its Ultimate Objective. Instead, it recommended that segregation be maintained, with the exception of proposing that small black units be placed into larger white divisions.

Specifically, the report recommended that the army maintain segregated educational, recreational, and dining facilities, that it not station black units in American towns where they would be unwelcome, and that it limit black enlistment to 10 percent of the army personnel. The report appeared to recognize that segregation in the army would and should eventually end, but, as editors of the *Chicago Defender* wrote, the entire report presented no "signs that the War Department is ending or will end racial segregation in the armed forces."[16] Roy Wilkins agreed, declaring, "The basic policy is still Jim Crow . . . Throughout the report the reference repeatedly to 'Negro units' shows that the board members never got out of the thought pattern of segregation."[17]

After two world wars and years of consistent protest, African Americans were surprised by the army's obtuse intransigence. The *Crisis* remarked that the Gillem report's " 'new' policy sounds like the same old stuff."[18] Editors of the *Pittsburgh Courier* concluded that "the Army command had undergone no real change of heart."[19] The Negro War Veterans of Alabama called the report "a gratuitous insult to the democratic aspirations of freedom that characterize the thinking and acting of the Negro people of America."[20]

The Gillem report did nothing to change the lives or status of most black soldiers. If anything, the document solidified segregation in the army. The secretary and undersecretary of war and the army chief of staff, General Eisenhower, spent more time reviewing the Gillem report than the board's members spent drafting it. Eisenhower refused to comment directly on the board's conclusions other than to pass it to Secretary Patterson with the tepid recommendation that the army accept the report "subject to such adjustment as experience shows is necessary."[21]

Although the status quo was inherently incompatible with the Gillem report's stated "Ultimate Objective," the report made clear that the status quo was largely acceptable. Commanders on the ground ignored the report's meager recommendations. A comprehensive army study on implementation of the Gillem board's proposals concluded that there was "no consistent enthusiasm for, and very often active opposition to, any positive measures for implementing the policies of the Gillem Board."[22]

IN THE MONTHS AFTER V-J Day, as it continued to integrate, the navy confirmed its position as the most progressive military branch. Secretary James Forrestal was committed to integrating the service. In August 1945, America's 165,000 black sailors accounted for 5.5 percent of the navy's manpower. Sixty-four African Americans, fifty-eight men and six women, served as commissioned officers.[23] The overwhelming majority of black sailors served in the Steward's Branch, but the 7,130 sailors in the regular service worked and lived with white sailors in submarines, on planes, and throughout the fleet.

The marine corps, under its Division of Plans and Policies director, Brigadier General Gerald C. Thomas, developed a postwar policy independent of Secretary Forrestal's integration objective. The marine corps's postwar plan of segregation was essentially the same as its wartime plan of segregation, except that, after the war, it was able to limit the number of black marines to 2,264. Believing that military integration policies were devised to "appease the Negro press and other 'interested' agencies," the marine corps's senior officers planned to solve what they called "the Negro question" by all but excluding Negroes from the corps.[24]

The navy's personnel needs decreased precipitously in the postwar years and Forrestal's efforts to integrate the service met the practical reality that the navy was becoming much smaller very quickly. Senior officials planned to reduce the wartime force of 3.4 million sailors to less than half a million. At regular attrition rates, the only black sailors soon would be, once again, those serving in the Steward's Branch. Forrestal implemented aggressive efforts to recruit more African Americans into the regular service. Even as the navy was downsizing, in just one year it tripled the number of black sailors in the regular service to 20,610.[25] The chair of the Bureau of Naval Personnel, Vice Admiral Louis E. Denfeld, told reporters, "I believe we will use Negroes more extensively as their training and experience would indicate. As they get to be chief petty officers, we will use them to the fullest extent of their capabilities." Denfeld confirmed that navy recruits would be accepted without regard to race.[26]

In February 1947, navy leaders issued a clearly worded directive: "Effective immediately, all restrictions governing the types of assignments for which Negro naval personnel are eligible are hereby lifted. In the utilization of housing, messing, and other facilities, no special or unusual provisions will be made for the accommodation of Negroes."[27] The order left no room for convenient misinterpretation by commanders opposed to the navy's progressive racial policies.

The Steward's Branch remained the primary source of the navy's image problem, and this greatly bothered Forrestal. The branch was open to all races, but there were no white stewards. (There were approximately 3,500 Filipino and Guamanian messmen.) The very existence of a nearly all-black Steward's Branch was sufficient evidence for many African Americans to conclude that, for all its rhetoric, the navy had not changed. As the army wrestled with political and morale fallout from the Gillem report, the Department of the Navy's problem was attracting black recruits, even as the only service in which they would be assigned according to their desires and capabilities.

The Noah's Ark Committee

America's fighting in World War II contributed to the desegregation of the armed forces in large part because of the dramatic changes that took place in black civilian life during the war. During World War I, African Americans had famously "closed ranks" with their countrymen. They had placed on hold their agitation against government-sanctioned inequality. During World War II, conversely, African Americans' struggle for equality at home actually became more intense.

During the war years, black Americans fought on several fronts. The NAACP's legal campaign against segregation, led by Charles Hamilton Houston and Thurgood Marshall, was winning cases with astonishing consistency. The two tireless attorneys traveled across the country speaking to crowds, investigating complaints of racial abuse, and educating black Americans about the legal battles under way. African Americans of all classes felt energized by Houston's and Marshall's historic judicial victories. As far back as 1936, when Houston and Marshall won their first desegregation case, which resulted in the integration of the University of Maryland law school, African Americans were so euphoric that Houston penned an article in the *Crisis* advising them, "Don't shout too soon." African Americans believed that their military service and sacrifice in World War II, combined with advocacy and protest on the homefront, would earn them their full rights as American citizens.

Like their civilian friends and family members back home, soldiers in the war viewed their battles against a white supremacist enemy abroad as related in some unspoken but logical way with the struggle against white supremacy in America. A navy steward first class from Baltimore named Willie W. Booth, Jr., explained to a reporter aboard the USS *Missouri*, "All of us, of course, are hoping that our service to country will be rewarded by better chances to live in our various communities as first class citizens . . . A chance to work where we show ability for the job, to continue our education in schools of choice, to have a vote in whatever community to which we return, [that] is what we've fought for and will continue to fight for when we go back home."[1] Booth and tens of thousands of soldiers and sailors like him believed that their service abroad was a vital contribution to black Americans' widening struggle for equality.

Indeed the struggle did widen during the war years. No longer was NAACP membership largely confined to middle- and upper-class African Americans and white progressives. In 1940 there were 50,556 NAACP members; in 1946 there were nearly 450,000 members in 1,073 branches across the country.[2] Working-class and outright poor black people came to view the struggle for equality as their own during World War II. Millions of them had migrated to Northern cities to take advantage of the expanding wartime defense industry.

After the war they found themselves laid off from those defense contractor jobs at a rate twice as high as white workers. The scant new job postings made clear that those jobs were for WHITES ONLY. It appeared as if their wartime struggles had been for naught. One commenter wrote that the NAACP's landmark Supreme Court victory *Smith v. Allwright*, which held that whites-only primaries violated the Constitution, was the only national "concrete gain" blacks achieved "during the almost four years of sacrifice, blood, sweat and tears both on the actual battlefield and on the home front."[3]

THE NATIONAL SECURITY ACT OF 1947 completely reorganized the armed forces and security apparatus of the United States. It established a separate Department of the Air Force and created the Central Intelligence

Agency and the National Security Council. The act reconstituted the Department of War as the Department of the Army and created the office of the secretary of defense.

President Truman selected James Forrestal to be the first secretary of defense. African American leaders lauded the promotion of the man who had proven to be an ally in his role as secretary of the navy. Each service branch had by now developed its own way of addressing African Americans' equality concerns. Leaders such as Walter White and A. Philip Randolph believed that the new secretary of defense, possessing authority over all the branches, would bring about uniformity and greater equality for African Americans in the military. Forrestal sought to quell their expectations, telling White in a letter, "The job of Secretary of Defense is one which will have to develop in an evolutionary rather than revolutionary manner."[4]

As concerned as Forrestal was about eliminating racist policies in the armed forces, the National Security Act of 1947 endowed the secretary of defense with limited authority over the military branches. Each branch's military and civilian leaders maintained control of their service branches. Future congressional legislation would empower the secretary of defense with greater authority over the military, but for now, any change in the policies of the army, navy or air force would have to come from the leaders of those individual service organizations.

ON CIVIL RIGHTS MATTERS Harry Truman had surprised nearly everyone since becoming president. He mortified progressives by appointing South Carolina's former senator James F. Byrnes as secretary of state, thereby placing a staunch segregationist in the line of succession for the presidency. African American leaders and reporters expressed their dismay in tones of resignation. They feared what the new Southern president might do next.

What Truman did next shook the Democratic Party. First, he asked House Rules Committee chairman Adolph J. Sabath to restore funding to the Fair Employment Practices Committee, telling the Illinois congressman, "To abandon at this time the fundamental principle upon which the Fair Employment Practices Committee was established is unthinkable."[5] Second, and more significant, Truman sent to Congress on September 6, 1945, a 16,000-word missive setting forth his twenty-one-point program for guiding the nation forward. The president called for tax reform, increased unemployment benefits, a permanent FEPC, and numerous other mandates for the common good as he saw it. If enacted in its entirety, Truman's plan would amount to an expansion of Roosevelt's New Deal. Southern senators successfully filibustered a bill to make the FEPC permanent. It appeared as if the man they had helped make president had turned on them.

Southern Democrats revolted against this apparent betrayal. As the 1946 elections approached they railed against Truman in public and in private. The president was quite irritated by their outrage. He presciently told an aide he wished "Southern Democrats could go where they belonged, into the conservative Republican Party."[6] Democrats lost many congressional seats in the 1946 election, and Truman's power to push legislation was drastically diminished.

Yet just one month after this disastrous midterm election, President Truman issued Executive Order 9808, establishing the President's Committee on Civil Rights. He tasked the committee with making "a very broad inquiry" in order to answer the question, "how can State, Federal and local governments implement the guarantees of personal freedoms embodied in the Constitution?"[7] In the wake of World War II, America was still very much a nation divided along the Mason-Dixon line. Twenty states mandated segregation in all public accommodations, while just eighteen states, nearly all of them in the North, prohibited racial discrimination in public facilities.[8] "I created this Committee with a feeling of urgency," Truman recounted. "No sooner were we finished with the war than racial and religious intolerance began to appear and threaten the very things we had just fought for."[9]

It seemed to Southern Democrats that their party's leader was not just a traitor to those who had worked to get him on the 1944 presidential ticket, but was politically suicidal—and intent on bringing the party down with him. Roosevelt had understood that, in order to maintain his New Deal coalition, he needed to keep white Southern voters in the Democratic fold by mostly ignoring state-sanctioned racism. Walter

White recalled how President Roosevelt "repeatedly told me that the time was not yet ripe for a head-on collision with the Southern Senators and Congressmen who, under the seniority rule . . . chaired important Senate and House Committees."[10] Truman would not even have become president of the United States without the efforts of the Southern politicians whose entreaties he now all but ignored.

Harry Truman had established himself in Washington by working on the Senate Special Committee to Investigate the National Defense Program before and during the war years. Just as his committee had uncovered facts, established a record, and produced results on which lawmakers and the president could act, he expected the President's Committee on Civil Rights to set forth concrete proposals to improve and protect the lives and property of America's historically vulnerable citizens. As stated in Executive Order 9808, the president expected to receive from the committee "recommendations with respect to the adoption or establishment by legislation or otherwise of more adequate and effective means and procedures for the protection of the civil rights of the people of the United States."[11]

The multiracial committee consisted of influential leaders in business, law, labor, education, and religion. Charles E. Wilson, the president of the General Electric Corporation, served as chairman. "We were so meticulous to get balance," one White House aide recounted, "that we wound up with two of everything: two women, two southerners, two business [leaders], two labor [leaders] . . ." Not for nothing did White House staffers dub the body the "Noah's Ark Committee."[12] Despite its geographic, racial, and gender inclusiveness, the committee was not at all ideologically diverse. Its members were progressives and moderates by design: The White House did not want to receive a civilian version of the army's Gillem report.★

Whatever Southern sympathies he held, Truman believed in the supremacy of the federal Constitution. As he explained to the committee's fifteen members, "I am a believer in the sovereignty of the individual

---

★The president appointed Sadie T. Alexander, James B. Carey, John S. Dickey, Morris L. Ernst, Roland B. Gittelsohn, Frank P. Graham, Francis J. Haas, Charles Luckman, Francis P. Matthews, Franklin D. Roosevelt, Jr., Henry Knox Sherrill, Boris Shishkin, Dorothy Tilly, Channing Tobias, and Chairman Charles E. Wilson.

and of the local governments. I don't think the Federal Government ought to be in a position to exercise dictatorial powers locally; but there are certain rights under the Constitution of the United States which I think the Federal Government has a right to protect."[13]

Truman insisted that the committee's fifteen members be given the resources and latitude they needed to provide him with a thoroughly substantive report. Twelve full-time staff members were assigned to the committee. Under Executive Order 9808, federal agencies were "authorized and directed to cooperate with the Committee in its work, and to furnish the Committee such information or the services of such persons as the Committee may require in the performance of its duties." Employees of federal agencies called to testify before the committee were required to do so.[14] The president basically granted the Committee on Civil Rights carte blanche to conduct its investigation. From December 1946 through October 1947, the committee met ten times as a group and more frequently in subcommittee hearings and meetings.

The whole affair made no sense to most Southern whites. Ernie Roberts, an old friend of Truman's from Kansas City, advised him in a letter, "Harry, let us the South take care of the Niggers . . . and if the Niggers do not like the Southern treatment, then let them come to Mrs. Roosevelt." The president wrote back to Roberts, chastising his "antebellum proslavery outlook." He took the time to elucidate:

The main difficulty with the South is that they are living eighty years behind the times and the sooner they come out of it the better it will be for the country and themselves. I am not asking for social equality, because no such thing exists, but I am asking for equality of opportunity for all human beings and, as long as I stay here, I am going to continue that fight . . .

When a Mayor and a City Marshal can take a negro Sergeant off a bus in South Carolina, beat him up and put out one of his eyes, and nothing is done about it by the State Authorities, something is radically wrong with the system . . . I can't approve of such goings on and I shall never approve it, as long as I am here, as I told you before. I am going to try to remedy it and if that ends up in my failure to be reelected, that failure will be in a good cause.[15]

This letter to an old friend, held in private until after Truman's death in 1972, revealed much about the president's thinking. The years following Truman's return home from World War I were the most uncertain years of his life. A new husband living with his in-laws, he struggled in business and often worried about money. He watched his war buddies who had fought in gruesome battles for their country strain to earn a living. His business partner filed for bankruptcy and Truman would have had to as well if he had not been saved by the Pendergast political machine.

As president, he hated the fact that once again many American veterans were returning home from a world war to face uncertainty and unemployment. He was horrified to learn that, once again, black veterans in the South were being brutally attacked and even killed, sometimes while still wearing their uniforms. The specter of these attacks and local law enforcement authorities' refusal to address them compelled Truman to act decisively on behalf of African Americans.

The Blinding of Isaac Woodard and the Signing of Executive Order 9981

THE DISCHARGE PROCESS HAD TAKEN longer than he had expected, what with the physical examination, interviews, and all the forms to complete, so army technical sergeant Isaac Woodard, Jr., was relieved to finally take his seat on the Greyhound bus that was boarding passengers at Camp Gordon, Georgia. It was afternoon by now, but even in Georgia on the twelfth day of February the afternoons swiftly passed. Nightfall was not far off. From the looks of it, nearly everyone aboard the coach was as tired as Isaac. The twenty-seven-year-old folded his tall, thin frame into a seat amid a group of fellow soldiers. His destination was his birthplace, the town of Winnsboro, South Carolina.

Woodard had lived in Winnsboro before the war. With just five years of formal education, he worked at a local lumberyard and had married his sweetheart in 1942. A few months later he was drafted into the army. Woodard underwent basic training in South Carolina and Georgia before serving in the Pacific theater. Like most African American soldiers, he was not trusted with combat duty. Instead Woodard worked as a military longshoreman. During his fifteen months in theater, Woodard received a meritorious citation for dangerous work in the line of fire on the island of New Guinea. Like the other soldiers on the Greyhound that afternoon, he was very much looking forward to getting home.

Despite having just been discharged at an army camp in the South, black and white soldiers sat together talking and laughing. Several white civilian passengers were noticeably offended by the integrated group even before a bottle of whiskey was revealed and passed around. Woodard, a known teetotaler, did not imbibe but did enjoy the revelry. Day became dusk. After a while, the coach stopped to exchange passengers in a town. Woodard rose, stretched his long legs, and made his way to the front of the bus. He asked the bus driver, a white man from Columbia, South Carolina, named A. C. Blackwell, if he could run to the men's room during this stop.

"Boy, go on back and sit down and keep quiet and don't be talking out so loud," Blackwell snapped.

"Goddamn it, talk to me like I'm talking to you," Woodard retorted. Three years of army training and service had planted in him a loathing for being called "boy." He told the bus driver, "I'm a man just like you." To the ears of a white South Carolinian like Blackwell, Sergeant Woodard's saying those words alone, could have made it seem as if he was drunk.

Many dark miles up the road, Blackwell stopped the Greyhound in a small South Carolina town called Batesburg. Still peeved over the black soldier's impudent manner of speaking to a white man, he asked Woodard to step off the coach for a moment to speak to two local police officers.

Woodard stepped out of the bus and into the hot night, where he met Chief Linwood Shull and Officer Elliot Long. They asked him what seemed to be causing the trouble aboard this Greyhound coach and began to beat him as soon as he began to answer. Woodard fought back. Chief Shull leveled him with a blackjack and dragged him behind a corner and out of view of the coach's passengers. Officer Long busied himself with questioning a white soldier.

Around the corner, Shull twisted Woodard's arm. Shull asked questions that Woodard answered without calling him "sir," so Shull beat him harder. Woodard gained his feet and tried to seize the blackjack until Officer Long arrived with his gun drawn. Shull then continued to beat Woodard in the face and head. With the short, blunt nightstick he ruptured both of Woodard's eyeballs. Then he arrested him. When he awoke in a jail cell the next morning, Sergeant Isaac Woodard was blind in both eyes.[1]

———————

"MY GOD, I had no idea it was as terrible as that!" President Truman exclaimed when Walter White, visiting the Oval Office with other civil rights leaders, told him of the attack on Isaac Woodard. "We've got to do something."[2] During their meeting, Truman had learned not just of the incident with Sergeant Woodard, but of the numerous black veterans who had been humiliated, beaten, and even murdered by white men since V-J Day. The next day he sent a memo to Attorney General Tom Clark describing the attack on Woodard. After commending Clark's unprecedented investigations of lynchings in Tennessee, Georgia, and Louisiana, Truman wrote, "I think it is going to take something more than the handling of each individual case after it happens—it is going to require the inauguration of some sort of policy to prevent such happenings."[3] It is impossible to discern precisely when President Truman decided to desegregate the armed forces, but it may have been on the morning he learned of the blinding of Isaac Woodard. As he later explained, "I took . . . action because of the repeated anti-minority incidents immediately after the war in which homes were invaded, property was destroyed and a number of innocent lives were taken."[4]

TRUMAN ACCEPTED WALTER WHITE'S INVITATION to address attendees of the thirty-eighth NAACP convention on the steps of the Lincoln Memorial on June 29, 1947. He would be the first president to speak to the organization. The president spoke for just twelve minutes on a stiflingly hot and humid summer Sunday, but his words to an integrated audience of ten thousand in the segregated nation's capital were broadcast live on the four major radio networks. The State Department transmitted the speech by shortwave radio to stations around the world.[5]

Like many presidential speeches in America's history, the significance of Truman's address was inversely proportional to its length. After being introduced by Walter White, the president quickly got to the point:

I should like to talk to you briefly about civil rights and human freedom. It is my deep conviction that we have reached a turning point in our country's efforts to guarantee freedom and equality to all our citizens. Recent events in the United States and abroad have made us realize that it is more important today than ever before to insure that all Americans enjoy these rights.

When I say all Americans, I mean all Americans.[6]

As Truman continued, speaking of "protection of people by the Government," the throngs of listeners gathered around the reflecting pool could scarcely believe their own ears. Never before had a president spoken so plainly about the responsibility of the federal government to protect black Americans just as it protected white Americans. To the crowd's audible approval, Truman declared, "We must make the Federal Government a friendly, vigilant defender of the rights and equalities of all Americans. And again I mean all Americans."[7]

The crowd roared at the end of the speech. Taking his seat, the president leaned over to Walter White and assured him, "I said what I did because I mean every word of it—and I am going to prove that I do mean it."[8]

FOUR MONTHS LATER, on October 29, 1947, the President's Committee on Civil Rights released its 178-page report. Titled *To Secure These Rights*, the paper was both a lamentation on the ways discrimination had harmed the country and a prescriptive policy paper with express recommendations on how to end the racism that it called "a kind of moral dry rot which eats away at the emotional and rational bases of democratic beliefs."[9] The report detailed the violence many black Americans suffered at the hands of white citizens and law enforcement officers. It boldly called for the federal government to implement measures to end segregation. *To Secure These Rights* set forth nearly three dozen proposals, including integrating Washington's school system and securing the right to vote for African Americans in the South. The *Washington Post* called it "social dynamite" and Walter White considered the report "explosive."[10]

When the committee members visited the White House to hand-deliver their report to the president, Truman told them, "I have stolen a march on you. I have already read the report and I want you to know that not only have you done a good job but you have done what I wanted you to." He called their report "an American charter of human freedom in our time," and predicted "that it will take its place among the great papers on Freedom."[11]

ON NOVEMBER 19, 1947, LESS than a month after Truman received the committee's report, he received a private memorandum written by the New Deal lawyer James Rowe and edited by Truman's personal confidant, the Washington, D.C. attorney Clark Clifford. The lengthy document, titled "The Politics of 1948," set forth what Rowe and Clifford called "a course of political conduct for the Administration extending from November, 1947 to November, 1948." The memorandum contrasted white Southerners' unwavering loyalty to the Democratic Party with the black voter's sudden potential "to swing back to his traditional moorings—the Republican Party." Thanks in large part to his "intelligent, educated and sophisticated leaders, the Negro voter has become a cynical, hardboiled trader . . . [who believes] that he can go no further by supporting the present Administration." Conversely, "the South," Rowe and Clifford counseled, "can be considered safely Democratic. And in formulating national policy, it can be safely ignored."[12]

The memorandum tacitly accepted as true black political leaders' loudening complaint about the Truman administration: For all his emboldened rhetoric, President Truman had not taken concrete steps to relieve the legal oppression under which millions of black Americans lived. He appeared beholden to the Southern Democratic congressmen and powerbrokers who secured his place on the national ticket nearly four years before. Rowe and Clifford flatly advised Truman, "Unless there are now real efforts (as distinguished from mere political gestures which are today thoroughly understood and strongly resented by sophisticated Negro leaders), the Negro bloc, which, certainly in Illinois and probably in New York and Ohio, does hold the balance of power, will go Republican."[13]

Truman realized that his reelection possibly hinged on whether he took action to end legalized discrimination in America. White Southerners already were furious about his civil rights rhetoric. If he backed his speeches with concrete action, white Southern Democrats might stage an electoral revolt at the Democratic convention. They would not support the likely Republican nominee, Governor Thomas E. Dewey of New York. A candidate supported exclusively by Southern segregationists would not win the presidency. Whether such a candidate could siphon off enough Democratic votes to affect the election was a presently unanswerable question.

Truman thought carefully about what concrete action he could take to help African Americans. He could not rely on congressional support, particularly in the Senate, where segregationists used the seniority system to stymie antidiscrimination measures. He could only do something only a president could do. Of the major proposals set forth in *To Secure These Rights*, the only one that Truman, as commander in chief of the army and navy, could implement without congressional approval was desegregating the armed forces.

THE AFRICAN AMERICAN ACTIVIST and labor leader A. Philip Randolph led the call for Truman to issue an executive order to end segregation in the armed forces. Randolph embodied more than any other public figure African Americans' fury at having been forced to serve, for two world wars, in a military that brutally discriminated against them. He gave voice to black veterans' bitterness even as he decided that the time for words had passed. Congress was debating yet another draft bill. Randolph determined that this was the season for action. If President Truman would not act, then Randolph would.

In the spring of 1948 Randolph testified before the Senate Armed Services Committee's hearing on the pending draft bill. He was speaking more to the White House than to the recalcitrant committee when he stunned the hearing room by pledging civil disobedience against any new draft law that did not expressly forbid segregation. Randolph vowed "to openly counsel, aid and abet youth, both white and Negro, to quarantine any Jim Crow conscription system . . . I shall call upon all Negro veterans to join this civil disobedience movement and to recruit their younger brothers in an organized refusal to register and be drafted . . ."

When Republican senator Wayne Morse admonished him that his words could amount to treason, Randolph retorted, "We have to face this thing sooner or later and we might just as well face it now."[14] No one in the hearing room had forgotten that, for all of Walter White's discreet influence, it had been Randolph who, by mobilizing many thousands of black Americans in his March on Washington movement, had forced President Roosevelt to issue an executive order banning discrimination in the defense industry. With Grant Reynolds, New York's commissioner of correction and a former army chaplain who was shocked by the racist treatment he had received during World War II, Randolph had recently formed the Committee Against Jim Crow in Military Service and Training. Their new group already enjoyed widespread support from young black Americans both in the workforce and in college. "In light of past official civil rights pronouncements," Randolph and Reynolds declared in a letter to the White House, "it is our belief that the President, as Commander in Chief, is morally obligated to issue an order now."[15]

Randolph and Reynolds's Committee Against Jim Crow in Military Service and Training found support in the report issued by the President's Committee on Civil Rights.

To Secure These Rights expressly called for the "enactment by Congress of legislation, followed by appropriate administrative action, to end immediately all discrimination and segregation based on race, color, creed, or national origin, in the organization and activities of all branches of the Armed Services. The injustice of calling men to fight for freedom while subjecting them to humiliating discrimination within the fighting forces is at once apparent . . ."

The president's committee directly refuted military leaders' most reliable retort, that the military was not a social laboratory: "During the last war we . . . found that the military services can be used to educate citizens on a broad range of social and political problems. The war experience brought to our attention a laboratory in which we may prove that the majority and minorities of our population can train and work and fight side by side in cooperation and harmony."[16]

Privately, President Truman's advisers had joined Randolph's call for an executive order to desegregate the armed forces. In the dawning cold war era, America's segregated military quickly had become a source of international embarassment. The United States was competing with the Soviet Union for allies among developing nations, many of which had majority nonwhite populations. Communist propagandists wrote derisively of an American military that purported to defend freedom while treating 10 percent of its men and women in uniform as second-class citizens. President Truman understood the foreign policy implications at stake. "The top dog in a world which is half colored ought to clean his own home," he quipped.[17]

ON JULY 26, 1948, with no great fanfare, President Harry Truman signed Executive Order 9981, which read in part:

ESTABLISHING THE PRESIDENT'S COMMITTEE ON EQUALITY OF TREATMENT AND OPPORTUNITY IN THE ARMED FORCES

WHEREAS it is essential that there be maintained in the armed services of the United States the highest standards of democracy, with equality of treatment and opportunity for all those who serve in our country's defense:

NOW THEREFORE, by virtue of the authority vested in me as President of the United States, by the Constitution and the statutes of the United States, and as Commander in Chief of the armed services, it is hereby ordered as follows:

1. It is hereby declared to be the policy of the President that there shall be equality of treatment and opportunity for all persons in the armed services without regard to race, color, religion or national origin. This policy shall be put into effect as rapidly as possible, having due regard to the time required to effectuate any necessary changes without impairing efficiency or morale.

2. There shall be created in the National Military Establishment an advisory committee to be known as the President's Committee on Equality of Treatment and Opportunity in the Armed Services, which shall be composed of seven members to be designated by the President.[18]

Public reaction to Executive Order 9981, in both black and white communities, was surprisingly muted. This is because it was not immediately clear what the order directed. A *Washington Post* reporter wrote what everyone who read the order immediately noted: Truman "did not call specifically for an end to segregation among American troops. It clearly authorized the committee to make recommendations for the ending of such segregation."[19] Segregationists in Congress all but ignored the order because, whatever it meant, there was nothing they could do to overturn it, and, more important, Harry Truman likely would not be president after the upcoming election.

No one knew what Truman's order meant. A president known for speaking plainly had issued a vaguely worded document at what appeared to be a moment of great significance. A federal official told the *New York Times* on background that, as he read it, integration was not the order's aim.[20] General Omar Bradley, the army chief of staff, felt comfortable telling reporters without reading the order that "the Army is not out to make any social reforms. The Army will put men of different races in different companies. It will change that policy when the nation as a whole changes it."[21]

African Americans decried Truman's equivocal order. A. Philip Randolph preached to a massive gathering at the Zion Baptist Church in Denver that Executive Order 9981 did not in any way alter the military's policy of separate but equal facilities and units.[22] African American newspapers likewise denounced the order for apparently allowing the military to separate its black and white service members.[23]

The day after Bradley made his statement, for which the general later apologized, Truman told reporters at a press conference that integration of the armed forces *was* the aim of Executive Order 9981. A. Philip Randolph received a personal assurance from Truman's chief spokesman that, as Randolph described it, "segregation as well as other discriminatory practices in the armed services are unequivocally banned under the Executive Order of July 26." He subsequently withdrew his calls for civil disobedience against the pending draft.[24]

On September 18, 1948, President Truman named the seven members of the President's Committee on Equality of Treatment and Opportunity in the Armed Services. They were former solicitor general Paul Fahy, serving as chairman; John Sengstacke, editor of the *Chicago Defender*, a leading African American newspaper; Lester Granger, National Urban

League executive secretary; William Stevenson, the president of Oberlin College; and the businessmen Alphonsus Donahue, Dwight Palmer, and Charles Luckman. The group, which became known as the Fahy committee, would begin its work in January 1949—if Harry Truman remained president, a condition not lost on African American voters. In the meantime, senior army officers maintained in no uncertain terms that, as New York National Guard brigadier general William H. Kelly wrote to Walter White regarding segregation, "the Army has not changed its policy with respect to this matter."[25] President Truman's Executive Order 9981 appeared to have changed nothing.

FREEDOM TO SERVE

PRESIDENT HARRY TRUMAN's 1948 REELECTION has become legendary. The president won a second term against significant political headwinds: He faced a resurgent Republican Party united behind a ticket composed of two popular governors, Thomas Dewey of New York and California's Earl Warren. Truman's own Democratic Party at last had split over civil rights issues, with Southern delegates storming out of the party's 1948 convention in Philadelphia to form the States' Rights Democratic Party, commonly called the Dixiecrats. Democratic liberals, led by the left-leaning former vice president Henry Wallace, also split from the party, forming the Progressive Party. Undaunted by political prospects that even his own administration officials admitted were bleak, Truman traveled 31,000 miles up and down and across the country in a furious campaign. Fuming like a faith-healing preacher, the sixty-four-year-old incumbent seemed never to tire. "Give 'em hell, Harry!" supporters would shout. "Oh, I'm going to give 'em the gun!" Truman yelled back to the crowd's delight. Unlike Dewey, who ran a subdued front-runner's campaign greatly concerned with avoiding controversy, Truman relished campaigning. Raucous crowds of working-class voters energized him. He blasted the Republicans. He lambasted what he called the "do-nothing, good for nothing Congress," and voters loved him for it.

In November, Harry Truman won 303 electoral college votes to

Thomas Dewey's 189 and Dixiecrat Strom Thurmond's 39. Henry Wallace received no electoral college votes. As he had throughout his career, Truman relied on and received solid support from African American voters, who overwhelmingly supported him, in no small part because he had signed Executive Order 9981. They did not think Henry Wallace could win, did not trust Thomas Dewey after his arms-length campaign, and obviously did not closely consider Strom Thurmond for president. African American voters and their allies hoped that Truman's order would fulfill its intended purpose in Truman's term.

WITH PRESIDENT TRUMAN now in office on the strength of his own electoral victory, he returned to work with renewed vigor. Addressing the Fahy committee at its first meeting on January 12, 1949, he stressed that the committee's work "is not a stunt. I want concrete results—that's what I'm after—not publicity on it." They were gathered in the Cabinet Room of the White House, a setting that emphasized the importance that Truman placed on the work of the seven-member committee. The secretaries of the navy, army, and newly independent air force attended this first meeting, and, perhaps for their benefit, Truman added, "I want the job done and I want it done in a way so that everybody will be happy to cooperate to get it done."[1]

The first secretary of the air force, a fellow Missourian named Stuart Symington, said as Truman prepared to leave, "Sir, I just want to report to you that our plan is to completely eliminate segregation in the Air Force."

The secretaries and senior officers of the air force and the navy had decided before the Fahy committee's first meeting that they would implement the full letter and intent of Executive Order 9981. The leaders had come to believe what activists such as Walter White and A. Philip Randolph had been contending for years—that segregation, in the military service at least, was fundamentally incompatible with equality. By the time the president called the committee to the Cabinet Room, black and white sailors and airmen were already training, working, and living together.

During the weeks after this first meeting, the Fahy committee's permanent staff, led by executive director Edwin W. Kenworthy, traveled to military bases and installations to investigate each branch's racial policy while committee members in Washington heard testimony from the branches' civilian and uniformed leaders. Staff members' fact-finding visits buttressed the testimony offered by senior officials. Each branch still had problems—marine corps officers were slow to accept the navy's desegregation directives, and the air force maintained a quota limiting black airmen to 10 percent of most units' manpower—but the army posed especially noteworthy resistance to President Truman's executive order. Committee members decided to address the army's issues in its report separately from the other branches.

The Fahy committee's final report, titled *Freedom to Serve: Equality of Treatment and Opportunity in the Armed Services*, recognized the extent to which the navy and air force had already met the terms and intent of Executive Order 9981. *Freedom to Serve* addressed the policies of the nation's oldest and newest branches together:

CONCLUSIONS

The following conclusions were borne out by the experience of the Navy and Air Force:

1. The range of individual Negro abilities is much wider than the services had assumed prior to the opening of all jobs in the Navy and Air Force.
2. Given sufficiently high enlistment standards, it does not follow that only a "relatively small percentage" of Negroes will be able to meet the competition of whites.
3. The services can not afford to waste these potential Negro skills.
4. There will be wastage and malassignment of manpower under segregation because there is no assurance that individual Negro skills can be, or will be, utilized in racial units.
5. Integration of the two races at work, in school, and in living quarters did not present insurmountable difficulties. As a matter of fact, integration in two of the services had brought a decrease in racial friction.
6. The enlisted men were far more ready for integration than the officers had believed.

7. The attitude of command was a substantial factor in the success of the racial policies of the Air Force and the Navy."[2]

The navy and air force in 1950 were not yet the incredibly diverse institutions they are today, but thanks to President Truman's executive order and the aggressive reforms both branches enacted after World War II, they already were very far from where they had been just ten years earlier.

WITH THE NAVY AND AIR FORCE well on their way to integrating their personnel (albeit with a recalcitrant marine corps), the Fahy committee turned its full attention to the army. Secretary of the Army Kenneth C. Royall testified before the committee on March 28, 1949, and did little more than reiterate the army's decades-old defenses and justifications for segregating its soldiers. The army, he testified, was "not an instrument for social evolution." More to the point, black soldiers had proven ill-suited for combat and were in fact "peculiarly qualified" for manual labor. The army segregated its soldiers according to race for efficiency's sake. "It follows that in the interest of efficient national defense," Royall contended, "certain types of units should be entirely or largely confined to white troops."[3]

General Omar Bradley testified that both efficiency and morale would suffer if the army were to integrate. Maintaining segregated units resulted in a fighting force in which "men have confidence in themselves, confidence in their fellow members of their unit and confidence in their leaders," Bradley told the committee. "If we try to force integration on the Army before the country is ready to accept these customs, we may have difficulty attaining high morale along the lines I have mentioned."[4]

Royall's and Bradley's testimony confirmed two realities: First, the army remained wholly committed to segregation despite President Truman's order. Second, most of the army's leaders and officers were convinced that, contrary to assertions made by the navy's and air force's leaders, segregation contributed to efficiency. Integration, they argued, would impede efficiency. Segregation and equality were entirely compatible in a disciplined fighting force.

Fahy committee staff executive director Edwin Kenworthy believed that segregation was immoral but knew better than to suggest that committee members appeal to army officials' moral sensibility. Kenworthy's tireless review of testimony transcripts and his travel to military bases across the country had led him to conclude that segregation impeded efficiency. On March 10, 1949, he wrote a letter to Chairman Fahy in which he prodded, "I wonder if the one chance of getting something done isn't to meet the military on their own ground—the question of military efficiency. They have defended their Negro manpower policies on the grounds of efficiency. Have they used Negro manpower efficiently? . . . Can it be that the whole policy of segregation, especially in large units like the 92nd and 93rd Division, ADVERSELY AFFECTS MORALE AND EFFICIENCY?"

Charles Fahy was intrigued by Kenworthy's proposition. The committee soon heard testimony from army officials who contradicted Royall's and Bradley's testimony by describing the ways in which segregation hindered military efficiency. Thousands of army positions were left empty because no soldiers had been trained to fill them. All of these positions, spread among 198 specialties, were reserved for white soldiers. Although there were black soldiers whose aptitude scores indicated that they were more than qualified to train for these positions, army regulations prohibited their doing so. Of the 106 army school courses offered to soldiers, only twenty-one were available to black soldiers. Untold scores of African American soldiers were confined to labor and service battalions when they could be serving in specialized, technical capacities. Segregation in the army resulted in vacant positions and wasted manpower—in a word, inefficiency.

Truman's new secretary of defense, a gifted Virginia lawyer named Louis Johnson, had no patience for the army's reluctance to adhere to a presidential executive order. In part because of "the President's direct interest" in the matter, Johnson issued a directive on April 6, 1949, instructing all the services to accept and assign personnel only "on the basis of individual merit and ability" and "without regard to race." Secretary Johnson rejected army officials' contention that efficiency and equality were possible under segregation. His directive was more specific than Truman's executive order. It left no question as to its purpose. Johnson's directive necessitated integration.

Secretary Johnson explained in a letter to Senator Lyndon B. Johnson of Texas that his integration policy had "the support of millions of citizens who feel strongly that segregation in the armed forces is sharply at variance with our democratic principles and ideals and who understand that its practice reduces the efficiency of our military strength." Members of the Fahy committee were surprised by Secretary Johnson's directive, but Kenworthy might as well have spoken for them when he wrote to Fahy, "In my opinion, man-to-man integration has got to come much sooner than I thought a month ago."[5]

On May 22, 1950, the Fahy committee presented its report, *Freedom to Serve*. Its recommendations to the army were concise:

1. Open up all Army jobs to qualified personnel without regard to race or color.
2. Open up all Army schools to qualified personnel without regard to race or color.
3. Rescind the policy restricting Negro assignments to racial units and overhead installations, and assign all Army personnel according to individual ability and Army need.
4. Abolish the racial quota.[6]

The army accepted all four recommendations with the caveat that they would take time to implement. When the Fahy committee adjourned in July 1950, the army had opened only seven more specialties to black soldiers. Senior army officials were determined to move slowly if at all. They believed that junior officers and base commanders would continue to segregate their soldiers even without being required to do so by official army policy. For a few months they were right: Segregation continued in the army as a matter of practice, not policy, until the army's draft and the next war proved the Fahy committee's conclusion that segregation impeded military efficiency.

On June 25, 1950, North Korea's premier Kim Il Sung invaded South Korea. With the Soviet Union refusing to participate, the United Nations Security Council adopted a resolution condemning the invasion. In support of the Security Council's goal of turning back the North

Koreans, President Truman ordered American forces to aid the belea-
guered South Koreans, first with air power and then with ground troops.
Despite the administration's attempt to characterize the intervention as a
"police action," America again was at war.

In just five months, the army doubled in size. By June 1951 there were
1.6 million American soldiers, and approximately 12 percent of them
were African Americans.[7] All-black units in the army swelled to more
than 160 percent of their allotted manpower. Crowding so many soldiers
into all-black units rather than using them to bolster smaller white units
was an example of the inefficiency that Fahy committee members contended was inevitable in a segregated military. Senior army officials remained largely uninterested in implementing the desegregation policy
they had resisted for so long. If the army was going to execute its new
desegregation policy, then local commanders would have to do it.

The army began to desegregate in the unlikeliest of states when local
commanders decided the issue for themselves. The commanding officer
of Fort Jackson, South Carolina, was faced with so many black and white
draftees that he found it "totally impractical to sort them out." So he
decided not to do so. In August 1950, lacking the resources and facilities
to "sort them out," that is, to segregate new inductees, Fort Jackson's
officers trained their men all together. Word rapidly spread among commanding officers nationwide: Fort Jackson in South Carolina had integrated its training units without any violence or trouble whatsoever. The
revolutionary transition had occurred without incident. Soon thereafter
the army integrated all of its basic training.[8]

TWO HUNDRED THIRTY THOUSAND ARMY TROOPS were serving in
Korea in the Eighth Army. Many of the segregated all-black units, replete with lesser-educated soldiers, were performing poorly. More black
soldiers, most from poor backgrounds, were arriving into theater each
week from Japan. What surprised most white commanders was that
many all-white units were performing poorly as well.[9] Soldiers who had
been stationed in Japan for months had gained weight and lost discipline
and morale.

As white combat soldiers began to suffer casualties in Korea, battle
commanders started replacing them with soldiers of both races. The

Korean War veteran and later New York congressman Charles Rangel explained, "They needed warm bodies in large numbers." Official army policy no longer mandated segregation, and commanding officers decided that the realities of combat no longer afforded them the option. The Eighth Army adopted what Rangel called "an unofficial policy of integrating African American troops into previously all-white units . . . Their need for as many replacements as they could get, as soon as they could get them, was suddenly as color blind as it was acute."[10]

Satisfied that the integration experiment was proceeding as well in theater as it had in training, Major General William B. Kean, commander of the Twenty-fifth Division, asked that the all-black units be disbanded. The issue did not lie in the individual soldiers, Kean concluded, but rather in the segregated unit itself. The problem was not that black soldiers could not fight effectively, it was that they could fight more effectively if they were not restricted to all-black units where half the soldiers scored in Classes IV or V of the army's aptitude test. Major General Kean was offering to his commanders the same rationale that had been proffered by civil rights activists since before World War II.[11] For all their blustery opposition to desegregation, army officers quietly commenced the task of desegregating their units.

After President Truman relieved General Douglas MacArthur of command on April 11, 1951, General Matthew B. Ridgway became America's Far East commander. Ridgway differed from his iconic predecessor in many ways, the most pertinent of which was that the Virginia native, born in 1895, believed that segregation in the military was "wholly inefficient, not to say, improper." For the new commanding officer of America's war in Korea, segregation was "both un-American and un-Christian."[12]

On May 14, 1951, General Ridgway formally requested authority to integrate his entire command. Army officials and officers in the Pentagon quickly approved his request. On July 26, 1951, three years to the day after President Truman issued Executive Order 9981, the army announced the integration of the entire Far East Command. Just as they had on training bases in the American South, black and white soldiers in Japan and Korea integrated without incident. Several wounded white soldiers returning from the Korean battlefields told one interviewer,

"Far as I'm concerned, [integration] worked pretty good . . . When it comes to life or death, race does not mean any difference . . . Had a colored platoon leader. They are as good as any people."[13]

In April 1952, army leaders ordered army commands in Europe that had not already done so to desegregate their soldiers. Again, desegregation occurred without incident. On October 12, 1953, Assistant Secretary of Defense John Hannah announced that 95 percent of African American soldiers were serving in integrated units. The remaining 5 percent would be transferring into integrated units during the next several months. In November 1954, six months after the Supreme Court issued its unanimous *Brown v. Board of Education* decision holding that segregated public schools violated the Constitution, the army disbanded the European Command's Ninety-fourth Engineer Battalion, its last segregated black unit. In a letter to Texas senator Lyndon B. Johnson, who received a great deal of mail from constituents inquiring about the military's evolving racial policies, Assistant Secretary Hannah wrote, "Official analyses and reports indicate a definite increase in combat effectiveness in the overseas areas . . . Army commanders have determined, also, that more economical and effective results accrue from the policies which remove duplicate facilities and operations based upon race."[14]

Hannah's note records the monumental fact that the army had desegregated not just its fighting units. It had desegregated itself entirely. Even in Southern states where local white residents violently enforced Jim Crow laws and customs, the United States Army integrated its schools, restaurants, and recreational facilities. Bases and posts became beacons of peaceful integration. America's military, integrated at sea and on land, was becoming an extraordinary demonstration of what was possible.

In the years to come, civil rights leaders turned their full attention to seeking justice and equality in the civilian world—in schools, on buses, at lunch counters, and at the voting booth. Although the American military remained a flawed institution, it had reformed itself because of African Americans' decades-long struggle. After two world wars, a president's executive order, and another war after that, victory at home at last had come for African American men and women who wore their nation's uniform.

THE MUSEUM AND THE MIRROR

TODAY THE UNITED STATES ARMY, Navy, Marine Corps, and Air Force together constitute, as retired air force colonel Alan Gropman succinctly noted, "the most racially integrated mass organization in the world."[1] African Americans serve in the military in proportions exceeding their 12 percent of the overall population. They comprise 22 percent of the army, 19 percent of the navy, 15 percent of the air force, and 11 percent of the marine corps. Each year tens of thousands of young African Americans join the military, and they reenlist at a rate 50 percent higher than white recruits. Nearly sixty-five years after President Truman issued Executive Order 9981, African Americans comprise one third of all senior enlisted personnel, 11 percent of officers, and 7 percent of generals and admirals.[2] Together with servicemen and -women of just about every other race, these soldiers, sailors, and marines make up a military that resembles the racially diverse nation it defends.

Contemporary military leaders defend diversity as fiercely as their predecessors defended segregation and racial exclusion. Television advertisements, recruiting posters, and even the recruiters themselves reflect the branches' policies of racial inclusion. Nothing so clearly demonstrated senior military commanders' wholehearted commitment to racial diversity as the amicus curiae brief they filed in the 2003 Supreme Court case *Grutter v. Bollinger.*

IN 1997, the white Michigan resident Barbara Grutter applied to the University of Michigan Law School. She had graduated from college with a 3.8 grade point average and scored 161 on the Law School Aptitude Test. Michigan's law school, which employed a form of racial affirmative action, rejected her. Believing that being white adversely affected her application, Grutter filed suit. She won her case in federal district court, lost in the court of appeals, and appealed to the Supreme Court of the United States.

The question before the high court was whether the University of Michigan Law School's consideration of applicants' race in student admissions violated the equal protection clause of the Fourteenth Amendment or Title VI of the Civil Rights Act of 1964. In a five-to-four ruling, a sharply divided court decided that it did not. Justice Sandra Day O'Connor wrote the majority opinion by which the court ruled that Michigan Law School's admissions policy was narrowly tailored to further the compelling state interest of educating students in a diverse student body.[3]

More than one hundred amicus curiae briefs were submitted to the court in the *Grutter* case. Members of Congress, the NAACP, and the Anti-Defamation League joined the governors and attorneys general of numerous states in presenting arguments for and against the University of Michigan's affirmative action policy.[4] A group of twenty-nine former high-ranking officers and civilian leaders of the army, navy, air force, and marine corps, including superintendents of the service academies, former secretaries of defense, and members of the U.S. Senate also filed a brief in which they argued that the University of Michigan's affirmative action program was constitutional. Commonly called "the military brief," it proved pivotal in the court's decision. Legal scholars have commented that it "well exemplifies what an amicus brief can and should be."[5] The court's opinion cited the military brief more than any other, including the briefs submitted by the parties themselves. Submitted less than two years after the attacks of September 11, 2001, and argued less than two weeks after American forces invaded Iraq, the brief can be regarded as the most influential amicus brief in Supreme Court history.

The court's opinion quoted liberally from the military brief, noting in part: "High-ranking retired officers and civilian leaders of the United

States military assert that, 'based on [their] decades of experience,' a 'highly qualified, racially diverse officer corps . . . is essential to the military's ability to fulfill its principal mission to provide national security.'" Because it recruited most of its officers during their college years, the leaders asserted in their brief, the military relied upon racially diverse college student bodies to maintain a racially diverse officer corps. In a declaration quoted in the court's opinion, the military brief declared that, if it is to maintain a diverse and selective officer corps, then "our country's other most selective institutions must remain both diverse and selective."[6]

Written by several prominent Washington lawyers, the military brief was signed by an array of three- and four-star admirals and generals, including Julius Becton, Wesley Clark, H. Norman Schwarzkopf, Hugh Shelton, and Anthony Zinni. Senators Carl Levin and Jack Reed were among the legislators who signed the brief, which began by recounting African Americans' struggle to desegregate the armed forces. The brief recounted how President Truman issued Executive Order 9981 in part "from a practical recognition that the military's need for manpower and its efficient, effective deployment required integration."[7]

Contemporary military commanders believe that "full integration and other policies combating discrimination are essential to good order, combat readiness and military effectiveness." Pentagon officials had learned "the lesson of history," specifically, "the lessons learned in the 1960s and 1970s."[8] During the tumultuous years of the Vietnam War, racial violence flared among enlisted soldiers, sailors, and marines.

In 1969 Corporal Edward G. Bankston had just returned to the marines' Camp Lejeune from Vietnam, where he had been wounded three times. On the night of July 20, he and a friend were walking back to barracks after seeing a movie when the two young white veterans were attacked by a large group of black and Puerto Rican marines. Bankston died of severe head injuries, and forty-two marines were charged in his death. *Life* magazine reported, "The crisis at Lejeune is as complex as the society outside that created it." Private Donner Tyson, a marine not involved with the killing, told a reporter off base that, in battle, white officers and senior enlisted men treated low-ranking black marines with respect: "Over in the Nam, you're treated better because they have to depend on you." As much as he longed to return home, Private Tyson admitted, "I hated to get off the plane." Back at Camp Lejeune, "you go to the washroom, and it's nigger this and nigger that, all over the wall . . . I think there's gonna be a bloodbath here someday."

As tense as the racial atmosphere was at Camp Lejeune in 1969, *Life* acutely reminded readers that "there is more official integration and equality of opportunity on the base than in society at large."[9] America's military bases certainly were more integrated than their surrounding communities, but according to the *Grutter* military brief, racial strife remained because there was an "absence of trust and communication between the predominately white officer corps and frustrated African American enlisted men." Racial violence became so endemic during the Vietnam War that it affected the troops' ability to fight.[10]

Commanders and civilian leaders learned during this time that racial diversity in the enlisted ranks mandated a diverse officer corps. One post-Vietnam report to the White House recounted, "Racial conflict within the military during the Vietnam era was a blaring wakeup call to the fact that equal opportunity is absolutely indispensable to unit cohesion and therefore critical to military effectiveness and our national security."[11]

After the military became an all-volunteer force in 1973, its leaders launched a decades-long recruitment and retention effort aimed at officers and officer candidates from racial and ethnic minority groups. At the end of the Vietnam War, 2.8 percent of military officers were African American. By March 2002, nearly 9 percent of officers were African Americans, and members of other racial and ethnic minority groups accounted for another 10 percent.

In conclusion, the *Grutter* military brief argued:

> In the interest of national security, the military must be selective in admissions for training and education for the officer corps, *and* it must train and educate a highly qualified, racially diverse officer corps in a racially diverse educational setting. It requires only a small step from this analysis to conclude that our country's other most selective institutions must remain both diverse and selective. [Emphasis in original.][12]

There are, of course, persuasive arguments for and against the military's support for limited racial preferences in college admissions. The morale and readiness justifications set forth in the *Grutter* military brief cannot be discounted by anyone who claims to care about the security of military personnel or the nation. Conversely, one can argue that the practice of accepting slightly lower test scores from nonwhite officer candidates does violence to the memory of servicemen like the Golden Thirteen, who, in the face of overt racial hostility, scored higher on the officer's examination than any group of candidates ever had. Justice Clarence Thomas has insisted that even minimal racial preference programs potentially cast a cloud over all successful black applicants, particularly those who would have been admitted without the preferential program.[13]

REGARDLESS OF ONE'S OPINION on the issue, however, it is indisputable that the armed forces' strong progressive stance on contemporary racial matters is remarkable. Like the nation it defends, America's military has traveled a difficult and sometimes bloody path to integration. The zeal with which the institution guards its racial and ethnic diversity is understandable. This diversity, aside from its morale and readiness benefits, helps connect service members with civilians. From exclusion and segregation to integration and diversity, the armed forces, for better or worse, have always reflected the country at large.

In this way, the military encompasses the history of our nation. It is both a museum of who we were and a mirror of who we are. From the runaway slave turned sailor who struck the first blow in the American Revolution to the first African American commander in chief, the history of our military is the story of our nation. Indeed, in a democracy, it should be no other way.

NOTES

CHAPTER 1: THE CAUSE OF LIBERTY

1. Robert F. Dorr, "Duty, Honor, Country: American 70 Years Late in Honoring WWI Soldier," *New York Times*, May 9, 2003.

2. Joseph J. DioGuardi, "More Blacks Deserve Honors as War Heroes" (letter to the editor), *New York Times*, January 21, 1997.

3. Donnie Radcliffe, "At Last, A Black Badge of Courage," *Washington Post*, April 25, 1991.

4. Gerald Astor, *The Right to Fight: A History of African Americans in the Military* (New York: Presidio Press, 1998), 110.

5. Ibid., 112–13.

6. Darren Staloff, *Hamilton, Adams, Jefferson: The Politics of Enlightenment and the American Founding* (New York: Farrar, Straus and Giroux, 2005), 244.

7. Alfred W. Blumrosen and Ruth G. Blumrosen, *Slave Nation: How Slavery United the Colonies & Sparked the American Revolution* (Naperville IL: Sourcebooks, 2005), 25–26.

8. Mary Miley Theobald, "The Monstrous Absurdity," *Colonial Williamsburg Journal*, Summer 2006.

9. Ibid.

10. Interview with Professor Betty Wood, Oxford University, *Africans in America*, WGBH Interactive, available at www.pbs.org/wgbh/aia/part2/2i1623.html.

11. Gail Buckley, *American Patriots: The Story of Blacks in the Military from the Revolution to Desert Storm* (New York: Random House, 2001), 16.

12. Robert A. Selig, *The Revolution's Black Soldiers*, available at www.american revolution.org, p. 5.

13. Ibid., 6.

14. James Roberts, "The Narrative of James Roberts, Soldier in the Revolutionary War," in Jay David and Elaine Crane, eds., *The Black Soldier from the American Revolution to Vietnam* (New York: Morrow, 1971), 18.

15. Blumrosen and Blumrosen, *Slave Nation*, 147.

16. Ibid., 149.

CHAPTER 2: THE FIRST TO COME AND THE LAST TO LEAVE

1. Gail Buckley, *American Patriots: The Story of Blacks in the Military from the Revolution to Desert Storm* (New York: Random House, 2001), 54.

2. Bernard C. Nalty, *Strength for the Fight: A History of Black Americans in the Military* (New York: Free Press, 1986), 26.

3. Frederick Douglass, "Men of Color, to Arms," March 2, 1863, in Jay David and Elaine Crane, eds., *The Black Soldier from the American Revolution to Vietnam* (New York: Morrow, 1971), 53–54.

4. Samuel P. Wheeler, "Alexander Stephens and His 'Cornerstone Speech,'" March 21, 2007, available at www.lincolnstudies.com.

5. Katharine Q. Seelye, "Celebrating Secession Without the Slaves," *New York Times*, November 29, 2010.

6. Abraham Lincoln, "Reply to Emancipation Memorial Presented by Chicago Christians of All Denominations," in Henry Louis Gates, Jr., and Donald Yacovone, eds., *Lincoln on Race and Slavery* (Princeton, NJ: Princeton University Press, 2009), xlviii.

7. Gates and Yacovone, *Lincoln on Race and Slavery*, 243.

8. Ibid., 248.

9. Ibid.

10. John T. Hubbell, "Abraham Lincoln and the Recruitment of Black Soldiers," *Journal of the Abraham Lincoln Association* 2, no. 1 (1980).

11. Buckley, *American Patriots*, 81.

12. Letter from John W. Crisfield to Abraham Lincoln, September 17, 1863, Abraham Lincoln Papers, Library of Congress.

13. David and Crane, *The Black Soldier*, 54.

14. War Department General Order 143, May 22, 1863, U.S. National Archives & Records Administration, Washington, DC.

15. Thomas Wentworth Higginson, "Army Life in Black Regiment," in David and Crane, *The Black Soldier*, 59.

16. Ibid.

17. Buckley, *American Patriots*, 109.

18. David and Crane, *The Black Soldier*, 78.

19. Jennifer Logan, "We Can, We Will," *Texas Park & Wildlife Magazine*, April 2006.

20. Ibid.

21. Ibid.

CHAPTER 3: THE ONLY REAL NEUTRAL

1. William G. Jordan, *Black Newspapers and America's War for Democracy, 1914–1920* (Chapel Hill: University of North Carolina Press, 2001), 41–44.
2. "Warned to Leave Their Homes," *Chicago Defender*, March 27, 1915.
3. "Midnight's Musings," *Baltimore Afro-American*, February 15, 1915.
4. "Alleged Thief Lynched," *Washington Post*, July 7, 1915.
5. "Two Lynched in Georgia," *Washington Post*, July 25, 1915.
6. "Lynched by Arkansas Mob," *Washington Post*, December 4, 1915.
7. "Race Man Lynched," *Chicago Defender*, December 4, 1915.
8. "Nine Human Beings Hanged in South Within 24 Hours," *Chicago Defender*, August 14, 1915.
9. "Nine Hanged in One Day," *Washington Post*, August 7, 1915.
10. "Nine Human Beings Hanged in South Within 24 Hours," *Chicago Defender*, August 14, 1915.
11. "Nine Hanged in One Day," *Washington Post*, August 7, 1915.
12. Woodrow Wilson, Message to Congress, 63rd Cong., 2d Sess., Senate Doc. No. 566.
13. Ibid.
14. "Loyalty to the Flag," *Chicago Defender*, April 17, 1915.
15. Gail Buckley, *American Patriots: The Story of Blacks in the Military from the Revolution to Desert Storm* (New York: Random House, 2001), 177.
16. "The Only Neutrals," *Baltimore Afro-American*, May 15, 1915.

CHAPTER 4: REPORT TO GOD THE REASON WHY

1. Woodrow Wilson, "Address to a Joint Session of Congress Requesting a Declaration of War Against Germany," April 2, 1917.
2. Woodrow Wilson, "Proclamation 1364—Declaring That a State of War Exists Between the United States and Germany," April 6, 1917; "Agree to Vote on War," *Washington Post*, April 4, 1917.
3. "Beginning the War," *Washington Post*, April 5, 1917.
4. "Pledge Loyalty," *Baltimore Afro-American*, April 14, 1917.
5. Ibid.
6. "Colored Citizens Show Patriotism," *Baltimore Afro-American*, April 28, 1917.
7. "Calls Colored Men to War," *Washington Post*, April 16, 1917.
8. "Attitude of the American Negro," *Baltimore Afro-American*, May 26, 1917.
9. "Colored Citizens Show Patriotism," *Baltimore Afro-American*, April 28, 1917.
10. "Call Their Race to Colors," *Washington Post*, April 14, 1917.
11. "No Disloyalty There," *Baltimore Afro-American*, April 14, 1917.
12. "Dr. Frissell Issues Call," *Baltimore Afro-American*, April 21, 1917.
13. Walter White, *A Man Called White* (Athens: University of Georgia Press, 1995), 36.
14. Ibid.
15. "Calls Colored Men to War," *Washington Post*, April 16, 1917.

16. "Pledge of Loyalty on Part of Negro," *Baltimore Afro-American*, April 21, 1917.

17. "Colored Race Is Loyal, Says Taft," *Washington Post*, April 29, 1917.

18. W.E.B. DuBois, "Close Ranks," *Crisis*, July 1918, 111.

19. "Dr. Frissell Issues Call," *Baltimore Afro-American*, April 21, 1917.

20. *Chicago Defender*, May 4, 1918.

21. Colonel Roscoe Conkling Simmons, "When There Is No Peace," *Chicago Defender*, October 12, 1918.

22. Lt. Col. (Ret.) Michael Lee Lanning, *The African-American Soldier: From Crispus Attucks to Colin Powell* (Secaucus, NJ: Birch Lane Press, 1997), 168.

23. Ibid., 131.

24. "South Opposes Negro Soldiers," *Baltimore Afro-American*, April 14, 1917.

25. "Pleads for Fair Play for Colored Soldiers," *Baltimore Afro-American*, September 15, 1917.

26. Ibid.

27. Bernard C. Nalty, *Strength for the Fight: A History of Black Americans in the Military* (New York: Free Press, 1986), 108.

28. Emmett J. Scott, *The American Negro in the World War* (Homewood Press, 1919), 71.

29. "Negro Soldiers Training Problem," *Washington Post*, August 4, 1917.

30. "Negro Troops to the South," *Baltimore Afro-American*, September 8, 1917.

31. "To Train Colored Troops Separate from Whites," *Baltimore Afro-American*, September 15, 1917.

32. Ibid.

33. Nalty, *Strength for the Fight*, 108.

34. Lanning, *The African-American Soldier*, 131.

35. Charles H. Williams, *Negro Soldiers in World War I: The Human Side* (New York: AMS Press, 1970, reprint of 1923 ed.), 21.

36. "Married Men Put on Exempt List for Purpose of Classification," *Washington Post*, June 8, 1917.

37. Scott, *The American Negro in the World War*, 70.

38. "Called Men Registering 'Slaves'; Is Fined a Dollar for Each Word," *Washington Post*, June 6, 1917.

CHAPTER 5: TRAGEDY AND TRIUMPH: HOUSTON AND DES MOINES

1. Lt. Col. (Ret.) Michael Lee Lanning, *The African-American Soldier: From Crispus Attucks to Colin Powell* (Secaucus, NJ: Birch Lane Press, 1997), 122.

2. Adriane Lentz-Smith, *Freedom Struggles: African Americans and World War I* (Cambridge, MA: Harvard University Press, 2009), 61–62.

3. Ibid., 64.

4. Lanning, *The African American Soldier*, 124.

5. William G. Jordan, *Black Newspapers and America's War for Democracy, 1914–1920* (Chapel Hill: University of North Carolina Press, 2001), 92.

6. "Charges of Murder Against 34 Negroes," *Washington Post*, August 25, 1917.

7. Lentz-Smith, *Freedom Struggles*, 63.

8. "Charges of Murder Against 34 Negroes," *Washington Post*, August 25, 1917.

9. Ibid.

10. Lentz-Smith, *Freedom Struggles*, 66.

11. Ibid., 67.

12. "Charges of Murder Against 34 Negroes," *Washington Post*, August 25, 1917.

13. Jordan, *Black Newspapers and America's War for Democracy*, 93.

14. Lentz-Smith, *Freedom Struggles*, 69.

15. "Our Position on the War Map," *Chicago Defender*, September 15, 1917.

16. Jordan, *Black Newspapers and America's War for Democracy*, 94.

17. "Charges of Murder Against 34 Negroes," *Washington Post*, August 25, 1917.

18. Jordan, *Black Newspapers and America's War for Democracy*, 94.

19. "In the Enemy's Camp," *Chicago Defender*, September 1, 1917.

20. Jordan, *Black Newspapers and America's War for Democracy*, 97.

21. Lentz-Smith, *Freedom Struggles*, 76.

22. Jordan, *Black Newspapers and America's War for Democracy*, 95.

23. Bernard C. Nalty, *Strength for the Fight: A History of Black Americans in the Military* (New York: Free Press, 1986), 105–06.

24. Emmett J. Scott, *The American Negro in the World War* (Homewood Press, 1919), 83.

25. "Jim Crow Training Camps—No!," *Chicago Defender*, April 28, 1917.

26. Charles H. Williams, *Negro Soldiers in World War I: The Human Side* (New York: AMS Press, 1970, reprint of 1923 ed.), 37.

27. "Spingarn Camp Taken Over by War Department," *Baltimore Afro-American*, April 28, 1917.

28. Scott, *The American Negro in the World War*, 83.

29. "Jim Crow Camp? Maybe. That or Nothing," *Baltimore Afro-American*, May 5, 1917.

30. Ibid.

31. Scott, *The American Negro in the World War*, 84.

32. "See Hampton Institute," *Chicago Defender*, April 21, 1917.

33. "U.S. Doesn't Want Negro Officers," *Baltimore Afro-American*, April 28, 1917.

34. "South Opposes Negro Soldiers," *Baltimore Afro-American*, April 14, 1917 (quoting Bradley Gilmont of the *Boston Globe*).

35. Scott, *The American Negro in the World War*, 90.

36. "War Secretary Approves Negro Officers Camp," *Baltimore Afro-American*, May 19, 1917.

37. Scott, *The American Negro in the World War*, 88.

38. "The President's 'Consideration,'" *Baltimore Afro-American*, November 29, 1918.

39. Robert H. Ferrell, *Woodrow Wilson and World War I: 1917–1921* (New York: Harper & Row, 1985), 214.

40. "O.R.T.C. Now a Fact," *Baltimore Afro-American*, May 19, 1917.

41. Scott, *The American Negro in the World War*, 88.

42. Ibid., 87.

43. Ibid., 88.

44. Ibid., 89.
45. Williams, *Negro Soldiers in World War I*, 46.
46. Ibid., 23.

CHAPTER 6: THE TRAVELS OF EMMETT J. SCOTT AND THE TRAVAILS OF
COLONEL CHARLES YOUNG

1. Adriane Lentz-Smith, *Freedom Struggles: African Americans and World War I* (Cambridge, MA: Harvard University Press, 2009), 94.

2. Ibid., 113.

3. Horace Slatter, "Some Men I Have Known," *Baltimore Afro-American*, July 22, 1916.

4. "The Cat Is Out of the Bag," *Baltimore Afro-American*, January 17, 1919.

5. Gail Buckley, *American Patriots: The Story of Blacks in the Military from the Revolution to Desert Storm* (New York: Random House, 2001), 179.

6. William G. Jordan, *Black Newspapers and America's War for Democracy, 1914–1920* (Chapel Hill: University of North Carolina Press, 2001), 101.

7. "Hon. Emmett Scott on Official Trip South," *Chicago Defender*, November 24, 1917.

8. "Burial of a Colored Soldier at Sea," *Baltimore Afro-American*, Decmber 6, 1918.

9. Bernard C. Nalty, *Strength for the Fight: A History of Black Americans in the Military* (New York: Free Press, 1986), 111.

10. "To Educate the Colored American on the War Aims of the United States," *Baltimore Afro-American*, May 31, 1918.

11. "Emmett Scott Makes Appeal for 'Mercy,'" *Baltimore Afro-American*, June 6, 1919.

12. "Emmett Scott Pleads for a Free Africa," *Baltimore Afro-American*, July 1, 1919.

13. "The Cat Is Out of the Bag," *Baltimore Afro-American*, January 17, 1919.

14. "Why Not?" (letter to the editor), *Baltimore Afro-American*, February 9, 1918.

15. "Democratic Ingratitude Shown by Secretary Baker," *Baltimore Afro-American*, September 17, 1920.

16. Emmett J. Scott, *The American Negro in the World War* (Homewood Press, 1919), 95.

17. Charles H. Williams, *Negro Soldiers in World War I: The Human Side* (New York: AMS Press, 1970, reprint of 1923 ed.), 69–70.

18. Ibid., 58.

19. Ibid., 60.

20. Scott, *The American Negro in the World War*, 95.

21. "A Jim Crow Democracy," *Baltimore Afro-American*, February 16, 1918.

22. Scott, *The American Negro in the World War*, 96.

23. Lt. Col. (Ret.) Michael Lee Lanning, *The African-American Soldier: From Crispus Attucks to Colin Powell* (Secaucus, NJ: Birch Lane Press, 1997), 132.

24. Buckley, *American Patriots*, 132.

25. Ibid., 176.

26. Nalty, *Strength for the Fight*, 110.

27. Buckley, *American Patriots*, 176.

28. "Exit Colonel Young," *Baltimore Afro-American*, August 11, 1917.

29. Lentz-Smith, *Freedom Struggles*, 114.

30. "Colonel Young on Retired List," *Baltimore Afro-American*, August 11, 1917.

31. Ibid.

32. Lanning, *The African-American Soldier*, 133.

33. "Exit Colonel Young," *Baltimore Afro-American*, August 11, 1917.

CHAPTER 7: FRANCE BY WAY OF CAROLINA

1. Bernard C. Nalty, *Strength for the Fight: A History of Black Americans in the Military* (New York: Free Press, 1986), 113.

2. "Defender Gets Real Story of Camp Funston Color Line Problem," *Chicago Defender*, May 11, 1918.

3. Emmett J. Scott, *The American Negro in the World War* (Homewood Press, 1919), 96.

4. Ibid., 97.

5. "What Does Breaking Mean?," *Baltimore Afro-American*, April 12, 1918.

6. Scott, *The American Negro in the World War*, 97–98.

7. "This Is No Soldier!," *Chicago Defender*, May 4, 1918.

8. Scott, *The American Negro in the World War*, 101.

9. Ibid., 96.

10. Michael L. Cooper, *Hell Fighters: African American Soldiers in World War I* (New York: Lodestar Books, 1997), 3.

11. Gail Buckley, *American Patriots: The Story of Blacks in the Military from the Revolution to Desert Storm* (New York: Random House, 2001), 191–93.

12. Cooper, *Hell Fighters*, 10.

13. "15th N.Y. Regiment Quietly Slips Away," *Chicago Defender*, October 20, 1917.

14. "Colonel Hayward Speaks a Word," *Chicago Defender*, September 8, 1917.

15. Views of World Travelers Met in Capital Hotel Lobbies," *Washington Post*, October 23, 1917.

16. Scott, *The American Negro in the World War*, 80.

17. Ibid.

18. Ibid.

19. Ibid.

CHAPTER 8: THE LOST CHILDREN

1. Charles H. Williams, *Negro Soldiers in World War I: The Human Side* (New York: AMS Press, 1970, reprint of 1923 ed.), 148.

2. Ibid., 27.

3. Lt. Col. (Ret.) Michael Lee Lanning, *The African-American Soldier: From Crispus Attucks to Colin Powell* (Secaucus, NJ: Birch Lane Press, 1997), 131.

4. Bernard C. Nalty, *Strength for the Fight: A History of Black Americans in the Military* (New York: Free Press, 1986), 112.

5. Lanning, *The African American Soldier*, 133.

6. Williams, *Negro Soldiers in World War I*, 27.

7. Ibid., 143.

8. Ibid., 144.

9. "Will Stay at Meade," *Washington Post*, November 7, 1917.

10. Williams, *Negro Soldiers in World War I*, 140.

11. Michael L. Cooper, *Hell Fighters: African American Soldiers in World War I* (New York: Lodestar Books, 1997), 26.

12. George Rothwell Brown, "Rush Docks in France," *Washington Post*, July 12, 1918.

13. "Colored Stevedores Doing Essential Work at Base Ports," *Baltimore Afro-American*, November 29, 1918.

14. Ibid.

15. George Rothwell Brown, "Rush Docks in France," *Washington Post*, July 12, 1918.

16. Williams, *Negro Soldiers in World War I*, 141.

17. "Only One Complaint of Food," *Washington Post*, March 18, 1918.

18. "Lighter Side of War," *Chicago Defender*, April 13, 1918.

19. Williams, *Negro Soldiers in World War I*, 148.

20. Emmett J. Scott, *The American Negro in the World War* (Homewood Press, 1919), 201.

21. Gail Buckley, *American Patriots: The Story of Blacks in the Military from the Revolution to Desert Storm* (New York: Random House, 2001), 200.

22. Cooper, *Hell Fighters*, 29–30.

23. Scott, *The American Negro in the World War*, 201.

24. Buckley, *American Patriots*, 201.

25. Ibid., 202.

26. Ibid., 163.

27. Peter N. Nelson, *A More Unbending Battle: The Harlem Hellfighters' Struggle for Freedom in WWI and Equality at Home* (New York: Basic Civitas, 2009), 150–51.

28. Buckley, *American Patriots*, 188.

29. Ibid., 212.

30. Cooper, *Hell Fighters*, 34.

31. Ibid., 31.

32. Buckley, *American Patriots*, 200.

33. Williams, *Negro Soldiers in World War I*, 198.

34. Cooper, *Hell Fighters*, 34.

35. Williams, *Negro Soldiers in World War I*, 198.

36. Scott, *The American Negro in the World War*, 208–10.

37. Ibid., 210.

38. Ibid.

39. "Our Boys Are Rough on Huns," *Baltimore Afro-American*, October 11, 1918.

40. Ibid.

41. "Soldier Routs Twenty Germans," *Chicago Defender*, August 31, 1918.

42. "Our Boys Are Rough on Huns," *Baltimore Afro-American*, October 11, 1918.

43. Scott, *The American Negro in the World War*, 212.

44. Nelson, *A More Unbending Battle*, 145.

45. Ibid.

46. "A Soldier Favored," *Baltimore Afro-American*, May 30, 1919.

47. Buckley, *American Patriots*, 188.

48. Ibid., 189.

49. Nelson, *A More Unbending Battle*, 147.

50. Buckley, *American Patriots*, 215.

51. "In the Enemy's Camp," *Chicago Defender*, September 1, 1917.

CHAPTER 9: DISILLUSIONED BY ARMISTICE

1. Charles H. Williams, *Negro Soldiers in World War I: The Human Side* (New York: AMS Press, 1970, reprint of 1923 ed.), 70–71.

2. Ibid., 71.

3. William G. Jordan, *Black Newspapers and America's War for Democracy, 1914–1920* (Chapel Hill: University of North Carolina Press, 2001), 122.

4. Ibid., 125.

5. Ibid., 128.

6. Williams, *Negro Soldiers in World War I*, 158.

7. Ibid.

8. Michael L. Cooper, *Hell Fighters: African American Soldiers in World War I* (New York: Lodestar Books, 1997), 47.

9. Williams, *Negro Soldiers in World War I*, 185.

10. Gail Buckley, *American Patriots: The Story of Blacks in the Military from the Revolution to Desert Storm* (New York: Random House, 2001), 218.

11. Cooper, *Hell Fighters*, 57.

12. Buckley, *American Patriots*, 221.

13. Gerald Astor, *The Right to Fight: A History of African Americans in the Military* (New York: Presidio Press, 1998), 125.

14. Emmett J. Scott, *The American Negro in the World War* (Homewood Press, 1919), 458.

15. Buckley, *American Patriots*, 221.

16. Arthur E. Barbeau, Florette Henri, and Bernard C. Nalty, *The Unknown Soldiers: African-American Troops in World War I* (Cambridge, MA: Da Capo, 1996), 175.

17. Ibid., 177.

18. Vincent Mikkelsen, *Coming from Battle to Face a War: The Lynching of Black Soldiers in the World War I Era* (Tallahassee: Florida State University Press, 2007), 145.

19. Ibid.

20. Chad L. Williams, *Torchbearers of Democracy: African American Soldiers in the World War I Era* (Chapel Hill: University of North Carolina Press, 2010), 239.

21. Ibid.

22. Mikkelsen, *Coming from Battle to Face a War*, 147.

23. Bernard C. Nalty, *Strength for the Fight: A History of Black Americans in the Military* (New York: Free Press, 1986), 124.

CHAPTER 10: OLD DRAFT IN A NEW DAY

1. Richard M. Dalfiume, *Desegregation of the U.S. Armed Forces: Fighting on Two Fronts, 1939–1953* (Columbia: University of Missouri Press, 1969), 31.

2. "Survey Shows Negro Still Leaving Farms," *New York Amsterdam News*, December 30, 1939.

3. Kelly Miller, "Wooing the Colored Vote," *Atlanta Daily World*, December 16, 1939.

4. William E. Leuchtenburg, *The White House Looks South: Franklin D. Roosevelt, Harry S. Truman, Lyndon B. Johnson* (Baton Rouge: Louisiana State University Press, 2005), 127.

5. "Most Negro Voters Still Democratic," *Washington Post*, February 4, 1940.

6. Walter White, *A Man Called White* (New York: Viking, 1948), 72.

7. "Boston Minstrel Show Insults Negro Citizens," *New York Amsterdam News*, November 11, 1939.

8. "Jim Crow in Chicago," *Chicago Defender*, November 11, 1939.

9. "Negro Must Keep Awake, Mrs. Bethune," *Atlanta Daily World*, December 26, 1939.

10. "Warns U.S. Against All Race Bias," *Chicago Defender*, November 11, 1939.

11. Ben Davis, Jr., "Nothing in War for Negroes—Paul Robeson," *Chicago Defender*, November 4, 1939.

12. "Draft Foes Ignore Upsets; Fight Police Interference," *Baltimore Afro-American*, September 21, 1940.

13. "City Sued as D.C. Halts Peace Parade," *Chicago Defender*, September 21, 1940.

14. "Randolph Opposes Draft in Nation," *Atlanta Daily World*, August 25, 1940.

15. "Buffalo NAACP Opposes Draft Measure," *Chicago Defender*, September 14, 1940.

16. Bernard C. Nalty, *Strength for the Fight: A History of Black Americans in the Military* (New York: Free Press, 1986), 136.

17. "Negroes Want Democracy," *Atlanta Daily World*, August 21, 1940.

18. "Senate Passes Amendment to Halt Army Jim Crow," *New York Amsterdam News*, August 31, 1940.

19. Nalty, *Strength for the Fight*, 137.

20. "House Bars Discrimination from Draft Bill," *Atlanta Daily World*, September 11, 1940.

21. Ibid.

22. Gail Buckley, *American Patriots: The Story of Blacks in the Military from the Revolution to Desert Storm* (New York: Random House, 2001), 263.

23. "36,000 Race Men Face Draft as FDR Signs Bill," *Chicago Defender*, September 21, 1940.

24. Ibid.

25. Buckley, *American Patriots*, 262.

26. "Few Negroes Are on Local Boards, Survey Finds," *Atlanta Daily World*, December 19, 1940.

27. "NAACP Protests South Carolina's All-White Draft Board," *Baltimore Afro-American*, October 12, 1940.

28. "Tennessee Governor Asserts Negroes Did Nothing for U.S.," *Atlanta Daily World*, October 29, 1940.

CHAPTER 11: POLITICS UNUSUAL

1. Bernard C. Nalty, *Strength for the Fight: A History of Black Americans in the Military* (New York: Free Press, 1986), 137–38.

2. Gail Buckley, *American Patriots: The Story of Blacks in the Military from the Revolution to Desert Storm* (New York: Random House, 2001), 263.

3. Richard M. Dalfiume, *Desegregation of the U.S. Armed Forces: Fighting on Two Fronts, 1939–1953* (Columbia: University of Missouri Press, 1969), 37.

4. "Only White Draft Officers OK'd by FDR," *Baltimore Afro-American*, October 12, 1940.

5. Dalfiume, *Desegregation of the U.S. Armed Forces*, 39.

6. "Only White Draft Officers OK'd by FDR," *Baltimore Afro-American*, October 12, 1940.

7. Dalfiume, *Desegregation of the U.S. Armed Forces*, 39.

8. Phillip McGuire, *He, Too, Spoke for Democracy* (New York: Greenwood, 1988), xii.

9. "White House Blesses Jim Crow," *Crisis*, November 1940.

10. "Roosevelt or Willkie," *Baltimore Afro-American*, October 19, 1940.

11. Roy Wilkins, "The Watchtower," *New York Amsterdam News*, October 19, 1940.

12. "Sees Willkie Victory Sure," *New York Amsterdam News*, October 26, 1940.

13. William B. Newsholme, "The Negro and Willkie," *New York Amsterdam News*, October 5, 1940.

14. William J. vanden Heuvel, "In Praise of Wendell Willkie, a 'Womanizer,'" *New York Times*, December 19, 1987.

15. "Wendell Willkie Says," *Baltimore Afro-American*, November 2, 1940.

16. "Wendell Willkie Invades Harlem," *New York Amsterdam News*, October 12, 1940.

17. J. Robert Smith, "Mrs. Willkie Tours Harlem," *New York Amsterdam News*, October 12, 1940.

18. "Sees Willkie Victory Sure," *New York Amsterdam News*, October 26, 1940.

19. "Leaders Predict Heavy Colored Vote for Willkie," *Baltimore Afro-American*, November 2, 1940.

20. William E. Leuchtenburg, *The White House Looks South: Franklin D. Roosevelt, Harry S. Truman, Lyndon B. Johnson* (Baton Rouge: Louisiana State University Press, 2005), 55, 60.

21. Ibid., 95–96.

22. Ibid., 58.

23. Roy Wilkins, "The Watchtower," *New York Amsterdam News*, October 19, 1940.

24. "Roosevelt Failed Race, Says Louis," *Washington Post*, October 31, 1940.

25. William Pickens, "If Colored, He'd Vote for Willkie," *New York Amsterdam News*, October 26, 1940.

26. W.E.B. DuBois, "As the Crow Flies," *New York Amsterdam News*, October 12, 1940.

27. "Roosevelt or Willkie," *Baltimore Afro-American*, October 19, 1940.

28. Dalfiume, *Desegregation of the U.S. Armed Forces,* 41.

29. McGuire, *He, Too, Spoke for Democracy,* 10.

30. "Colonel Davis Named General," *Baltimore Afro-American*, November 2, 1940.

31. "Two Howard U. Men to Plan Defense Aid by Colored," *Washington Post*, October 26, 1940.

32. McGuire, *He, Too, Spoke for Democracy*, 8.

33. Ibid., 11.

34. "Colonel Davis Named General," *Baltimore Afro-American*, November 2, 1940.

35. McGuire, *He, Too, Spoke for Democracy*, xii, 12.

36. Ibid., 13.

37. Ibid.

38. Ibid., 10.

39. "The Inquiring Reporter," *Baltimore Afro-American*, November 2, 1940.

40. "Roosevelt Is Our Choice," *New York Amsterdam News*, October 26, 1940.

41. David Woolner, "African Americans and the New Deal: A Look Back into History," Franklin and Eleanor Roosevelt Institute, available at www.roose veltinstitute.org.

42. Ralph Matthews, "Watching the Big Parade," *Baltimore Afro-American*, October 26, 1940.

43. Bishop R. R. Wright, Jr., "Bishop Sees No Hope for Race in Willkie," *Chicago Defender*, October 26, 1940.

44. "Roosevelt Is Our Choice," *New York Amsterdam News*, October 26, 1940.

45. "United Front Is Asked by Negro Leaders," *Atlanta Daily World*, November 12, 1940.

46. Frank Freidel, *F.D.R. and the South* (Baton Rouge: Louisiana State University Press, 1966), 81.

47. "Mo. Voters Cut Stark for Stand on School Case," *Baltimore Afro-American*, August 17, 1940.

48. William C. Berman, *The Politics of Civil Rights in the Truman Administration* (Columbus: Ohio State University Press, 1970), 9.

CHAPTER 12: FOLLOW THE GLEAM

1. David McCullough, *Truman* (New York: Simon & Schuster, 1992), 36–37.

2. Mrs. W.L.C. Palmer, Oral History interview, January 18, 1962, Harry S. Truman Library and Museum (hereafter cited as HSTL).

3. McCullough, *Truman*, 61.

4. Palmer interview, HSTL.

5. Ibid.

6. Harry S. Truman, *The Autobiography of Harry S. Truman*, ed. Robert H. Ferrell (Columbia: University of Missouri Press, 1980), 12.

7. "National Affairs: Follow the Gleam," *Time*, March 24, 1952.

8. Palmer interview, HSTL.

9. McCullough, *Truman*, 54.

10. William C. Berman, *The Politics of Civil Rights in the Truman Administration* (Columbus: Ohio State University Press, 1970), 10.

11. McCullough, *Truman*, 86.

12. William E. Leuchtenburg, *The White House Looks South: Franklin D. Roosevelt, Harry S. Truman, Lyndon B. Johnson* (Baton Rouge: Louisiana State University Press, 2005), 151.

13. Ibid., 147–49.

14. Ibid., 147.

15. Harry S. Truman, "The Military Career of a Missourian," circa 1940, Senate and Vice Presidential File, HSTL.

16. Ibid.

17. Ibid.

18. Leuchtenburg, *The White House Looks South*, 150.

19. Truman, *Autobiography*, 34.

20. McCullough, *Truman*, 49.

21. Truman, *Autobiography*, 34.

22. Report of Physical Examination of Harry S. Truman, August 9, 1917, Subject Files, RG407: Records of the Adjutant General's Office: Military Personnel File of Harry S. Truman, HSTL.

23. Acceptance of Commission, First Lieutenant by Harry S. Truman, September 14, 1917, Subject File, RG407: Records of the Adjutant General's Office: Military Personnel File of Harry S. Truman, HSTL.

24. McCullough, *Truman*, 111.

25. Ibid., 113.

26. Harry S. Truman to Bess Wallace, May 12, 1918, HSTL.

27. Harry S. Truman to Bess Wallace, May 19, 1918, HSTL.

28. Ibid.

29. Harry S. Truman to Bess Wallace, September 1, 1918, and September 15, 1918, HSTL.

30. Truman, *Autobiography*, 45.

31. McCullough, *Truman*, 122–23.

32. Ibid., 132.

33. Truman, *Autobiography*, 51.

34. Robert H. Ferrell, *Harry Truman: A Life* (Columbia: University of Missouri Press, 1994), 73.

35. Ted Marks, Oral History interview, 1962, HSTL.

36. Harry E. Murphy, Oral History interview, 1970, HSTL.

37. Frederick J. Bowman, Oral History interview, 1972, HSTL.

38. Ibid.

39. Harry S. Truman, autobiographical manuscript, 1945, HSTL.

Chapter 13: Some Minor County Office

1. Harry L. Abbott, Oral History interview, April 4, 1990, HSTL.

2. "Hoodlum Politics," Editorial, *Life*, October 20, 1952.

3. Robert H. Ferrell, *Truman and Pendergast* (Columbia: University of Missouri Press, 1999), 6.

4. David McCullough, *Truman* (New York: Simon & Schuster, 1992), 160.

5. "Hoodlum Politics," Editorial, *Life*, October 20, 1952.

6. William Reddig, *Tom's Town* (Columbia: University of Missouri Press, 1986), 265.

7. David Blumenthal and James A. Morone, *The Heart of Power: Health and Politics in the Oval Office* (Berkeley: University of California Press, 2009), 61.

8. Mrs. W.L.C. Palmer, Oral History interview, January 18, 1962, HSTL.

9. Theodore Alford, "New Faces in the Senate—Harry Truman of Missouri," *Washington Post*, November 12, 1934.

10. McCullough, *Truman*, 181.

11. Robert H. Ferrell, *Harry S. Truman: A Life* (Columbia: University of Missouri Press, 1994), 127.

12. McCullough, *Truman*, 204.

13. Ferrell, *Harry S. Truman*, 128–29.

14. Ibid., 129–30.

15. McCullough, *Truman*, 208.

16. Brian Burnes, *Harry S. Truman: His Life and Times* (Kansas City, MO: Kansas City Star Books, 2003), 118–19.

17. Ferrell, *Harry S. Truman*, 131.

18. William E. Leuchtenburg, *The White House Looks South: Franklin D. Roosevelt, Harry S. Truman, Lyndon B. Johnson* (Baton Rouge: Louisiana State University Press, 2005), 156–57.

19. McCullough, *Truman*, 213.

20. Ibid., 214.

21. Palmer interview, HSTL.

22. "Pendergast Faces New U.S. Charge," *Washington Post,* July 14, 1940.

23. Burnes, *Harry S. Truman*, 119–20.

24. "Governor Stark Leads Senator Truman in Missouri Vote," *Washington Post,* August 7, 1940.

25. "Truman Leads Missouri Race by 7,000 Votes," *Washington Post,* August 8, 1940.

26. Leuchtenburg, *The White House Looks South*, 157–58.

27. McCullough, *Truman*, 247.

28. Leuchtenburg, *The White House Looks South*, 158.

29. "Roosevelt, Top of Ticket, Ride Crest in Missouri," *Washington Post*, November 6, 1940.

CHAPTER 14: THUNDERING RESENTMENT IN THE VOICE OF GOD

1. A. Philip Randolph, "Why F.D. Won't End Defense Jim Crow," *Baltimore Afro-American*, April 12, 1941.

2. Gail Buckley, *American Patriots: The Story of Blacks in the Military from the Revolution to Desert Storm* (New York: Random House, 2001), 270.

3. "10,000 Should March on D.C., Says Randolph," *Baltimore Afro-American*, January 25, 1941.

4. A. Philip Randolph, "The Randolph Plan," *Chicago Defender*, March 15, 1941.

5. "10,000 Plan March on D.C. to Protest J.C.," *Baltimore Afro-American*, May 10, 1941.

6. "100,000 to March to Capital," *New York Amsterdam Star-News*, May 31, 1941.

7. Ibid.

8. "Plan All-Out March to D.C.," *New York Amsterdam Star-News*, April 12, 1941.

9. "10,000 Plan March on D.C. to Protest J.C.," *Baltimore Afro-American*, May 10, 1941.

10. A. Philip Randolph, "Let the Negro Masses Speak," *New York Amsterdam Star-News*, April 12, 1941.

11. "10,000 Plan March on D.C. to Protest J.C.," *Baltimore Afro-American*, May 10, 1941.

12. A. Philip Randolph, "March of 10,000 Workers on Washington Called Way to Get Jobs," *Baltimore Afro-American*, March 15, 1941.

13. Buckley, *American Patriots,* 271.

14. "First Lady Is Not For Hike to Capital," *New York Amsterdam Star-News*, June 21, 1941.

15. A. Philip Randolph, "Let the Negro Masses Speak," *New York Amsterdam Star-News*, April 12, 1941.

16. "10,000 Should March on D.C., Says Randolph," *Baltimore Afro-American*, January 25, 1941.

17. Buckley, *American Patriots*, 271.

18. "President Roosevelt Orders Jim Crow Ban Lifted on National Defense Jobs," *New York Amsterdam Star-News*, June 21, 1941.

19. "Rep. Day Says FDR Can Halt Defense Bias," *Chicago Defender*, June 14, 1941.

20. "Washington March Postponed," *Atlanta Daily World*, June 28, 1941.

21. "LaGuardia Hails Order Barring Race Bias in Arms Plants," *Washington Post*, July 2, 1941.

22. "Says F.D.'s Order Won't Stop J.C.," *Baltimore Afro-American*, July 5, 1941.

23. "Harlemites Divided on Value of F.D.R. Order," *New York Amsterdam Star-News*, July 5, 1941.

24. "Wait, Watch, Check, Marchers Told in Radio Broadcast," *Atlanta Daily World*, June 29, 1941.

CHAPTER 15: THE USS *MILLER*

1. Memorandum from the Senior Surviving Officer, USS *West Virginia*, to the Commander in Chief, Pacific Fleet, December 11, 1941.

2. "N.A.A.C.P. Alert in Case of Navy Hero," *Chicago Defender*, April 11, 1942.

3. "Willkie Scores Navy Race Policy," *Chicago Defender*, March 28, 1942.

4. "Navy Discloses Name of Heroic Mess Attendant," *Atlanta World*, March 13, 1942.

5. "Congressional Medal Urged for Pearl Harbor Hero," *Baltimore Afro-American*, March 21, 1942.

6. "Senate Kills Bill for Medal to Dorie Miller," *Baltimore Afro-American*, May 16, 1942.

7. "Congress Hears Honors Pleas for Navy Hero," *Atlanta Daily World*, March 23, 1942.

8. "Messman Awarded Navy Cross by FDR," *Chicago Defender*, May 16, 1942.

9. "Asks FDR, Knox to Officially Recognize Hero," *Atlanta Daily World*, March 18, 1942.

10. "Parents of Naval Hero to Be Feted," *Atlanta Daily World*, April 16, 1942.

11. "Dorie Miller, Naval Hero, in California," *New York Amsterdam Star-News*, May 9, 1942.

12. "Says Navy Should Lift Ban in Tribute to Dorie Miller," *Atlanta Daily World*, March 22, 1942.

13. "Willkie Scores Navy Race Policy," *Chicago Defender*, March 28, 1942.

14. "Navy Cross Awarded to Dorie Miller," *Baltimore Afro-American*, May 16, 1942.

15. "Three Cheers for Roosevelt," *Chicago Defender*, May 23, 1942.

16. Gail Buckley, *American Patriots: The Story of Blacks in the Military from the Revolution to Desert Storm* (New York: Random House, 2001), 275.

17. Richard M. Dalfiume, *Desegregation of the U.S. Armed Forces: Fighting on Two Fronts 1939–1953* (Columbia: University of Missouri Press, 1969), 28.

18. Ibid., 26.

19. Ibid., 31.

20. Clifton S. Hardy, "Road to War, from the Diary of Clifton S. Hardy," *Baltimore Afro-American*, January 13, 1940.

21. "Raps War Department for Discrimination," *Chicago Defender*, April 13, 1940.

22. Morris J. MacGregor, Jr., *Integration of the Armed Forces, 1940–1965* (Washington, DC: U.S. Government Printing Office, 1981), 17.

23. "Race Soldier Dissatisfied Says Ex-Vet," *Chicago Defender*, March 23, 1940.

24. "German Jim Crow," *Baltimore Afro-American*, January 27, 1940.

25. Alfred Martin, "Racial Hatred," *Chicago Defender*, January 20, 1940.

26. Nancy Cunard, "Says Colonials Hate Nazi Ideal," *Atlanta Daily World*, January 28, 1940.

27. "Still Cannon Fodder," *Baltimore Afro-American*, April 20, 1940.

28. Franklin Roosevelt, "Address to Congress Requesting a Declaration of War with Japan," December 8, 1941, FDR Presidential Library and Museum.

CHAPTER 16: THE DOUBLE V

1. Phillip McGuire, *He, Too, Spoke for Democracy* (New York: Greenwood, 1988), 30.

2. "Army, Navy Agreed on Blood Ban," *Baltimore Afro-American*, November 29, 1941.

3. "Red Cross Solves Problem: Will Accept and Segregate Negro Blood," *Chicago Defender*, January 31, 1942.

4. "Red Cross Turns Down Negro Blood," *Chicago Defender*, January 17, 1942.

5. McGuire, *He, Too, Spoke for Democracy*, 74.

6. "Red Cross Turns Down Negro Blood," *Chicago Defender*, January 17, 1942.

7. "Army, Navy Agreed on Blood Ban," *Baltimore Afro-American*, November 29, 1941.

8. Ibid.

9. Roy Wilkins, "The Watchtower," *New York Amsterdam Star-News*, January 17, 1942.

10. "Randolph Says Red Cross Bias Reeks of Nazism," *Baltimore Afro-American*, January 24, 1942.

11. Albert Deutch and Tom O'Connor, "Red Cross Bias Called Hindrance to War Effort—Luxury We Can't Afford," *Baltimore Afro-American*, January 17, 1942.

12. "Red Cross Exposed; Will Have to Give Up Bias," *Baltimore Afro-American*, January 31, 1942.

13. "Blood Policy of Red Cross Ill-Founded," *Baltimore Afro-American*, February 14, 1942.

14. McGuire, *He, Too, Spoke for Democracy*, 75.

15. Ibid.

16. "Blast New Jim Crow Policy of Red Cross," *Baltimore Afro-American*, February 7, 1942.

17. McGuire, *He, Too, Spoke for Democracy*, 76.

18. Gail Buckley, *American Patriots: The Story of Blacks in the Military from the Revolution to Desert Storm* (New York: Random House, 2001), 273.

19. McGuire, *He, Too, Spoke for Democracy*, 30.

20. "Agitation for the Impossible," *Atlanta Daily World*, May 12, 1942.

21. Roy Wilkins, "The Watchtower," *New York Amsterdam Star-News*, June 13, 1942.

22. Buckley, *American Patriots*, 257.

23. Roy Wilkins, "The Watchtower," *New York Amsterdam Star-News*, June 13, 1942.

24. "Agitation for the Impossible," *Atlanta Daily World*, May 12, 1942.

25. "White Scribes Say MacLeish Is Wrong," *Baltimore Afro-American*, February 21, 1942.

26. Richard M. Dalfiume, *Desegregation of the U.S. Armed Forces: Fighting on Two Fronts, 1939–1953* (Columbia: University of Missouri Press, 1969), 47.

27. McGuire, *He, Too, Spoke for Democracy*, 16.

28. "Miss Victory Will Be Crowned at Double V Dance Friday Evening," *Atlanta Daily World*, April 29, 1942.

29. "She's the Double V Queen of A & T," *Atlanta Daily World*, June 2, 1942.

30. George F. McCray, "C.I.O. Auto Workers Make Strong Demands on Negro Job War Issue," *Chicago Defender*, August 15, 1942.

31. "Willkie Urges Navy to Drop Bar Against Negro Recruits," *Washington Post*, March 20, 1942.

32. McGuire, *He, Too, Spoke for Democracy*, 55.

CHAPTER 17: HARVEST OF DISORDER: THE ARMY

1. Richard M. Dalfiume, *Desegregation of the U.S. Armed Forces: Fighting on Two Fronts, 1939–1953* (Columbia: University of Missouri Press, 1969), 45.

2. Ibid.

3. Ollie Stewart, "U.S. Bows to Virginia Prejudice," *Baltimore Afro-American*, December 13, 1941.

4. Dalfiume, *Desegregation of the U.S. Armed Forces*, 49.

5. Morris J. MacGregor, Jr., *Integration of the Armed Forces, 1940–1965* (Washington, DC: U.S. Government Printing Office, 1981), 20–21.

6. Gerald Astor, *The Right to Fight: A History of African Americans in the Military* (New York: Presidio Press, 1998), 159.

7. Dalfiume, *Desegregation of the U.S. Armed Forces*, 47.

8. Ibid., 56.

9. Walter White, *A Man Called White* (New York: Viking, 1948), 221–22.

10. "Negro, White Volunteer Army Unit Proposed," *Atlanta Daily World*, January 14, 1942.

11. "Southerners Endorse Negro and White Army Divisions," *Chicago Defender*, January 24, 1942.

12. MacGregor, *Integration of the Armed Forces*, 31.

13. White, *A Man Called White*, 222.

14. Phillip McGuire, *He, Too, Spoke for Democracy* (New York: Greenwood, 1988), 16.

15. "Varied Groups in D.C. Pledge Loyalty to U.S. President," *Washington Post*, December 8, 1941.

16. "Pullman Porters Pledge Support in U.S. War Effort," *Baltimore Afro-American*, December 20, 1941.

17. "Mr. President, Count on Us," *Baltimore Afro-American*, December 13, 1941.

18. "Negro Troops Made Excellent Record in First Year of War, Reports Army," *Chicago Defender*, December 19, 1942.

19. MacGregor, *Integration of the Armed Forces*, 32.

20. Ibid., 39.

21. Michael Robert Patterson, Arlington National Cemetery biography of Vernon Joseph Baker, First Lieutenant, United States Army, July 16, 2010.

22. Astor, *The Right to Fight*, 289–90.

23. Ibid., 290.

24. Vernon Baker and Ken Olsen, *Lasting Valor* (New York: Random House, 1999), 203.

25. Gail Buckley, *American Patriots: The Story of Blacks in the Military from the Revolution to Desert Storm* (New York: Random House, 2001), 483.

26. Courtland Milloy, "WWII Hero Vernon Baker Fought Fascism Over There, Racism at Home," *Washington Post*, July 21, 2010.

27. "Famed Black Buffaloes Activated in Alabama," *Atlanta Daily World*, October 18, 1942.

28. "Race Officers Seen for 92d," *Atlanta Daily World*, September 1, 1942.

29. "Second Negro Division Activated in Alabama," *Atlanta Daily World*, October 18, 1942.

30. "In the Camps," *Chicago Defender*, December 18, 1943.

31. "Transition . . . A Case In Point," *Atlanta Daily World*, December 29, 1943.

32. "Sgt. Barrow (Joe Louis) Makes Tour of Huachuca," *Chicago Defender*, June 5, 1943.

33. "Learn to Fight Dirty, 93rd Division Is Told," *Atlanta Daily World*, October 1, 1942.

34. "New York Medics Oppose Jim-Crow Army Hospital," *Baltimore Afro-American*, March 28, 1942.

35. MacGregor, *Integration of the Armed Forces*, 40.

36. Dalfiume, *Desegregation of the U.S. Armed Forces*, 71.

37. Ibid., 68.

38. "Negro Troops Made Excellent Record in First Year of War, Reports Army," *Chicago Defender*, December 19, 1942.

39. "Southern U. Has Given Army Four Lieutenants," *Baltimore Afro-American*, August 29, 1942.

40. MacGregor, *Integration of the Armed Forces*, 48.

41. Ibid., 47–49.

42. "Army Schools Reflect FDR Democratic Policy," *Chicago Defender*, June 13, 1942.

43. "Race Officers Seen for 92d," *Atlanta Daily World*, September 1, 1942.

44. William Hastie, Oral History interview, pp. 16–17, HSTL.

45. Dalfiume, *Desegregation of the U.S. Armed Forces*, 65.

46. "Negro Militancy Outstanding in 1941, White Says at Meet," *Atlanta Daily World*, January 6, 1942.

47. Walter White, "People and Places," *Chicago Defender*, April 17, 1943.

48. Dalfiume, *Desegregation of the U.S. Armed Forces*, 67.

49. "Gen. Davis Spends Four Days in Visit to Camp Atterbury," *Chicago Defender*, January 30, 1943.

50. Lt. Col. (Ret.) Michael Lee Lanning, *The African-American Soldier: From Crispus Attucks to Colin Powell* (Secaucus, NJ: Birch Lane Press, 1997), 173.

51. Astor, *The Right to Fight*, 175.

52. Dalfiume, *Desegregation of the U.S. Armed Forces*, 68.

53. "Negro Army Officers Are Limited, Report," *Atlanta Daily World*, February 24, 1943.

54. "Is the 93rd a Token Outfit?," *Baltimore Afro-American*, March 6, 1943.

55. Ibid.

56. "Army Rule Bars Promotions," *New York Amsterdam Star-News*, February 27, 1943.

57. "In the Camps," *Chicago Defender*, December 18, 1943.

58. Walter White, "People and Places," *Chicago Defender*, April 17, 1943

CHAPTER 18: THE ARMY AIR CORPS

1. "Identify Body of Soldier Found Near Camp," *Chicago Defender*, April 19, 1941.

2. Walter White, *A Man Called White* (New York: Viking, 1948), 226–27.

3. William Hastie, Oral History interview, pp. 17–18, HSTL.

4. Gerald Astor, *The Right to Fight: A History of African Americans in the Military* (New York: Presidio Press, 1998), 176–77.

5. Richard M. Dalfiume, *Desegregation of the U.S. Armed Forces: Fighting on Two Fronts, 1939–1953* (Columbia: University of Missouri Press, 1969), 74.

6. Morris J. MacGregor, Jr., *Integration of the Armed Forces, 1940–1965* (Washington, DC: U.S. Government Printing Office, 1981), 39.

7. Dalfiume, *Desegregation of the U.S. Armed Forces*, 74–75.

8. Christopher Paul Moore, *Fighting for America: Black Soldiers—The Unsung Heroes of World War II* (New York: Presidio Press, 2006), 38–39.

9. Ibid., 40.

10. Astor, *The Right to Fight*, 162–63.

11. MacGregor, *Integration of the Armed Forces*, 38.

12. Phillip McGuire, *He, Too, Spoke for Democracy* (New York: Greenwood, 1988), 90.

13. Ibid., 89.

14. Ibid., 92.

15. Bernard C. Nalty, *Strength for the Fight: A History of Black Americans in the Military* (New York: Free Press, 1986), 167.

16. White, *A Man Called White*, 255.

17. MacGregor, *Integration of the Armed Forces*, 42–43.

18. White, *A Man Called White*, 254.

19. Nalty, *Strength for the Fight*, 168.

20. Dalfiume, *Desegregation of the U.S. Armed Forces*, 94.

21. "75,000 Colored Men Overseas—Stimson," *Baltimore Afro-American*, April 17, 1943.

22. "Stimson Assures Race Army Officers Higher Promotions," *Atlanta Daily World*, April 16, 1942.

23. MacGregor, *Integration of the Armed Forces*, 43.

24. Nalty, *Strength for the Fight*, 151–52.

25. Ibid., 169.

26. "Ninety-third Division to See Combat Soon, Says MacArthur," *Chicago Defender*, March 10, 1945.

27. John L. Newby, "The Fight for the Right to Fight and the Forgotten Negro Protest Movement: The History of Executive Order 9981 and Its Effect Upon Brown v. Board of Education and Beyond," *Texas Journal on Civil Liberties & Civil Rights* 10 (Winter 2004): 83–110.

28. Hastie interview, p. 19, HSTL.

29. MacGregor, *Integration of the Armed Forces*, 27.

30. "Negro Flyers Equal to Any, Says Teacher," *Atlanta Daily World*, May 14, 1942.

31. Walter White, "People and Places," *Chicago Defender*, February 20, 1943.

32. "Judge Hastie's Resignation," *Atlanta Daily World*, February 3, 1943.

33. McGuire, *He, Too, Spoke for Democracy*, 83.

34. Charles P. Howard, Sr., "The Observer," *Atlanta Daily World*, February 9, 1943.

35. Gail Buckley, *American Patriots: The Story of Blacks in the Military from the Revolution to Desert Storm* (New York: Random House, 2001), 280.

36. Ibid., 279.

37. White, *A Man Called White*, 264.

Chapter 19: "Entitled to a Showdown": The Navy Under Secretary Knox and the Truman Committee

1. Yvonne Latty, *We Were There: Voices of African American Veterans from World War II to the War in Iraq* (New York: HarperCollins, 2004), 46.

2. Morris J. MacGregor, Jr., *Integration of the Armed Forces, 1940–1965* (Washington, DC: U.S. Government Printing Office, 1981), 58.

3. "We Can Cook in the Most Prejudiced Branch of the U.S. Navy," *Baltimore Afro-American*, March 13, 1943.

4. "Frank Knox," Naval Historical Center Online Library, www.history.navy.mil.

5. MacGregor, *Integration of the Armed Forces*, 59–60.

6. "NAACP Asks Navy to End Segregation," *Chicago Defender*, December 20, 1941.

7. "FDR Asked to Abolish Navy's Jim Crow Policy," *Baltimore Afro-American*, December 27, 1941.

8. "A Plea to Secretary Knox," *Chicago Defender*, December 27, 1941.

9. "Navy Jim Crow Flag Flies Despite War," *Baltimore Afro-American*, December 13, 1941.

10. "Navy Officer Answers," *Baltimore Afro-American*, April 17, 1943.

11. "'Awful Sight'—Liberty Ship Aflame after Enemy Bombing," *Baltimore Afro-American*, October 16, 1943.

12. "FDR Asked to Abolish Navy's Jim Crow Policy," *Baltimore Afro-American*, December 27, 1941.

13. Gail Buckley, *American Patriots: The Story of Blacks in the Military from the Revolution to Desert Storm* (New York: Random House, 2001), 305.

14. MacGregor, *Integration of the Armed Forces*, 64.

15. "The Negro and the Navy," *New York Times*, April 9, 1942.

16. "What the Daily Press Thinks of the New Jim-Crow Navy Rules," *Baltimore Afro-American*, April 18, 1942.

17. MacGregor, *Integration of the Armed Forces*, 66–67.

18. Bernard C. Nalty, *Strength for the Fight: A History of Black Americans in the Military* (New York: Free Press, 1986), 191.

19. Gerald Astor, *The Right to Fight: A History of African Americans in the Military* (New York: Presidio Press, 1998), 215.

20. "Negro Navy Volunteers Continue to Increase," *Atlanta Daily World*, September 10, 1943.

21. "400 S.C. Men Enter Navy in May," *Atlanta Daily World*, June 11, 1943.

22. MacGregor, *Integration of the Armed Forces*, 70.

23. Ibid., 71–72.

24. "No Colored Sailors on Seagoing Vessels," *Baltimore Afro-American*, July 3, 1943.

25. Ibid.

26. "Hawaii Hate!" *Chicago Defender*, January 9, 1943.

27. MacGregor, *Integration of the Armed Forces*, 70.

28. "Proudly We Served: The Story of USS Mason and Her Crew," www .ussmason.org.

29. Ibid.

30. Jim Hewlitt, "Destoryer Escort Commissioned," *New York Amsterdam News*, March 25, 1944.

31. Thomas W. Young, "Reporter Describes Exploits of 1st Negro-Manned Warship," *New York Amsterdam News*, September 2, 1944.

32. "Proudly We Served: The Story of USS Mason and Her Crew," www .ussmason.org.

33. Ibid.

34. Gregory Lind, "Saga of Convoy NY 119," *Minnesota's Greatest Generation*, www. people.mnhs.org.

35. "Proudly We Served: The Story of USS Mason and Her Crew," www .ussmason.org.

36. Ibid.

37. Ibid.

38. "Who's in Charge—FDR or the Navy?" *Baltimore Afro-American*, November 20, 1943.

39. "Navy Day for Whom?" *Baltimore Afro-American*, October 23, 1943.

40. "Navy Boss Bars Mixed Crews in Navy," *Chicago Defender*, November 20, 1943.

41. "Who's in Charge—FDR or the Navy?" *Baltimore Afro-American*, November 20, 1943.

42. Nalty, *Strength for the Fight*, 190.

43. "Navy Day for Whom?" *Baltimore Afro-American*, October 23, 1943.

44. MacGregor, *Integration of the Armed Forces*, 81.

45. "Navy Plans to Commission First Race Officers," *Chicago Defender*, October 16, 1943.

46. Astor, *The Right to Fight*, 222.

47. Ibid., 223.

48. Buckley, *American Patriots*, 307.

49. MacGregor, *Integration of the Armed Forces*, 82.

50. Walter White, *A Man Called White* (New York: Viking, 1948), 220.

51. "Navy Now Has 34 Commissioned Negro Officers," *Chicago Defender*, January 27, 1945.

52. Roy Wilkins, "The Watchtower," *New York Amsterdam-News*, June 3, 1944.

53. "Girl Called for Exam in WAVES by Error," *Baltimore Afro-American*, November 27, 1943.

54. "WAVES Put Ban on Negro Officers," *Chicago Defender*, August 15, 1943.

55. "Navy to Admit WAVES, But Strictly Jim Crow," *Chicago Defender*, August 1, 1943.

56. "AKAs Launch Drive Against WAVE Plan," *Atlanta Daily World*, July 26, 1943.

57. Nalty, *Strength for the Fight*, 191.

58. Andrew Dunar, *The Truman Scandals and the Politics of Morality* (Columbia: University of Missouri Press, 1984), 17–18.

59. Ibid., 19.

60. Ibid.

61. Ibid., 20.

62. Seymour Morris, Jr., *American History Revised: 200 Startling Facts That Never Made It into Textbooks* (New York: Crown, 2010), 76.

63. "See Move to Kill Truman Committee Efforts as Hearings Again Hit Snag," *Chicago Defender*, August 16, 1941.

64. "Fear Truman Committee Is Ducking Probe," *Chicago Defender*, August 2, 1941.

65. "Hit Postponement of Defense Jim Crow Probe," *Chicago Defender*, July 5, 1941.

CHAPTER 20: THE NAVY AND MARINE CORPS UNDER SECRETARY FORRESTAL

1. "SecDef Histories—James V. Forrestal," available at www.defense.gov.

2. Gail Buckley, *American Patriots: The Story of Blacks in the Military from the Revolution to Desert Storm* (New York: Random House, 2001), 308.

3. Morris J. MacGregor, Jr., *Integration of the Armed Forces, 1940–1965* (Washington, DC: U.S. Government Printing Office, 1981), 85.

4. *Time*, December 7, 1942.

5. Buckley, *American Patriots*, 308.

6. Bernard C. Nalty, *Strength for the Fight: A History of Black Americans in the Military* (New York: Free Press, 1986), 194.

7. Buckley, *American Patriots*, 310.

8. J. Robert Smith, "Navy Blast Dead Mount; No Bodies Found in Ruins," *Chicago Defender*, July 29, 1944.

9. Ibid.

10. Richard Goldstein, "Freddie Meeks, 83, Ex-Sailor Who Was Pardoned, Dies," *New York Times*, June 30, 2003.

11. Ibid.

12. Ibid.; Erin Hallissy, "Freddie Meeks—Pardoned in Port Chicago Mutiny," *San Francisco Chronicle*, June 21, 2003.

13. MacGregor, *Integration of the Armed Forces*, 86.

14. Ibid., 194.

15. Nalty, *Strength for the Fight*, 196.

16. MacGregor, *Integration of the Armed Forces*, 87.

17. "Thomas Holcomb, General, United States Marine Corps," Arlington National Cemetery, www.arlingtoncemetery.net.

18. MacGregor, *Integration of the Armed Forces*, 100.

19. Lt. Col. (Ret.) Michael Lee Lanning, *The African-American Soldier: From Crispus Attucks to Colin Powell* (Secaucus, NJ: Birch Lane Press, 1997), 211.

20. Buckley, *American Patriots*, 312.

21. Lanning, *The African-American Soldier*, 211.

22. Buckley, *American Patriots*, 312.

23. MacGregor, *Integration of the Armed Forces*, 205.

24. Nalty, *Strength for the Fight*, 200.

25. Buckley, *American Patriots*, 315.

26. Alfred A. Duckett, "1350 Race Leathernecks Graduate at N.C. Camp," *Chicago Defender*, March 20, 1943.

27. Ibid.

28. "Race Marines Set for Action," *Chicago Defender*, May 15, 1943.

29. "Civilians Made into Marines at LeJeune," *Baltimore Afro-American*, November 27, 1943.

30. "Four N.C. Marines Promoted to Sergeant's Rank," *Baltimore Afro-American*, May 22, 1943.

31. Duckett, "1350 Race Leathernecks Graduate at N.C. Camp," *Chicago Defender*, March 20, 1943.

32. "First Colored Marines on Duty Overseas," *Baltimore Afro-American*, May 15, 1943.

33. "Combat Marines Head for the Pacific," *Chicago Defender*, February 12, 1944.

34. Buckley, *American Patriots*, 319.

35. "Our Black Marines," *Chicago Defender*, August 19, 1944.

36. Buckley, *American Patriots*, 319.

37. "First Colored Marines on Duty Overseas," *Baltimore Afro-American*, May 15, 1943.

38. Walter White, *A Man Called White* (New York: Viking, 1948), 262.

39. "Race to Discard Party Labels in 1944 Vote," *Chicago Defender*, May 22, 1943.

CHAPTER 21: FROM SENATOR TO VICE PRESIDENT IN ONE HUNDRED DAYS

1. Harry S. Truman, *The Autobiography of Harry S. Truman*, ed. Robert H. Ferrell (Columbia: University of Missouri Press, 1980), 87.

2. William E. Leuchtenburg, *The White House Looks South: Franklin D. Roosevelt, Harry S. Truman, Lyndon B. Johnson* (Baton Rouge: Louisiana State University Press, 2005), 159.

3. Ibid.

4. Harry McAlpin, "Truman Says Negroes Will Lose Nothing," *Atlanta Daily World*, July 25, 1944.

5. Ibid.

6. Leuchtenburg, *The White House Looks South*, 161.

7. Drew Pearson, "The Washington Merry-Go-Round," *Washington Post*, April 16, 1945.

8. Leuchtenburg, *The White House Looks South*, 160.

9. McAlpin, "Truman Says Negroes Will Lose Nothing," *Atlanta Daily World*, July 25, 1944.

10. Ibid.

11. "GOP to Use Truman's Nomination as Weapon," *Baltimore Afro-American*, August 5, 1944.

12. Ibid.

13. "Says Truman Committee Wouldn't Probe Jim Crow," *Baltimore Afro-American*, July 29, 1944.

14. "Howard Says Truman Indifferent to Problems Faced by Negro People," *Atlanta Daily World*, August 4, 1944.

15. "Pledge Justice in Postwar Plans," *Atlanta Daily World*, September 10, 1944.

16. Harry S. Truman, *Letters Home by Harry Truman*, ed. Monty M. Poen (Columbia: University of Missouri Press, 1984), 106.

17. Leuchtenburg, *The White House Looks South*, 152.

18. "Truman Denies Klan Membership in Answer to NAACP Telegram," *Atlanta Daily World*, October 31, 1944.

19. "Vice-President Truman," *Atlanta Daily World*, November 18, 1944.

20. Franklin Delano Roosevelt, "Address to Congress on Yalta," March 1, 1945, available at www.millercenter.org/president/speeches/detail/3338.

21. Jon Meacham, *Franklin and Winston: An Intimate Portrait of an Epic Friendship* (New York: Random House, 2003), 343.

22. Arthur Krock, "President Roosevelt Is Dead; Truman to Continue Policies," *New York Times*, April 12, 1945.

23. Ibid.

24. "Truman's First Day as Nation's Chief Executive," *New York Amsterdam News*, April 21, 1945.

25. David McCullough, *Truman* (New York: Simon & Schuster, 1992), 415, 417.

26. Drew Pearson, "The Washington Merry-Go-Round," *Washington Post*, April 16, 1945.

27. Robert H. Ferrell, ed., *Off the Record: The Private Papers of Harry S. Truman* (New York: Harper & Row, 1980), 23.

28. Ibid., 16.

29. "F.D.R. Dies!," *Atlanta Daily World*, April 13, 1945.

30. Leuchtenburg, *The White House Looks South*, 162.

31. Bernard John Poll, "President Truman in National Unity Plea," *New York Amsterdam News*, April 21, 1945.

32. Leuchtenburg, *The White House Looks South*, 162.

33. "Chicagoans Mourn FDR, Pledge to Aid Truman," *Chicago Defender*, April 21, 1945.

34. Carolyn Dixon, "Harlem Weeps with World Remembering a Great Man," *New York Amsterdam News*, April 21, 1945.

35. Poll, "President Truman in National Unity Plea," *New York Amsterdam News*, April 21, 1945.

36. Ferrell, *Private Papers of Harry S. Truman*, 20.

37. "F.D.R. Dies!," *Atlanta Daily World*, April 13, 1945.

38. Ferrell, *Private Papers of Harry S. Truman*, 16.

39. McCullough, *Truman*, 355.

40. Truman, *Autobiography*, 100.

41. Poll, "President Truman in National Unity Plea," *New York Amsterdam News*, April 21, 1945.

42. McCullough, *Truman*, 359.

CHAPTER 22: V-DAY DEFERRED

1. Harry S. Truman, *The Public Papers of the Presidents: Harry S. Truman, 1945* (Washington, DC: U.S. Government Printing Office, 1961), 48.

2. Ibid., 48–49.

3. David McCullough, *Truman* (New York: Simon & Schuster, 1992), 438.

4. Robert H. Ferrell, ed., *Off the Record: The Private Papers of Harry S. Truman* (New York: Harper & Row, 1980), 55–56.

5. "PEACE! Japan Officially Gives Up," *Atlanta Daily World*, August 15, 1945.

6. Venice T. Spragg, "V-J Brings U Street Whoopee in D.C.," *Chicago Defender*, August 25, 1945.

7. McCullough, *Truman*, 462–63.

8. Spragg, "V-J Brings U Street Whoopee in D.C.," *Chicago Defender*, August 25, 1945.

9. "695,264 in Army on V-J Day," *Chicago Defender*, November 10, 1945.

10. McCullough, *Truman*, 469.

11. "White Only Jobs Back in Ads, NAACP Finds," *Chicago Defender*, September 1, 1945.

12. "Our Workers Fired Twice as Fast as Whites in NY," *Baltimore Afro-American*, October 20, 1945.

13. Richard M. Dalfiume, *Desegregation of the U.S. Armed Forces: Fighting on Two Fronts, 1939–1953* (Columbia: University of Missouri Press, 1969), 150.

14. Ibid., 155.

15. "Text of Gillem Report on Negro GIs," *Chicago Defender*, March 9, 1946.

16. "The Gillem Report," *Chicago Defender*, March 23, 1946.

17. "Gillem Report Called Failure by Roy Wilkins," *Chicago Defender*, April 20, 1946.

18. "Army's 'New' Policy," *Crisis*, September 1946.

19. A. James Fuller and Lawrence Sondhaus, eds., *America, War and Power: Defining the State, 1775–2005* (New York: Routledge, 2007), 95.

20. "Alabama Vets Parley Blasts Gillem Report," *Chicago Defender*, March 23, 1946.

21. Fuller and Sondhaus, *America, War and Power*, 95.

22. Dalfiume, *Desegregation of the U.S. Armed Forces*, 153–54.

23. Morris J. MacGregor, Jr., *Integration of the Armed Forces, 1940–1965* (Washington, DC: U.S. Government Printing Office, 1981), 235.

24. Ibid., 173–74.

25. Ibid., 238.

26. Ernest E. Johnson, "Peacetime Navy to Have Full Quota of Negro Volunteers," *Chicago Defender*, November 17, 1945.

27. Gail Buckley, *American Patriots: The Story of Blacks in the Military from the Revolution to Desert Storm* (New York: Random House, 2001), 340.

CHAPTER 23: THE NOAH'S ARK COMMITTEE

1. Charles H. Loeb, "Japs give Up and Negroes Are Up Front," *New York Amsterdam News*, September 8, 1945.

2. Richard M. Dalfiume, *Desegregation of the U.S. Armed Forces: Fighting on Two Fronts, 1939–1953* (Columbia: University of Missouri Press, 1969), 123.

3. Dan Gardner, "V-J Day Rejoicing But What Did American Negroes Gain?" *New York Amsterdam News*, September 8, 1945.

4. Morris J. MacGregor, Jr., *Integration of the Armed Forces, 1940–1965* (Washington, DC: U.S. Government Printing Office, 1981), 299.

5. Harry S. Truman, *The Public Papers of the Presidents: Harry S. Truman, 1945* (Washington, DC: U.S. Government Printing Office, 1961), 104.

6. William E. Leuchtenburg, *The White House Looks South: Franklin D. Roosevelt, Harry S. Truman, Lyndon B. Johnson* (Baton Rouge: Louisiana State University Press, 2005), 164.

7. Ibid., 165.

8. Michael R. Gardner, *Harry Truman and Civil Rights: Moral Courage and Political Risks* (Carbondale, IL: Southern Illinois University Press, 2002), 47.

9. Ibid., 43.

10. Ibid., 60.

11. Harry S. Truman, Executive Order 9808, December 5, 1946, HSTL.

12. Gardner, *Harry Truman and Civil Rights*, 23.

13. Harry S. Truman, "Remarks to Members of the President's Committee on Civil Rights," January 15, 1947, HSTL.

14. Truman, Executive Order 9808, December 5, 1946, HSTL.

15. Michael R. Gardner, "A President Who Regarded Civil Rights as a Moral Imperative," in Raymond H. Geselbracht, ed., *The Civil Rights Legacy of Harry S. Truman* (Kirksville, MO: Truman State University Press, 2007), 25.

CHAPTER 24: THE BLINDING OF ISAAC WOODARD AND THE SIGNING OF EXECUTIVE ORDER 9981

1. Andrew Myers, "Resonant Ripples in a Global Pond: The Blinding of Isaac Woodard," prepared for the 2002 American Studies Association Conference.
2. Walter White, *A Man Called White* (New York: Viking, 1948), 331.
3. Michael R. Gardner, *Harry Truman and Civil Rights: Moral Courage and Political Risks* (Carbondale, IL: Southern Illinois University Press, 2002), 17.
4. William C. Berman, *The Politics of Civil Rights in the Truman Administration* (Columbus: Ohio State University Press, 1970), 57.
5. Gardner, *Harry Truman and Civil Rights*, 34.
6. "Gov't Must Insure Rights to All—Truman," *Atlanta Daily World*, July 1, 1947.
7. Ibid.
8. Gardner, *Harry Truman and Civil Rights*, 41.
9. *To Secure These Rights: The Report of the President's Committee on Civil Rights*, HSTL.
10. Gardner, *Harry Truman and Civil Rights*, 49–50.
11. William E. Leuchtenburg, *The White House Looks South: Franklin D. Roosevelt, Harry S. Truman, Lyndon B. Johnson* (Baton Rouge: Louisiana State University Press, 2005), 173.
12. Memorandum from Clark Clifford to President Truman, "The Politics of 1948," November 19, 1947, HSTL.
13. Ibid.
14. Morris J. MacGregor, Jr., *Integration of the Armed Forces, 1940–1965* (Washington, DC: U.S. Government Printing Office, 1981), 303–04.
15. Raymond H. Geselbracht, ed., *The Civil Rights Legacy of Harry S. Truman* (Kirksville, MO: Truman State University Press, 2007), 110.
16. *To Secure These Rights*, Chapter 4, HSTL.
17. Leuchtenburg, *The White House Looks South*, 169.
18. Harry S. Truman, Executive Order 9981, July 26, 1948, HSTL.
19. Mary S. Spargo, "Truman Orders Equal Rights in U.S. Jobs, Armed Forces," *Washington Post*, July 27, 1948.
20. Richard M. Dalfiume, *Desegregation of the U.S. Armed Forces: Fighting on Two Fronts, 1939–1953* (Columbia: University of Missouri Press, 1969), 172.
21. Berman, *The Politics of Civil Rights*, 119–20.
22. "Randolph, League Not Satisfied by Truman's Order," *Chicago Defender*, August 7, 1948.
23. Dalfiume, *Desegregation of the U.S. Armed Forces*, 173.
24. "Randolph Drops Fight on Civil Disobedience," *New York Amsterdam News*, August 21, 1948.

25. "NAACP Asks Secretary of Defense Forrestal to End Military Jim Crow Now," *Atlanta Daily World*, September 9, 1948.

CHAPTER 25: FREEDOM TO SERVE

1. Transcript of meeting of Fahy committee with President Truman, January 12, 1949, HSTL.

2. Fahy committee, *Freedom to Serve: Equality of Treatment and Opportunity in the Armed Services* (Washington, DC: U.S. Government Printing Office, 1950), 45.

3. Richard M. Dalfiume, *Desegregation of the U.S. Armed Forces: Fighting on Two Fronts, 1939–1953* (Columbia: University of Missouri Press, 1969), 181.

4. Morris J. MacGregor, Jr., *Integration of the Armed Forces, 1940–1965* (Washington, DC: U.S. Government Printing Office, 1981), 351.

5. Dalfiume, *Desegregation of the U.S. Armed Forces*, 183–85.

6. Fahy committee, *Freedom to Serve*, 60–61.

7. MacGregor, *Integration of the Armed Forces*, 430.

8. Dalfiume, *Desegregation of the U.S. Armed Forces*, 203.

9. Bernard C. Nalty, *Strength for the Fight: A History of Black Americans in the Military* (New York: Free Press, 1986), 256.

10. Charles B. Rangel and Leon Wynter, *And I Haven't Had a Bad Day Since: From the Streets of Harlem to the Halls of Congress* (New York: Thomas Dunne Books, 2007), 60.

11. William T. Bowers, William M. Hammon, and George L. MacGarrigle, *Black Soldier, White Army* (Washington, DC: Center of Military History, United States Army, 1996), v.

12. MacGregor, *Integration of the Armed Forces*, 439.

13. Ibid., 447.

14. Ibid., 455–56.

CHAPTER 26: THE MUSEUM AND THE MIRROR

1. Alan L. Gropman, "Blacks in the Military," *National Interest*, no. 48, Summer 1997.

2. Ibid.

3. *Grutter* v. *Bollinger*, 539 U.S. 306 (2003).

4. Mark K. Moller, "Race, 'National Security,' and Unintended Consequences: A Sideways Glance at *Brown v. Board of Education* at Fifty," *Loyola University Chicago Law Journal* 36 (2004).

5. Sylvia H. Walbolt and Joseph H. Lang, Jr., "Appellate Advocacy Symposium, Part II: Amicus Briefs Revisited," *Stetson Law Review*, Fall 2003.

6. *Grutter* v. *Bollinger*, 539 U.S. 306 (2003).

7. Consolidated brief of Lt. Gen. Julius W. Becton, Jr., et al., *Grutter* v. *Bollinger*, p. 6.

8. Ibid., 14.

9. Paul Goode, "A Proud Esprit Soiled by Racial Hate," *Life*, September 26, 1969.

10. Consolidated brief of Lt. Gen. Becton, p. 16.

11. Ibid., 17.

12. Ibid., 29.

13. See, for example, *Grutter* v. *Bollinger*, 539 U.S. 306 (2003), Thomas, dissenting.

INDEX